OMAR M. McROBERTS

STREETS OF GLORY

CHURCH AND COMMUNITY

IN A BLACK URBAN

NEIGHBORHOOD

THE UNIVERSITY OF CHICAGO · CHICAGO AND LONDON

OMAR M. MCROBERTS is assistant professor of sociology at
the University of Chicago.

The University of Chicago Press, Chicago 60637
The University of Chicago Press, Ltd., London
© 2003 by The University of Chicago
All rights reserved. Published 2003
Printed in the United States of America
12 11 10 09 08 07 06 05 04 03   1 2 3 4 5
ISBN: 0-226-56216-6 (cloth)

A portion of this work has been previously published in "Understanding the 'New' Black Pentecostal Activism: Lessons from Boston
Ecumenical Ministries" *Sociology of Religion* 60, no. 1 (spring 1999):
47–70. © Association for the Sociology of Religion, Inc.
All rights reserved.

Library of Congress Cataloging-in-Publication Data

McRoberts, Omar Maurice.
  Streets of glory : church and community in a Black urban
neighborhood / Omar Maurice McRoberts.
    p.   cm. — (Morality and society series)
Includes bibliographical references and index.
  ISBN 0-226-56216-6 (cloth : alk. paper)
  1. African American churches—Massachusetts—Boston—
History. 2. City churches—Massachusetts—Boston—History.
3. Boston (Mass.)—Church history.   I. Title. II. Morality and society.
  BR563.N4 M38 2003
  77.44'61—dc12

                                           2002009612

My eyes fail from weeping, I am in torment within,
my heart is poured out on the ground because my people are
destroyed, because children and infants faint in
the streets of the city.

LAMENTATIONS 2:11

Your people will rebuild the ancient ruins
and will raise up the age-old foundations; you will
be called Repairer of Broken Walls, Restorer of
Streets with Dwellings.

ISAIAH 58:12

CONTENTS

ACKNOWLEDGMENTS

In countless ways, many people, more than I could ever list, have helped me get through this project. Among these are the members of my dissertation committee, whose guidance proved indispensable at every turn. Christopher Winship introduced me to Four Corners and strongly encouraged me to make the study of religion a central part of my sociological sojourn. Were it not for his initial and subsequent support, this project would never have been conceived, let alone completed. He has probably heard me say, "Thanks, Chris" a hundred times. Chris, here's one more. Nancy Ammerman provided consistently sharp and insightful critiques of my work and offered marvelous advice at every phase of the project. Also, during the final hours of my dark night of the dissertative soul, Professor Ammerman's votes of confidence were vital psychic buoys. William Julius Wilson has been a source of sage, candid scholarly advice since my undergraduate days at the University of Chicago. His enthusiasm about this project, along with his active mentoring and personal example, have impacted me and my work immeasurably.

My entire family has sustained me in many, many precious ways. My parents, Minnie and William McRoberts, have nurtured my intellectual inclinations from childhood through the present. Their high expectations, warmly textured with unconditional love, have given me the confidence to pursue this work and, indeed, all meaningful work. My younger sister, Ochanya, is the vision of the future that gives me hope. I strive always toward her rich intelligence, awesome creativity, and all-around boundless potential.

Shelley Davis, my wife and partner in all things good and beautiful, has kept me grounded and sane in more ways than she probably knows. Our energetic discussions about power, policy, and justice have kept my mind sharp, yet open. Shelley's interest in my ideas and occasional kicks in the pants helped me to keep writing when I was convinced that my words made absolutely no sense. She also read the entire text and pointed out sections that really did need to be articulated more clearly. At other times, Shelley helped me to sustain a life outside of academic obsessions. At all times, Shelley is a true inspiration.

Several colleagues kindly read the manuscript in its entirety and offered guidance, encouragement, or both: Nancy Eiesland, Aldon Morris, Robert J. Sampson, Winnifred Sullivan, Andrew Greeley, Manuel Vasquez, Evelyn Brodkin, Lowell Livezey, Alan Wolfe, R. Scott Hanson, Martin Riesebrodt, Gerald Suttles, Mark Warren, Richard Wood, and Richard Taub (who introduced me to both sociology and public policy in my undergraduate days). Parts of this book have also benefited greatly from feedback I received at various scholarly gatherings: the Harvard Sociology Colloquium, the Louisville Institute, the Northwestern University Ethnography Workshop, the Project on Theology and Community, the Hauser Center for Nonprofits at Harvard, the Chicago Area Group for the Study of Religious Communities, and the University of Chicago Urban Social Processes Workshop.

This work has been generously supported by a number of research grants and fellowships. The material in this book is based on research supported by a National Science Foundation Graduate Research Fellowship, a Harvard Graduate Society Summer Research Grant, a Ford Foundation Dissertation Fellowship, a Hauser Center for Nonprofit Organizations Dissertation Fellowship, and a Louisville Institute Dissertation Fellowship. I am grateful to the Association for the Sociology of Religion for granting permission to include portions of my article "Understanding the 'New' Black Pentecostal Activism," published previously in *Sociology of Religion* (1999).

Deep thanks to the neighborhood workers, organizers, and residents who shared their views about the neighborhood, its churches, and the meaning of revitalization. I hope this book will make a difference for the better by bringing attention to Four Corners and to scores of neighborhoods like it in urban centers around the country.

Finally, I have found it profoundly humbling to study and write about institutions that perennially, audaciously take up the ancient matter of human ultimacy. I can only begin to do justice to these remarkably complex entities. Still, to the clergy and congregants who so graciously opened their churches to me and so generously shared their time, thoughts, and experiences— thank you. I hope this book will communicate my respect for you and my reverence for the many paths you walk.

ONE

Introduction

Most observers will agree that religious institutions are woven deeply into the physical and social fabric of the city. In nearly every neighborhood and downtown we find temples, churches, mosques, and synagogues. Places of worship house what is perhaps the oldest and most ubiquitous form of urban community—the religious congregation. Yet, these places of worship and the communities that gather within them are not always entirely *at home* in the city. Sometimes religious minds perceive the city—with its stark juxtaposition of rich and poor, its dazzling mosaic of lifestyles and moral cultures, and the seemingly inevitable violations that occur in its streets and halls of power—as the sign and symbol of humanity's spiritual waywardness.

At the same time, developers, public officials, and city dwellers themselves do not always act as if religious functions were as vital to urban life as residential, commercial, industrial, or recreational ones. Indeed, people sometimes view places of worship as social and economic malignancies. Congregations, whether housed or searching for homes, may therefore encounter the same degree of local resentment as homeless shelters, institutions for mentally ill persons, public and low-income housing, smoke-belching factories, and toxic dumps. In numerous instances, urbanites have even attempted to zone places of worship out of residential and commercial areas.[1]

In 1997, the Boston Redevelopment Authority announced plans to rezone Dorchester.[2] The rezoning effort would incorporate residential input through a series of Planning and Zoning Advisory Committee meetings. At one meeting, convened on a crisp October evening, the committee would discuss properties along the segment of Washington Street that cuts through Four Corners: a 0.6-square-mile, economically depressed, predominantly African American neighborhood.

Fourteen people, including myself, attended the meeting. Among the attendants were Four Corners residents and representatives of community development groups in Codman Square and Mt. Bowdoin. A Boston Redevelopment Authority (BRA) representative served as guide and scribe. He distributed a packet of parcel maps covering several segments of Washington

Street. Each parcel, represented by a little polygon, had an identification number and street address printed inside it. The facilitator also distributed a lengthy table describing the use for which each parcel had been zoned. Tonight, committee members would comb through the materials, checking the BRA records against their own mental maps. Participants made sure each parcel had the right address, noted when a property zoned for one purpose was being used for another, and debated the "highest and best use" of particular properties.

During one of these debates, a Four Corners resident raised the issue of parasitic churches. She was disappointed that a particular church met, quite legitimately, in a space zoned for "public assembly." If the parcel had been zoned for some other use, perhaps the church could be ousted from the space. After all, church members take up a good deal of parking space on Washington Street. Shouldn't these parking spaces be available for patrons of the few businesses in Four Corners?

Sandra,[3] a member of another congregation in Four Corners, frowned when she heard these remarks. Without revealing her affiliation, she mentioned, dryly, that her church was listed erroneously as a residential property. "I would say it should be listed as 'CS': a community space." An awkward silence followed. Sandra's point of correction implied that not every church could be dismissed as a mere "public assembly" leeching away the neighborhood's last precious drops of economic lifeblood in the name of God. This church—her church—was a *community space*. The man sitting next to Sandra resisted her subtle attempt to give the church issue a positive spin. The church in question, he impugned, might deliberately be ignoring the property's use designation or operating with a conditional usage permit. The committee should find out which was the case and make sure that the space reverted to residential use when the church inevitably died.

With that remark, the negative spin on churches gained considerable torque; it lost inertia only as the meeting itself wound to a close. At one point, someone lumped churches and auto body shops (reputed as "chop shops," where thieves strip stolen cars) into the same "nuisance" category. "Well, I wouldn't put them *all* in the same category," replied a man representing the Codman Square Community Development Corporation. "I think of churches as being somewhat different." Other attendants nodded reluctantly, as if in deference to some particularly petty point of political correctness. Another man complained that the second floor of the triple-decker next to his home was being used as a church, "so every Sunday I have to put up with their singing!" Then came the retort: "At least they were inside!"

Finally, a representative from Mt. Bowdoin asked if there might be a more effective way to highlight religious institutions operating in places zoned for other purposes. The BRA facilitator responded, helplessly:

> The problem is, churches can be *anywhere*. We ran into this problem when we zoned Blue Hill Avenue. We counted about twenty-one churches on Blue Hill Ave. alone. We put in a recommendation that churches with one hundred seats or more must have at least ten parking spaces. But they said we could not target churches. So we decided to go after all public assemblies.

Some readers will find it odd, if not alarming, that a public discussion about urban land use should "target" churches in this way. One might not expect churches to be discussed in such decisively negative terms. The crux, however, was that churches, like auto body shops, appeared as obstacles to planned economic revitalization. Religious institutions might somehow be useful for members, but they were not useful for the neighborhood. Churches may function as communities, but what do they do for the community?

Debate over the role, the *usefulness,* of religion and religious institutions in urban life is hardly confined to local zoning processes. Such debate has become a prominent feature of the national public discourse on urban poverty. For instance, since 1996 people have debated the merits of the Charitable Choice clause, the portion of the 1996 Wefare Reform Act that makes local churches eligible to receive federal money to provide welfare services to poor people. Feature articles on the role of churches in addressing "inner-city" problems keep appearing in popular magazines. One *Newsweek* cover story even proclaimed "A New Holy War" of churches against the urban ills of violence and drugs (Woodward 1998). Another cover story, appearing in the *American Prospect,* asked, "Can the Churches Save the Cities?" (Kramnick 1997).

From a sociological standpoint, the actual and potential roles of churches in "inner-city" neighborhoods like Four Corners are far from obvious. In fact, sociological studies of life in depressed urban neighborhoods often take for granted the *absence* of voluntary associations, churches included. According to some of these studies, such institutions historically helped to socialize "ghetto" residents, thus buffering poor people against the negative social consequences of their poverty (Wilson 1987; Wacquant and Wilson 1990). Middle-class out-migration, however, is thought to have drained inner-city Black neighborhoods of such associations. Other studies acknowledge the continuing presence of churches and other associations but focus on individual rather than institutional behaviors (Anderson 1990, 1999). In short, despite the ascendancy of church-talk in the world of social welfare policy, not to mention the many local conflicts over the literal place of religion in the urban landscape, the sociological literature has yet to pay sufficient attention to the countless religious congregations that literally line the streets of even the poorest urban areas.

The pressing need for such attention became evident to me in the summer of 1995, when I began visiting Four Corners. I ventured into the neighborhood as a part of a small team of Harvard graduate students evaluating a summer youth program at the Azusa Christian Community. Prior to my first visit, I possessed a statistical understanding of what the neighborhood was like. I knew, for example, that this neighborhood was composed mostly of Black, working poor people. I knew that the neighborhood had high violent crime rates. But there was something else about Four Corners that would reveal itself only after repeated visits. Each time I returned to the neighborhood I noticed more churches, mostly in commercial storefronts. The cliché about depressed neighborhoods containing little other than churches and liquor stores came to mind. I wondered what it could mean for so many churches to be concentrated in such a compact area. These concerns evolved into a four-year, primarily ethnographic study of religion and community revitalization in Four Corners.

The thriving religious presence in countless poor urban neighborhoods and the ambiguous status of these churches in the public imagination raise some crucial questions: 1) Why do some poor neighborhoods contain so many congregations, and how do these neighborhoods sustain so much religious activity? 2) Assuming these churches are not identical to each other (despite the currency of sweeping euphemisms like "storefront churches"), how do they vary meaningfully as social institutions? and 3) What roles do churches play or fail to play in collective efforts to address neighborhood problems? This book will begin to answer these questions by presenting an ethnographic study of Four Corners, which in 1999 hosted twenty-nine congregations.

THE NEIGHBORHOOD OF FOUR CORNERS

In the mid-1980s, Four Corners began to gain a national reputation as a "rough" neighborhood. A thriving, gang-driven drug market and rising violent and property crime rates kept residents in perpetual fear. A spate of drive-by shootings drew wide media attention to the neighborhood and its problems and put the name "Four Corners" on the proverbial map, albeit under less than flattering circumstances. On the literal map, Four Corners is a 0.6-square-mile community area straddling the neighborhood districts (also called city planning districts) of Roxbury and Dorchester (map 1). In 1990, it had a population of 14,519.[4] The median family income in Four Corners was $21,250, a full $13,250 below the city median. With a poverty rate of 29 percent, Four Corners could be located just below the threshold of high poverty.[5] The neighborhood unemployment rate of 14 percent well exceeded the city rate of 8 percent. During the period of study (1995–99) Four Corners was also the least economically developed neighborhood on Washington Street, the major thoroughfare that cuts through most of Dorchester. Vacancy rates soared. Businesses were relatively rare and lacked diversity—the most numerous commercial establishments were corner quick shops, auto repair garages, and hair salons.

Although Four Corners was 81 percent African American,[6] there was some ethnic diversity in the neighborhood. Most of the non–African American residents were immigrants from Latin America. Immigrants from Haiti and the Caribbean islands were a smaller, but visible, presence. Altogether, immigrants made up roughly thirteen percent of the population. There was also a small White population, making up about 6 percent of Four Corners residents. Most of these were older persons who got "left behind" (Cummings 1998) when the neighborhood tipped from White and Jewish to

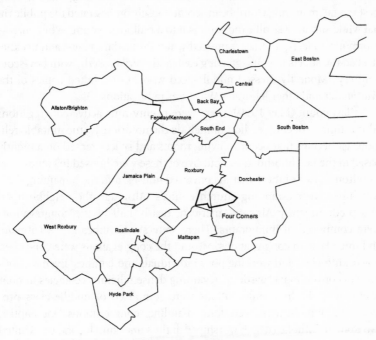

Map 1 City of Boston

Black. A few, however, were young gentrifiers. On rare occasions, they could be seen moving new furniture into rickety Victorian houses or jogging down Washington Street.

Four Corners also contained myriad organizations. These were not community development corporations (CDCs) and community health centers, the kinds of institutions that spearheaded revitalization in adjacent neighborhoods. They were churches. In fact, Four Corners teemed with lush religious life. The religious presence was most conspicuous on Sunday mornings, when the storefronts, dark and deserted most of the week, came alive with the movements and sounds that accompany vigorous worship and warm fellowship. Religion, however, was not invisible during the workweek, either. There were a few "community churches"; these were conspicuous because their doors were perpetually open, their lights were always on, and there were always people going in and out and milling around outside. In the meantime, a variety of evangelists, some based in other neighborhoods, roved the streets and occasionally held worship in outdoor common spaces. A half dozen white-robed members of a nearby Spiritual Baptist church regularly convened on Washington Street at the edge of a small park; for hours they would sing hymns, beat tambourines, dance, and sing praises. Their pastor, a tall man with a Caribbean accent, loosely orchestrated the public ritual while shouting shrill exhortations into a bullhorn. Young White men— Mormons, in fact—in freshly pressed white shirts, dark pants, and neckties strolled the streets in pairs, greeting each and every passerby with boy-scout courtesy.[7] Modestly dressed middle-aged women distributed copies of the *Watchtower* and other Jehovah's Witnesses publications.

At last count (May 1999), there were twenty-nine active congregations (this estimate, of course, did not include the notoriously uncountable religious gatherings that occur in living rooms and spaces rented on a nightly basis) in the neighborhood. All but five of these were housed in commercial storefronts. Two of these met in converted houses, and the remaining three worshiped in freestanding church edifices. Although the neighborhood was predominantly African American, nearly half of the congregations were composed of immigrants. There were six Caribbean, five Latina/o, and three Haitian congregations. Most of the congregations were composed of working-class and working poor individuals and families. Even so, contrary to conventional "wisdom" regarding dense religious ecologies in poor neighborhoods, five congregations were composed of middle-class professionals. Finally, there were four "mainline" congregations: one Baptist, two Roman Catholic (which worshiped at the same church), and one United Methodist. In addition, there was one Jehovah's Witnesses hall containing six congregations and one Seventh-day Adventist congregation. These eleven congregations were conspicuous minorities in an overwhelmingly Holiness-Pentecostal-Apostolic organizational field—although the term "organizational field" never quite captured the nature of religious activity in this neighborhood. Four Corners was a religious *district,* where the most commonplace and the most unusual faith communities existed literally side by side.

Thus, as the neighborhood changed from a once thriving commercial junction to a place known for its economic depression and violence, residents witnessed the peculiar irony that eventually inspired this book. This is the irony of religious generation in the midst of neighborhood decay. Aware of this irony, Reverend Eugene Rivers, Four Corners resident and pastor of the Azusa Christian Community, warned that unless local religious institutions intervened, "in a decade it will be Welcome to the Terror Dome. All that's going to be left of the Black community is crack houses, churches, and twelve-year-old girls prostituting themselves on the streets to survive. Everything else will be gone."

UNDERSTANDING THE RELIGIOUS DISTRICT

This is not the first study to explore aspects of religious life in an African American urban context. It is, however, the first study since 1940 to show how a dense religious ecology emerged within a Black neighborhood, to explore in ethnographic detail the diversity of churches in that ecology, and to explain how churches have impacted the locale. In their classic sociological works, Mays and Nicholson (1969 [1933]), Gunnar Myrdal (1944), and E. Franklin Frazier (1974 [1963]) pondered the abundance of churches in urban Black areas but adopted a national perspective rather than a more intimate local one. Each of their treatises traced the phenomenal post–Civil War growth of urban Black churches to three factors: 1) the great migration, during which millions of southern Blacks moved to urban, usually northern, centers; 2) their continued exclusion from the political, economic, and associational institutions of White society, which forced Blacks to establish parallel institutions in their own areas; and 3) class and cultural differentiation within the Black populace.

All of these scholars further agreed that Blacks were "overchurched"—that is, that African Americans possessed far more churches than they could keep up or that could be useful in ameliorating the social and economic conditions of the Black population. Moreover, each predicted that as racial barriers to the wider urban society crumbled, Blacks would attain higher levels of education, cultural sophistication, and professional status. Subsequently, Black churches would become *less numerous* through consolidation and the death of countless tiny storefront churches lacking social, political, and economic relevance. These studies, aside from lacking local context, have thus far proved wrong in their prognosis for Black religion: churches—especially storefronts—are still numerous in Black urban areas.

Another crucial early work, Vattel Daniel's (1942) "Ritual and Stratification in Chicago Negro Churches," took a local perspective but focused entirely on the ways churches varied by "function." After studying forty congregations in Chicago's "Black Belt," Daniel concluded that churches could be divided into four ritual groups, each of which served the needs of a particular population: "ecstatic sects or cults," "semidemonstrative groups," "deliberative churches," and "liturgical denominations"(354). Moreover, "the type of ritual engaged in, reflects the life of the society of which the worshiper is a member." Daniel was uncommonly sensitive to the ways churches could differ in a particular place. He also usefully emphasized how people *sought out* congregations that suited their tastes and needs. Yet, he did not explain how so many churches had come into existence in that place. Nor did he explore the broader implications of this dense ecclesial presence for politics and social life in Chicago's Black Belt.

A number of ethnographers have produced marvelous studies of individual churches. These works mainly are concerned with the psychological benefits particular churches bestow upon poor congregation members. Some pivotal studies in this vein argue that churches compensate poor people for their lack of accomplishment in the "mainstream" social world (Paris 1982; Williams 1974). Writing more recently and in direct response to the neglect of religious organizations in "underclass" studies, anthropologist Francis Kostarelos explained how a single Chicago church continued to buffer poor individuals against the consequences of their poverty (Kostarelos 1995). Moreover, rather than simply consoling or buffering poor people, this church offered a worldview that emphasized self-worth while exposing the societal roots of personal suffering.

Still, since they do not take as analytical units the neighborhoods in which churches are located, these ethnographies do not shed much light on the nature of multicongregational religious life in particular places. For example, in his meticulous study of three Mount Calvary Holy churches in Boston, Paris (1982:38) observed that "Shawmut Avenue [in Boston's South End] is noteworthy for its large number of churches. At the time of this study, there were four other churches within a block of the Alpha church." Since his study was not about religion in the South End per se, Paris understandably does not tell us much about the churches operating in such close proximity to the Alpha church, let alone about how all of these religious communities managed to coexist. Other ethnographies similarly lack discussions of how churches fit into neighborhood life and religious ecologies. In short, they offer deep insight into the lives of people in particular churches but do not enlighten us about the place of churches in particular neighborhoods.

I am aware of only one prior investigation into the origins, internal diversity, and impact of a religious ecology in a Black neighborhood: St. Clair Drake's *Churches and Voluntary Associations in the Chicago Negro Community*, a Works Projects Administration (WPA) document published in 1940.[8] Drake showed that Black churches not only grew but multiplied as migrants arrived in Chicago in the thousands. Moreover, the Black religious ecology grew quite dense as blacks themselves largely were confined to a single overcrowded area. As he illustrated with a series of hand-colored thematic "pin" maps, churches were especially concentrated in "less desirable" quarters of the Black Belt, where vacant commercial spaces abounded. In this dense religious ecology congregations diversified, each drawing membership from a distinct stratum in an increasingly complicated Black class system. Finally, Drake turned to "the role of the church and associations in the solution of community problems . . . with emphasis upon the manner in which community leaders 'mobilize the community'"(163). The presence of large numbers of congregations proved especially consequential during the depression, when churches served as relief distribution centers. Congregations also offered a mass base for protests, such as the "'Spend your money where you can work' campaign"(247). Nonetheless, the great *diversity* among churches sometimes thwarted strategic unity by calling attention not to a common Black plight but to cultural and economic fault lines running through the Black Belt.

Drake's narrative makes an implicit statement about the relationship between urban contexts and organized religion: local urban contexts give rise to particular religious ecologies, which in turn condition the process of local urban change. In presenting the case of Four Corners, this book makes a similar, but much more explicit, conceptual statement about the origins, anatomy, and impact of the phenomenon I call the religious district. This phenomenon, which is the empirical grain of truth at the center of the "churches and liquor stores" cliché, embodies and extends existing ideas about the nature of religious ecology, voluntary religious practice, and religious influence on urban environments.

Religious Ecology

The idea that urban forms give rise to religious forms originated in the religious ecological tradition of congregational studies (Douglass 1927; Kincheloe 1964, 1989; Ammerman 1997a). This tradition, in turn, grew out of the Chicago school of urban sociology, which understood the city as a system analogous to a natural ecology, with concentric "zones" and local communities serving unique functions within an organic whole (Burgess 1969 [1925]; see also Park et al. 1969 [1925]). Thus, moving from the core of the city to the periphery, there was a central commercial zone, a "zone of transition" characterized by illicit activity, rooming houses, and slum conditions, a "zone of workingmen's homes," a more generic "residential zone," and a near-suburban "commuter's zone." Ethnic groups were thought to progress through communities and zones as they integrated into mainstream urban social and economic life. An immigrant from Italy, then, might initially live in the worn down "zone of transition" where the settlement houses were located. He might then move into a homogenous ethnic enclave, a "little Italy" in the "zone of workingmen's homes." And finally, after a period of acculturation, the immigrant would move into one of the presumably generic quarters in the peripheral zones.

Students of religion in the Chicago school inherited the urban ecological model's sensitivity to the fluctuating nature of racial and ethnic settlement in the city. Churches, they theorized, must extract resources from the local environment in order to survive. Resources include membership, money, legitimacy, and information. When the resources in a neighborhood change due to the exodus and/or influx of a particular population group, churches have four options: 1) alter their products to satisfy new local consumers, 2) follow familiar populations and resources to new neighborhoods, 3) become "niche" churches—that is, abandon the geographical parish focus and create metropolitanwide ministries, or 4) die of resource starvation.

In short, shifting local environments *select* for the most appropriate congregations. This is an extremely useful understanding of the congregation, for it opens the way for studies of the connectedness of religious life to the immediate social environment. It lays bare the ways congregations are subject to the demography and economy of local communities. Importantly, despite the empirical focus of most religious ecological studies, this understanding need not apply solely to isolated congregations in changing neighborhoods. Drake stretched the ecological theory to show how the density, diversity, and economic depression of the postmigration Black Belt gave rise to a dense, diverse multicongregational ecology where people often worshiped in commercial spaces. He demonstrated that the environment affected not only individual churches but also the contours and textures of the entire local religious field.

I, too, assume that religious ecological forms respond to shifts in the local environment. I recognize, though, that the ecological perspective fails on two counts. First, the ecological metaphor, which casts patterns of urban settlement and land usage as the results of natural processes, obscures the "wizards"—the powerful political and economic actors and institutions—working behind the scenes in the urban Oz. For example, consider the Chicago Black Belt. As Drake and Cayton (1945) astutely observed, the segregated Chicago Black Belt was not a "natural" ethnic enclave but a result of deliberately racist, exclusionary housing practices that kept Blacks from living elsewhere. Nor is Four Corners a "natural area." As I will argue in chapter 3, its depressed economic state, which facilitated its transformation into a religious district, is a result of uneven resource distribution in a municipal system that acknowledges the development needs of certain neighborhoods and ignores those of others.

Second, religious ecology does not consider fully the *voluntary* nature of religious life. The dense religious ecology Drake observed relied not only on the density and diversity of the population and the intense economic depression of certain quarters but also on the ability of people to *choose* which church they would attend. This oversight renders the ecological approach unable to explain neighborhoods like Four Corners, which are not so diverse residentially yet host a great diversity of congregations. People of diverse regional, national, and class backgrounds choose to worship in Four Corners despite the fact that many do not live in the neighborhood.

Religious Voluntarism

The religious voluntarism literature traces the decline of ascriptive religious practices, such as the geographically defined parish, and observes the rise of elective, voluntary forms of adherence that transform congregations into cultural forums for specific social groups (Rowe 1924; Roof and McKinney 1987; Bellah 1985). People tend to "shop" for religious communities that suit their tastes and interests rather than submit to traditions that assign individuals to congregations according to some prior familial, geographical, or denominational affiliation (Wuthnow 1988).

Congregations are becoming what Nancy Ammerman (1997a; see also Warner 1993) calls "particularistic spaces of sociability." This means that people congregate around common ethnicity, gender, social status, sexual orientation, and other dimensions of difference. Territorial identity, however, rarely is the basis for coming together. Thus, churches tend toward de facto congregationalism," where

> the local religious community is in fact constituted by those who assemble together (which is the etymological root of "congregation") rather than by the geographic units into which higher church authorities divide their constituents, which is what "parishes" historically are. (Warner 1993:1066–1067)

In this highly voluntaristic context, uniqueness becomes one of the local church's most precious assets; it is this asset that distinguishes one church from another in what is basically a demand-driven religious market. In such markets, according to organizational ecology theory, organizations compete to corner niches (this kind of niche is not to be confused with the niche church of religious ecology), composed of populations with particular needs and interests (Hannan and Freeman 1977). The most competitive churches, or denominations for that matter, are those that corner the right niche and strike just the right balance between costs demanded from and novel benefits delivered to members. Meanwhile, less impeccable religious organizations fade into obscurity or die.[9] In this model, churches respond not to urban environments but to competition within the religious field itself.

The voluntarism perspective is helpful in making sense of diversity in religious districts old and new. Still, in all its excitement about competition between churches, religious particularism, and personal choices, this perspective neglects the ways *localities* present opportunities for and place constraints on the flowering of religious markets. Although the churches in Four Corners are particularistic spaces of sociability, particularism alone cannot explain why Four Corners became a religious district and not some other neighborhood. It seems that the ecological and voluntarism perspectives can benefit from cross-pollination. Sensitivity to the voluntary aspects of participation can extend the explanatory power of religious ecology. Meanwhile, the place-oriented insights of religious ecology can make voluntarism theory more applicable to local contexts.[10]

How Churches Impact the "Environment"

What both the voluntarism and ecological perspectives fail to consider is how local congregations can alter the urban environment and each other through various modes of "religious presence" (Roozen et al. 1988). Congregations change the environment through the symbols, rituals, ideas, and activities they generate (Wuthnow 1988); this may be acutely true of churches that worship in public spaces or proselytize on front stoops and street corners. Church leaders may also impact city politics by defining and representing local community interests (Hunter 1953; Demerath and Williams 1992). By acting on religious understandings of and attachments to local places, churches can actually reconfigure the urban patchwork quilt of racial and ethnic neighborhoods. As John McGreevy (1996) and Gerald Gamm (1999), respectively, contend, Roman Catholic and Jewish religious organizations have shaped the course of ethnic residential settlement and mobility in major cities. Religious presence may also alter local economies when churches mobilize to build single-family housing (Rooney 1995) or to attract business franchises to their neighborhoods. Such alterations may spur demographic turnover, as when revitalization attracts middle-class Blacks or young White professional couples to a formerly poor, Black neighborhood.

Even a church that intentionally does *nothing* to impact the environment still does so by virtue of its presence. For example, a storefront church by definition occupies a commercial space (indeed, this is the only accurate generalization about storefront churches). If the church were not there, the space would probably lie vacant. Even so, especially if it owns the storefront, the church impacts the locale by reducing the number of spaces available for commercial purposes.

Also, the clergy and congregations in a local community are usually aware of each other, even when they do not formally interact (Ammerman 1997a:360–362; see also Foster and Seidman 1982). They may *actively compete* for resources and develop alliances, antagonisms, and spatial or demographic "turf" (Eiesland 1999). They may also entirely lack relations within a given locale. As I will show in chapter 7, both interaction and noninteraction can impact social organization in neighborhoods. It is important, then, to recognize that congregations do not exist in isolation; other congregations constitute the "environment" as much as residents and physical conditions.

A MAP OF THE BOOK

The next two chapters present a historical view, describing the "patterned sequence" (Abbott 1995) of urban events that gave rise to this religious form. Chapter 2 shows how this characteristically dense, diverse religious environment emerged first not in Four Corners but in the South End and Roxbury during the period of the great migration. Churches, even at this point in history, were "particularistic spaces of sociability," where people congregated according to affinity.

Chapter 3 shifts the focus to the neighborhood of Four Corners. I pick up the story in the 1960s, when Blacks began moving into Dorchester and other previously White parts of the city. The subsequent downward spiral of economic disinvestment, which produced a glut of cheap vacant commercial storefronts, made this a prime area for the emergence of a new religious district. It is significant that most of congregations were assembled around ethnic and class affinity, not shared residential territory. As a result, the churches that moved into these storefronts tended to draw membership from beyond the confines of the neighborhood. This, in addition to the abundance of vacant commercial space, explains how a 0.6-square-mile neighborhood managed to sustain twenty-plus congregations.

I then explore dimensions of difference among churches in Four Corners, for our appreciation of religious choice requires an appreciation of what people have to choose *from*.I focus, nonetheless, on aspects of particularism other than the ethnic or racial composition of congregations; previous studies have highlighted these dimensions of difference to the virtual exclusion of church mission and of the many ways the faithful apply religious ideas to human experiences. Thus, chapters 4–6 trâeat religious ideas themselves and how religious people interpret these ideas to varying consequence.

It is my concern with the content of religious belief and practice that perhaps most distinguishes this book from Drake's. *Churches and Voluntary Associations* considered churches mainly as organizations serving different functions for different populations. *Streets of Glory* certainly is concerned with the organizational dimension of religious life. Even so, I, like anthropologist Clifford Geertz (1973:90), take religions as "cultural systems," whose symbols are arranged and presented in ways that motivate human action, inspire emotion, give order to existence and, for the believer, constitute realities in themselves. Chapter 4, then, explains how migrant churches and immigrant churches used the theme of religious exile to speak to their target populations. By creatively applying religious ideas to project a sense of "peoplehood" and authenticity, churches further elaborated particularisms in the religious district.

Chapter 5 explores another dimension of difference in the district: how churches variously attached religious meaning to the immediate urban environment, or "the street." Churches conceived of "the street" in one of four ways: as an evil other, as a recruitment ground, as the place where the faithful demonstrate their "worldly" concern for persons at risk, or as some combination of the latter two. In each case, the street was more than just a physical place—it was a trope embodying complex assigned meanings. The meanings that church people assigned to the street in turn helped them define what it meant to be religious. By making sense of the immediate urban space, religious people made sense of themselves.

Regardless of how they characterized their immediate environs, nearly all of the clergy felt their churches should leave an indelibly positive imprint on the world and could therefore be called "activist." Still, as chapter 6 explains, churches expressed "activism" in multiple ways, and this multiplicity further distinguished congregations in the religious district. This chapter complicates our understanding of what it means for a church to have social impact. In Chapter 7, I return the analytical focus to the neighborhood of Four Corners. This chapter examines the relationships and ties *among* organizations in order to explain how the religious district impacted social organization in Four Corners and, by extension, the course of neighborhood revitalization.

The concluding chapter revisits and further specifies the religious district concept, elaborating on the two-way model of church-context interaction presented above. It also considers the broader implications of this study. Specifically, I address the budding urban sociological literature on diversity in urban neighborhoods and the challenges diversity poses for neighborhood collective action. I also address the ongoing "civil society" debate and push for a more purpose-oriented, place-sensitive understanding of how civil society actually functions. Finally, I discuss the implications of the study for social policy, which has become quite church-friendly but tends to lack awareness of the actual behaviors and orientations of churches in depressed urban areas.

TWO

Birth of the Black Religious District

The Great Migration brought about changes in the religious
landscape of the urban North far beyond the expansion, proliferation,
and relocation of existing churches and the efforts of national
denominations and local congregations to respond to the new institutional
demands placed upon them. Uprooted but not without roots,
the migrants brought cultural gifts, though an appreciation of
this religious treasure was not always evident. By the end
of the Great Migration era African American religious culture
in northern cities was much more diverse and resistant to easy
generalization than at the end of the nineteenth century.
—Sernett 1997:180

Reverend Robert Jameson, founder and pastor of the Church of the Holy Ghost in Four Corners, arrived in Boston from South Carolina in 1954. He had left the South in search of work—his older brother had already found plentiful employment as a laborer in Boston. Jameson settled in a Lower Roxbury apartment not far from where his brother lived. He immediately noticed that here, "there were lots of little storefronts." Having found Pentecostal religion in South Carolina, Jameson set out among the many storefronts to find a new church home, only to find himself bewildered by the sheer range of choices. His brother eventually pulled him into one of the three Church of God in Christ congregations in the South End. The church was composed almost entirely of Black migrants like himself.

Reverend Jameson's story is not unusual. It resembles the experiences of millions of Black Southerners who, between the end of the Civil War and the end of the Second World War, set out for Boston and other northern centers in search of a higher standard of living and a reprieve from the relentless, often violent racial repression of the South. Especially telling, though, is Jameson's impression of religious life in 1950s Black Boston. Like him, many migrants were used to a more sparse and homogeneous religious landscape. Those migrants arriving at the close of the Second World War must have been especially amazed at the panoply of religious organizations that lined the major arteries of Black Boston.

Jameson's recollections indicate that the "religious district" is not unique to Four Corners in Boston history. Instead, as I will argue in this chapter, the template for the contemporary religious district, with its high concentration of churches characterized by their shifting, percolating particularisms and

16

their handiness with untraditional (especially commercial) worship spaces, has its origins in early twentieth-century Black Boston. It emerged in direct response to the Black population, which was being transfigured numerically, socially, and spatially by the great migration. As the Black population grew more diverse and more concentrated in space, more churches appeared, each appealing to a certain social group. In other words, religious particularism grew more refined as churches multiplied within the Black area.

The chapter contains four sections. The first section explains how the great migration, coupled with severely restricted housing opportunities, created a dense, fairly contiguous Black residential area: the Boston Black Belt. The second section describes the social diversity that developed within this dense Black area. Diversity emerged along two dimensions: socioeconomic class and place of origin. The third section shows how the density and diversity of the Black population gave rise to a dense, diverse "religious district." I first chart the proliferation of churches in the Black Belt and then explore the major dimensions of difference, of particularism, among these churches. As I will argue in the chapter's conclusion, the sociohistorical process uncovered here illuminates an important point of contact between the notion of religious particularism and sociological theorizing on the nature of urban subcultures.

GEOGRAPHIC SHIFT AND CONSOLIDATION

Between the Civil War and the turn of the century, Boston was one of the top migrant destinations in the urban North. By 1900, migration had increased the number of Blacks in the city to 11,591, nearly fivefold the number in 1865. Blacks were 2.1 percent of Boston's population in 1900; only in Philadelphia did Blacks constitute a larger portion (4.8 percent) of a major city's population (Thernstrom 1973:179).[1] After 1900, though, Boston would never be as popular a destination point as cities like New York, Chicago, and Detroit. Between 1910 and 1930, Boston's Black population grew by little more than half. Meanwhile, Detroit registered a staggering gain of 1900 percent; Cleveland, 800 percent; Chicago, 430 percent; New York, 250 percent;, and Philadelphia, 160 percent (Thernstrom 1973:180; see table 1). Until around 1890, Boston Blacks were concentrated in Ward 9 of the West End, an area known to its residents as Beacon Hill and to many white nonresidents as "Nigger Hill."

The Black West End materialized and persisted as a matter of proximity to work. Before the Civil War many Black Bostonians worked as domestic laborers for wealthy whites and resided in servants' quarters behind the great mansions on the Hill. Later, as moneyed Whites fled the core city for newer

Table 1   Growth of the Black Population of Boston, 1900–1970

Year	Population	Percent Increase	Percent of City Population
1900	11,591	43	2.1
1910	13,564	17	2.0
1920	16,350	20	2.2
1930	20,574	26	2.6
1940	23,679	15	3.1
1950	40,157	70	5.0
1960	63,165	57	9.1
1970	104,596	66	16.3

Adapted from Thernstrom (1973:179) table 8.1. Data are from the U.S. Census, 1900–1970.

housing stock in streetcar suburbs (Warner 1976), Black people, including some southern migrants, remained in the West End for its access to nearby docks and food markets. Here, in formerly White-owned mansions also lived a portion of the Black elite. The other portion, the highly educated "Black Brahmins," lived and worshiped among whites as a matter of principle. The West End hosted all five of Boston's Black churches: First Baptist (originally the First African Meeting House), North Russell A. M. E. (African Methodist Episcopal) Zion, Union United Methodist, Twelfth Baptist, and Charles Street A. M. E.

As the Black population grew, the geographic center of sacred and secular Black life shifted from the West End to areas further south. In 1904, only 3,000 of 11,591 Blacks lived in the West End. Five thousand Blacks lived in the South End, and the remainder resided in Lower Roxbury and elsewhere (*Colored American* 1904). In 1910, only 1,500 Blacks remained in the West End, and 7,000 lived in a predominantly Black quarter of the South End (Daniels 1914; see map 2). By the opening of the First World War, the South End had become the center of Boston's Black community (map 3). Here, according to an article in *Our Boston,* a magazine published by the Women's Municipal League of Boston, is where the first "colored" business district developed "between Northampton and Ruggles Streets, chiefly on Tremont St. . . . It is here that there are established not only the businesses, but most of the churches, and social welfare organizations" (Ridley 1927: 17–18). The article also depicts the South End as the seat of Black poverty, and "although on its fringe, and often within its border, live many leaders—doctors, ministers, lawyers, etc." (18). What accounted for this shift? Migrants were settling disproportionately in the South End, convenient as it was to the hotels and railroads where many Black newcomers worked (Pleck 1979:77). Meanwhile, Blacks who could afford to do so were abandoning the rapidly dilapidating housing of the West End for more desirable lodging in Lower Roxbury and the South End.

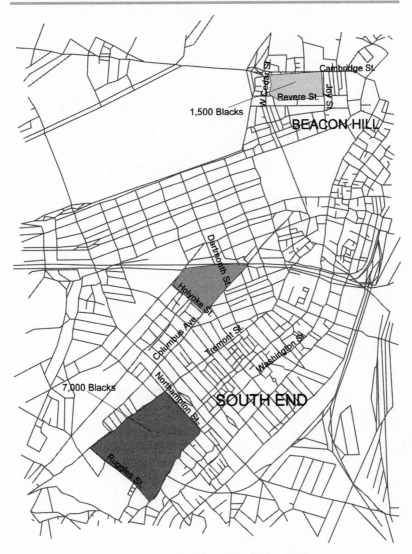

Map 2 Centers of Black Residential Life in 1910
as described by John Daniels (1914)

The new Black residential area did not grow without limit. A de facto program of Black containment effectively denied Blacks free access to neighborhoods other than the South End and Lower Roxbury (Daniels 1914:153).
Black existence thus became not only more segregated but also more concentrated in space: while the Black residential area had expanded, containment kept it from expanding enough to keep up with Black population

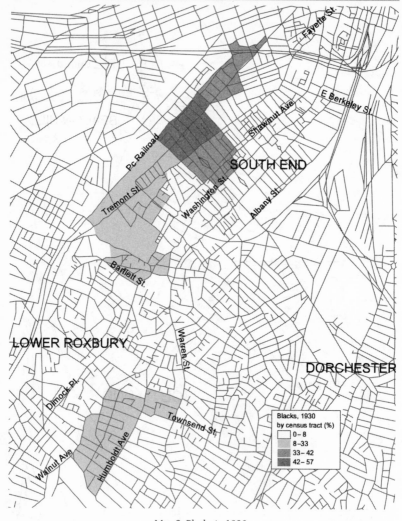

Map 3 Blacks in 1930

growth. Boston's residential segregation never reached the proportions it did in other northern cities. A few Black families always managed to secure homes in Brookline, Dorchester, Upper Roxbury, and the suburbs. Nevertheless, de facto segregation ensured that the bulk of the swelling Black community, including its middle and upper classes, would remain concentrated in a small, overcrowded portion of the city through the 1950s, when "block-busting" real estate practices and urban renewal, respectively, allowed, then forced Blacks to explode their narrow confines (map 4).

SOCIAL DIVERSITY IN POSTMIGRATION BLACK BOSTON

As Blacks grew more numerous and began to take up more space in the city, charitable White liberals, used to a smaller, more manageable Black community, grew indifferent to the Black predicament. White retraction "left the Negro superficially enjoying great freedom but slowly and surely experiencing alarm over growing restrictions" (Cromwell 1994:72). Blacks faced no discrimination on public transportation or in theaters yet found it difficult to

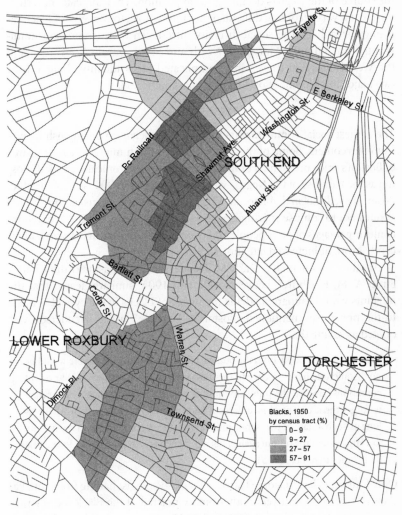

Map 4 Blacks in 1950

establish a foothold in the professions. An insidious White taste for segregated accommodations made it increasingly difficult for Blacks to secure adequate housing and hotel rooms. Meanwhile, the geographic expansion of the Black population, fed by the continual influx of migrants and immigrants, loosened their political foothold in the West End.

The sudden shift in racial climate, coupled with increasingly visible Black poverty, unemployment, disease, and overcrowding, occasioned the first attempts to classify Black Bostonians according to social and economic status. Invariably, these social taxonomies aimed to locate within the Black populace the source of the Negro's declining social position. They indicate, nevertheless, that it was becoming difficult, if not impossible, to conceive of Blacks as a singular public. The social diversity introduced by migrants and immigrants from Virginia, Maryland, North and South Carolina, Georgia, and the West Indies had irreversibly complicated Black identity along at least two major lines: point of origin and socioeconomic class.

Place of Origin

The earliest social commentators thought it sufficient to distinguish natives from newcomers. Some of these identified southern migrants as the source of Boston's "race problem." For instance, in an article ironically entitled "Boston as the Paradise of the Negro," which appeared in a 1904 issue of the elite, Boston-based *Colored American Magazine,* the anonymous author urged Whites not to confuse striving Blacks with "lower types" (a double entendre conjuring images of poor people and people of southern origin) who had recently brought increased attention to Blacks as a group.

Another commentator, Dr. J. M. Henderson, who pastored the Charles Street A. M. E. Church between 1900 and 1905, similarly feared that the migrants would irreparably defile the image of Blacks in the eyes of Whites. In the previously mentioned "Boston as Paradise" article, Henderson was quoted as saying that

> had no colored people from the outside come to New England, there would be no disquietude here . . . An evil that has come about in Boston is that present conditions have led the public to think of colored people as a race rather than to forget the accident of race descent and to think only of the individual. As long as such a state of the public mind exists, the best colored man must share to a large extent the odium against his race which is provoked by the lower type that comes to notice. (315)

Only four years later, George Harris, a Black sociologist hailing from Topeka, Kansas, would present yet another binary portrait of the Black social structure (Harris 1908). Nevertheless, unlike Henderson, who decried the tarnished reputation of the native, Harris celebrated the upward struggle of the newcomer.[2] He also speculated that the native Black elite was being overtaken by thrifty, hard-working migrants.

Journalistic slants aside, native Bostonians had indeed become a minority of the Black population. Indeed, as early as 1870 native Massachusetts Blacks made up only 37 percent of Boston's Black population. The remaining 63 percent were composed of southern migrants (38 percent), arrivals from other U.S. states including the Midwest (14 percent), and foreign immigrants (11 percent). By 1900, the proportion of Boston Blacks actually born in the state had fallen to 25 percent. The proportion rose steadily after this low point, although much of the increase can be attributed to the offspring migrant and immigrant families (Thernstrom 1973:181; see table 2).

It was not until 1914 that attention to Black foreigners entered the analysis of Black points of origin. Most of the Black immigrants were from the British West Indies, especially Jamaica and Barbados. A smaller contingent of immigrants hailed from Nova Scotia and New Brunswick, both Canadian territories to which enslaved Blacks had escaped decades earlier via the underground railroad; and Cape Verde, then a Portuguese territory off the west coast of Africa. By 1940, according to the U.S. Census, 11.3 percent of Black Bostonians were immigrants (cited in Cromwell 1994:73).

Socioeconomic Class

Sociologist John Daniels produced the most nuanced take on the emerging Black class structure. His 1914 work, *In Freedom's Birthplace*, a treatise on Black Boston indubitably patterned after Dubois's 1899 *Philadelphia Negro*,[3] delineates no less than five socioeconomic classes. At the "bottom of the scale," Daniels wrote, were a "devious," "shiftless" lower class. This group, representing 10 percent of the population, "live generally in questionable

Table 2   Nativity (Percent) of Boston Black Population, 1900–1970

Year	Place of Birth			
	Massachusetts	South	Other U.S.	Foreign
1900	25	53	12	10
1910	29	n.a.	n.a.	13
1920	30	n.a.	n.a.	18
1930	38	37	9	16
1960	43	n.a.	n.a.	8
1970	49	29	16	6

Adapted from Thernstrom (1973:181), table 8.3. Data on 1900 are from Daniels (1914: 468–469). Data on 1910, 1920, and 1930 are from the U.S. Bureau of the Census (1935: 32, 74, 75, 216–218); *Negroes in the United States, 1920–1932*. Figures on 1960 and 1970 are from Massachusetts *Population* volumes of the 1960 and 1970 Censuses.

lodging-house sections in the downtown parts of the city" (175). Distinct from this lumpenproletariat was the "rank-and-file, the common people," who made up 70 percent of Black Bostonians. These were the hotel workers and janitors, the domestic servants and porters. Cromwell, applying the terminology of Warner and Lunt (1949), describes this group as the "upper-lower" and "lower-middle" classes. This population in turn passed into a solid middle class, making up approximately 18 percent. The middle class was itself composed of three substrata: a lower stratum of financially secure waiters, janitors, porters, and artisans; a middle stratum of clerical employees, small businessmen, and "the minor professional element"; and a home-owning upper stratum of higher-salaried employees, important business proprietors, and leading professionals.

Finally, there was the Black upper class, among which could be found a truly elite set and a "smart set" of poseurs. "Smart set," as Daniels describes with amusement, refers to "an excrescence growing out of the several classes which have been noted. There are a host of Negroes who labor to create an impression of superiority by dressing far beyond their means and by attempting to assume the ways of culture . . . Many a Negro, who sports a silk hat and stick on Sunday 'totes' quarters of beef in the market on Monday" (180). Daniels was at pains to distinguish this charlatan elite from the genuine article upper class, which was "made up of lawyers, physicians, business proprietors, literary and musical people, and the like who are distinguished by superior education and refinement. This class comprises the remaining small quota of two percent of the Negro population" (181).

Daniels also attempted a cross-classification of Blacks by place of origin and class. "Not all, but the larger number of [elite] members are of Northern birth or long Northern residents, have a considerable strain of White blood and are of light complexion" (Daniels 1914:181). Southern migrants, by contrast, made up the majority of the lower classes, with limited representation among middle-class merchants. Immigrants from the West Indies were a unique case. Like Blacks born in the United States, West Indians faced racial discrimination in Boston and other northern cities, making it difficult to infiltrate the trades and labor unions. Unlike their migrant counterparts, however, West Indians often arrived preeducated and preapprenticed in the trades. For this reason, he explained, West Indians clustered primarily in the middle classes.

Accounts from the early twentieth century thus testify that the waves of migration and immigration that swept Boston in the early part of the twentieth century not only augmented but complicated the Black population. Immigrants and southern migrants supplanted natives, thereby raising the question of whether the latter constituted the "real" Black Boston. Meanwhile, a complex class structure developed among laborers, entrepreneurs, professionals, and the chronically unemployed. The Black residential area that crystallized during the great migration was therefore not only densely populated but diversely populated. It is from this spatially compact and socially complex Black milieu that the religious district emerged.

UNDER THEIR OWN VINE AND FIG TREE: THE ELABORATION OF RELIGIOUS PARTICULARISM

Of Black Boston in the first half of the twentieth century, Cromwell writes, "The effects on the Negro structure of other Negroes who differ from the natives in speech, in attitudes toward the White world, often in religion, and frequently also in patterns of behavior and class naturally have been divisive" (1994:73). Such division became evident as Black civil society grew more complex. The early 1900s witnessed a boom in voluntary associations, each attempting to carve a niche in the Black social scene. In his autobiography, Walter J. Stevens (1946), a Black Brahmin who described himself only as "an old Bostonian," described a Black social terrain speckled with social clubs often segregated by regional origin and social status. If migrants had their Florida and Virginia clubs, Brahmins had their Society of the Descendants of Early New England Negroes. Many clubs were gender-specific, with some wearing "the mantle of masculine social superiority" (Cromwell 1994:75), and others, like the elite Women's Era Club, seeking "'to awaken in our women an active interest in the events of the day and giving to them through such an organization an opportunity of hearing and participating in the discussion of current topics'" (78). Churches were critical to this boom, for they too provided social havens for Blacks of particular class, regional, and national backgrounds.

It is not surprising that as the Black population grew and diversified, the demand for churches grew as well. Between 1910 and 1950, just after the close of the Second World War, the number of Black churches rose from fifteen to more than fifty.[4] Most of the religious district stretched along Tremont and Shawmut Streets, the two major commercial thoroughfares in the Black Belt (maps 5–7). The churches in the district represented a far greater number of religious traditions than could have been found in Black Boston at the turn of the century. In 1900, there were only Baptist, Methodist, Episcopalian, and Congregationalist churches; in 1950, there were at least thirteen different kinds of churches, the largest group of which belonged to the Holiness-Pentecostal-Apostolic constellation. Only Baptist churches came close to keeping up with these newer religious groups, mainly because migrants, mostly Baptist themselves, were establishing southern-style Baptist enclaves.

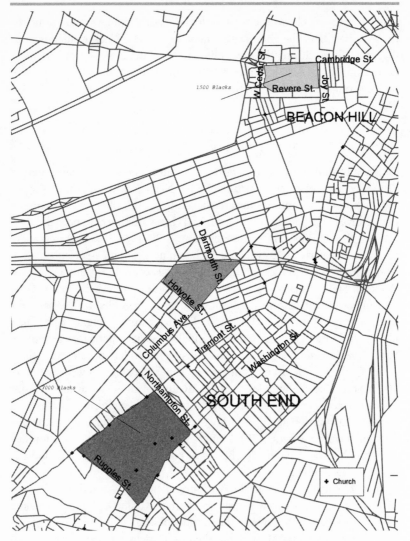

Map 5 Centers of Black Residential Life in 1910 as described by
John Daniels (1914) with Churches

By midcentury the number and variety of churches in the Black Belt was
so impressive that H. Paul Douglass (1944), in a commissioned report on
mainline mission activity in Boston, could offer only the vaguest speculations
about the vast majority of Black churches in the South End and Roxbury. His
treatment of the South End included twenty-two churches, but only four of
these were "Negro," because "most of the Negro churches are of a somewhat
impermanent sort. They have never been adequately studied and are not in-

cluded in the list" (27). In Roxbury, Douglass studied thirty-six churches, "[s]even of which are Negro, but the list entirely fails to enumerate the great multitude of the Negro store front churches representing the more or less irregular sects" (31).

The number of persons in the ministerial profession also increased dramatically. Boyd (1998:325) reports that between 1900 and 1920 the number of professional clergy (as recorded in federal censuses) rose from 13 to 25. Thus, while the Black population increased by only 41 percent during

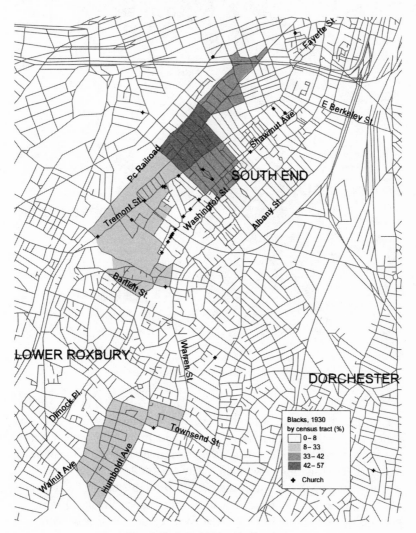

Map 6 Blacks in 1930, with Churches

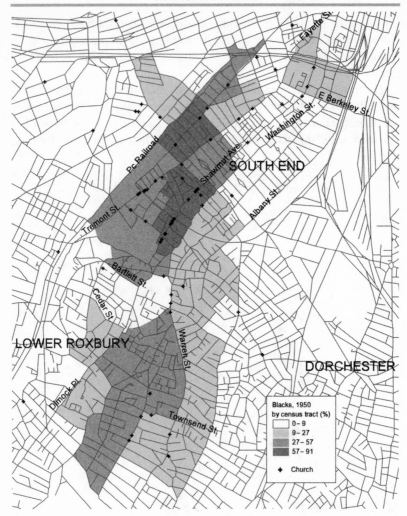

Map 7 Blacks in 1950, with Churches

the period in question, the number of ministers increased by 92 percent. Meanwhile, the Black clerical pool expanded comparatively more in Boston than in most other major migrant destinations. In order to compare cities, Boyd constructed an index relating the proportion of Blacks in the ministry to that of Blacks in the city workforce. Between 1900 and 1920, Boston's index increased by 0.55. Out of the twelve northern cities in Boyd's study, Boston registered the fifth largest increase, even though it ranked last in proportional growth of the Black population. (Detroit ranked first, with a 73 minister increase and a 1 point change in index).

The disproportionate growth of the ministerial profession in Boston probably reflected a demand for different kinds of churches more than a simple desire for more churches. Churches and clergy multiplied during the great migration in order to satisfy a newly expanded range of spiritual and social needs. In other words, churches not only grew more numerous but more particularistic in terms of the range of social groups they targeted. The postmigration and postimmigration Black religious landscape in Boston offered a panoply of decidedly southern, northern, West Indian, elite, and poor churches—not to mention churches representing an array of political and ecclesiastic tendencies. In short, when it came to congregations and denominations, the various Black social groups lived "every man under his vine and his fig tree" (1 Kings 4: 25; an irony of the anachronistic "man" and "his" in this passage is that the majority of Black churchgoers were, and still are, women). One could no longer speak of a singular "Black church" as such, just as it had become difficult to locate a seamless Black public. The next section traces the contours of this pluralistic "Black church." I describe the three major kinds of particularistic churches: those of northern Blacks, migrants, and West Indians.

Old Churches of Northern Blacks

To be certain, migrants and immigrants did not introduce religious particularism to Boston; rather, they refined it exponentially. The secession of Black communicants from White congregations in the early nineteenth century reflected a yearning among Black Bostonians for racially homogeneous religious spaces free of the indignities, such as segregated seating and the denial of voting rights, that accompanied worship with Whites. In 1805, Black Baptists withdrew their memberships from two major White congregations to form the African Meeting House, the first Black church in Boston. In 1818, Black Methodists followed suit and formed the Union United Methodist Church. By 1900, Black churches themselves reflected considerable social and political diversity, thus elaborating a religious particularism initially based solely on race and denomination. This diversity grew in part out of the churches' roles as public spheres (Higginbotham 1993) where people formulated and debated opinions on race advancement. Churches had long been pivotal organizing centers for Black Bostonians. The nineteenth-century abolition struggle, which earned Boston its liberal reputation, was based in churches. Even after the arrival of the secular NAACP and Urban League in 1910 and 1919, respectively, churches and clergy continued to weigh in on race issues. Rather than resolving political differences internally, however, public sphere churches were amoebalike: they were prone to split over the contentious politics of slavery and over the relative strategic merits of protest and accommodation, integration and separation. The African Meeting House itself underwent mitosis in 1840 following an internal dispute most likely over the church's role in the abolition movement (Hayden 1983). The products of that split, People's Baptist and Twelfth Baptist, survive to this day.

As the great migration ensued and the Black population settled new parts of the city, these older churches faced the familiar predicament described in religious ecological studies of congregational change. With the bulk of their members moving to the South End and Lower Roxbury, old churches could either remain in one place and pray for their members to return for worship, reach out to new populations, follow old members to new locales, or enact some combination thereof.

Only one church chose the first option: Charles Street A. M. E. As most of its membership left the West End, Charles Street became Boston's first Black commuter church, or niche church, in the religious ecological sense of a congregation that relinquishes its parish identity and attempts to draw members from all over a metropolis. "When I assumed charge of Charles Street Church," wrote Reverdy Ransom in 1930, "there were not more than a score of families of our group living in the West End. To get to my church it was necessary for most of my congregation to pass by every colored church in Boston to reach it" (1930:151). For three decades the church fought to retain its membership and in the thirties even sent busses around to Roxbury and the South End on Sunday mornings to pick up members. Only in 1939 did the church finally give in and build a church in the South End. Charles Street would be the last Black institution to leave Beacon Hill.

Most churches took the third route, moving to those sections of the Black Belt that they felt would give them the greatest access to the particular people they were used to serving. I emphasize "sections" by way of complicating the traditional religious ecological perspective, which might take the entire Black Belt (it was, after all, Black) to have been a seamless, homogeneous ethnic enclave, ready to accommodate a couple of large Black churches. Yet the Lower Roxbury and southernmost South End of "gilded palaces" clearly was a different species than the depressed South End, closer to Boston's downtown, whose tenements "were overcrowded three- and four-story wooden and brick buildings, housing eight families in what had been a comfortable dwelling for one" (Pleck 1979:79). Churches that relocated from the West End understood as much. In an attempt to hold on to their particularistic northern membership, they moved with calculated savvy into those sections of the Black Belt that would grant them access to the populations they intended to target.

Thus writes the Black Brahmin and West End native Walter J. Stevens: "It didn't take long before the Twelfth Baptist Church was gone from its original place on Phillips Street where it had always drawn such large crowds to worship" (1946:84). Twelfth Baptist in fact moved to the corner of Shawmut Avenue and Madison Street in Lower Roxbury, where 85 percent of its elite membership had moved by the early 1900s (Hayden 1983:30). Likewise, First Baptist moved to the corner of Camden and Tremont in Lower Roxbury in 1898.

In one case, a church relocation actually spurred Blacks to settle a new residential area, rather than the other way around (Hayden 1983). From its 1895 founding in the South End, St. Mark's Congregational was an influential liberal forum and a haven of the intellectual elite. In its role as public sphere, St. Mark's operated a very popular musical and literary union. Organized in 1902, the union's stated objective was, innocuously enough, "the moral and intellectual improvement of the community." In practice, though, the union's activities were hardly so neutral. In its early years the union revealed its civil rights slant by inviting speakers such as W. E. B. Dubois and Mrs. William Monroe Trotter, wife of the political activist and publisher of the radical civil rights organ, the *Boston Guardian*. Indeed, due to its potential influence on elite opinion, the political thrust of the union itself became an object of hot contestation. In 1908, when the union was usurped by more accommodationist leadership, George Harris remarked with characteristic ire that "such literary organizations as the St. Mark's Literary, now under the leadership of the square and thoughtful Mr. William Rahn, formerly rife with the declarations and hubbub of the mal-contents and hot-heads, now conduct sane, helpful and deliberate discussions on all subjects" (Harris 1908).

In the spirit of particularism, St. Mark's was partial to a certain population and actually used its public activities to attract prized constituencies. Union event announcements proclaimed, of course, that "meetings are open to everybody." Yet, at least until the depression, union activities were targeted at educated young socialites and the children of Boston's Black elite. Adelaide Cromwell (1994) speculates that a primary function of the union and similar clubs was "to provide a much-needed liaison between the Negro elite and the Boston area's transient student population. These organizations' regular forums became meeting places for the Negro town-and-gown elements and set up associational ties that often endured through the years" (80). In this way, the church's public activities were intended not only to uplift the race but also to attract specific Black populations into church life.

The church furthered its particularistic aims when it apparently anticipated the movement of Blacks into Upper Roxbury. In reality, the church would initiate the movement. In 1926, the church purchased a Quaker worship house in the still White area and slowly built a Black community around itself by encouraging its members to make the move as well. In this way,

St. Mark's used a parish ethic to create an elite Black enclave in Upper Roxbury (Hayden 1983; Gamm 1999).

As migration altered the cultural and geographic face of the Black populace, not all of the oldest churches would remain havens of northern-born Blacks. After the post–Civil War wave of migration, several long-established churches found themselves swamped by southern communicants. Two of these churches, North Russell A. M. E. Zion and Union United Methodist, had always fancied themselves as missionary institutions, and made the southern newcomers the focus of a new, migrant particularism. They left the West End in 1902 and 1911, respectively, but relocated not to Lower Roxbury or the gilded South End but among the migrants in that South End known for tenements and tuberculosis.

Most of the older churches did not adapt so easily, preferring instead to hold on to familiar, northern patterns of worship and membership. In her study of Black migration to Boston between 1865 and 1900, Elizabeth Pleck (1979) revealed that two elite churches, Charles Street A. M. E. and Twelfth Baptist, had memberships that were more than 50 percent southern. Churches such as these found it difficult to appease both populations, for the intimate, demonstrative worship style that appealed to Southerners tended to ruffle Northerners, and the relatively decorous and anonymous northern religious style often bored, if not alienated, Southerners. Southerners, if welcomed, might fill pews to the brim; welcoming them, however, might introduce a cultural flavor unsavory to the Northern elites who had long ago helped build the churches. Both Charles Street and Twelfth Baptist would attempt to appease northern members. In order to supplement the elite, educated core of the Charles Street congregation, Reverdy Ransom, pastor of the church from 1905 to 1907, took to setting aside a special pew for area college students, not all of whom were Black:

> I selected a well-placed pew in the auditorium of Charles Street Church, and reserved it for students from Harvard and Boston Universities. It was generally well filled each Sunday morning, sometimes to overflowing, with students from these schools, both white and colored, quite frequently with a Japanese, a Hindu, or a Chinaman added for good measure.

The presence of the young elites helped preserve the decorum of the church not only by their example but by giving Ransom a reason to continue in the cranial style of ministry favored by educated Northerners:

> The presence of these young men in my congregation acted as a great stimulant to me in the range and substance of my sermons. The eagerness with which they frequently surrounded me at the close of the service and sought

advice and counsel, and also plied me with many questions, kept me constantly on the alert. (Ransom 1930:153)

Likewise, Twelfth Baptist resisted the relaxation of rigid liturgical norms well into the twentieth century. Recalls John White, a third-generation member of the church:

> You never clapped if there was any sort of good music . . . you waved your handkerchief. Things were very reverent . . . young people had to follow rules and regulations. That was the church . . . Very few people even said "Amen" except the deacons who had the "Amen corner" up front. And they never dispensed with those seats. It was sacrilegious to sit up there. (Hayden 1983:31)

Clergy who succumbed to the preferences of southern worshipers risked mutiny. St. Paul's Baptist, not included in Pleck's list of northern churches with southern majorities, was one place where the reluctant introduction of emotive southern styles resulted in heated controversy. St. Paul's is one of several Boston churches that can trace its origin to the First African Baptist Church, founded by Black New Englanders in 1805. Until the first awesome wave of southern migrants hit Boston after the Civil War, St. Paul's was a refuge for Black New Englanders of Baptist persuasion. By the time the wave abated, around 1900, the church contained a critical mass of Southerners, who apparently were used to a livelier Baptist liturgy. Internal tension over the fate of this historic refuge reached a head in 1902, when the deacon board of St. Paul's ousted its recently installed pastor, Simon P. W. Drew. The debacle, elevated to scandalous proportions in the *Boston Globe,* resulted partly from a dispute over church finances but also from Drew's penchant for preaching "in a southern revival style." This style, according to the *Globe,* "often aroused his congregation to such a pitch of enthusiasm that they vented their feelings in weird howls" (*Boston Globe,* June 15, 1902).

Migrant Churches

The fact that some native Bostonian churches early on managed to attract so many Southerners would seem to imply that regional contrasts were not so important. Yet it is well documented that in other cities these contrasts caused considerable tension within churches and often spurred Southerners to start their own congregations. In this way, Southerners further diversified, or further particularized, the religious landscape. Sernett, writing about Chicago, contends that the diversification of the religious landscape

> was in large part brought about by the religious preference of migrants from the South and by attempts of the mainline churches to reach out to them. Many migrants found it difficult to adjust from the southern religious ethos to that

of the large city churches . . . While we should not exaggerate the cultural differences between migrants and Chicago's established black churches, they are important for understanding why some newcomers sought to organize their own congregations or felt like spectators rather than family in the established churches. (1994:162)

Even Pleck ultimately observes that Southerners in Boston, despite their heavy early involvement with indigenous Baptist and A. M. E. churches, tended toward "institutional completeness" (Breton 1964); that is, migrants created homogeneous spaces where distinctive group needs, including spiritual, material, and social ones, could be met. Institutional completeness was made possible by extensive family and friendship networks, which pulled migrants northward in chainlike fashion, then introduced them to widening communities of Southerners in Boston. Pleck describes this process:

> In the initial stages of chain migration migrants simply relied on friends and relatives and on informal patterns of visiting in neighborhoods. After a few years businesses were established (pool halls, gyms, taverns, even brothels) that served a migrant clientele. The migrants founded a church and affiliated with already established black churches and lodges . . . Because black migrants from the South created a separate institutional life as well as an informal network of association, they were less likely to have white friends, to belong to white organizations, or to intermarry. For the same reasons, their contacts with blacks born outside the South were limited. (84–85)

Thus, migrants not only attended established Black churches but also organized many of their own in order to invoke familiar modes of worship and facilitate mutual support. As migrants established more and more churches, recent arrivals found that they literally could "shop" for the right spiritual home. Boston, like Sernett's Chicago, "offered migrants a far greater choice in religious affiliation than did the South where most churchgoing African Americans were either Baptists or Methodists. After settling in . . . newcomers could shop around for a church in which they felt comfortable" (1994:161). Shoppers lacking familial or friendship connections to existing churches needed only to stroll the Black quarter, especially along Shawmut and Tremont Streets, where such churches were appearing with great frequency in commercial storefronts. If that approach failed, newcomers could simply peruse a Black newspaper. A few southern-style churches advertised in the religion sections of the *Guardian* and *Chronicle,* Boston's primary Black news organs, next to the most popular northern churches. Embedded in these ads were peculiar codewords and catchphrases, which would tip off fellow Southerners in search of a familiar church flavor. For example, a Church of God in Christ (a Pentecostal body not to be confused with the Church of God and Saints of Christ [CGSC]) advertised a "down home revival." More subtly, another church described itself as "homelike."

The earliest migrant churches were Baptist, as were the bulk of migrants themselves. Yet, as Dorothy West (1948) dramatized in her novel *The Living Is Easy*, tensions between southern and northern ways emerged even among Baptists of southern origin. In the following passage, Bart, a successful banana merchant, Southerner, and "shouting Baptist," is miffed by the curious religious preferences of his wife Cleo, a Southerner with Brahmin pretensions:

> He rarely went to the South End church of his faith because Cleo would never go with him. The congregation was largely composed of transplanted Southerners, hard-working simple worshipers, who broadly hinted, to Bart's embarrassment, that his wife considered herself too good for them. He was a shouting Baptist, and Cleo thoroughly disapproved. She had never felt the spirit, and he supposed she never would. Her Episcopalian friends were persuading her to their wishy-washy way of worship. They really believed you could get to heaven without any shouting. (64)

A similar conflict emerged within the first entirely migrant congregation to appear in Boston after the Civil War. Ebenezer Baptist began in 1868 as a prayer meeting in the kitchen of Mrs. Martha Jones, a South End resident of Ottawa Court. All of the original members were formerly enslaved Virginians (and one North Carolinian), who had come to Boston to find work as porters, domestic servants, laborers, waiters, and janitors. Services among the Ebenezerites were jubilant affairs—as one early member described: "We come together to sing the praises to the Lord, and to Jesus Christ, his son, who came to do us good and to save us, and then we feel so thankful, that we sing the tunes pretty loud, and the 'glory to God' comes out very full and strong." Apparently the worship was so "full and strong" that urbanized Blacks began referring to the church as "the Jay Bird Tabernacle" (Massachusetts, Bureau of Statistics of Labor 1870:180–181).

Ebenezer acquired formal church status in 1871, when it began renting a hall on Washington Street for $37.50 per month. Later, as the church grew popular among migrants and their children, the congregation purchased a large brick edifice, abandoned by fleeing White Presbyterians, which seated three hundred persons. Its first pastor was the Reverend Peter Randolph, a former Virginian who had arrived in Boston in 1847. The founding members of the Ebenezer community undoubtedly saw in Randolph both familiarity and opportunity: a surefire recipe for institutional completeness. He was clearly from "down home"; yet he also could read and write, was an ordained Baptist minister, had helped fellow Virginians find jobs and education in

Boston, and had earned a reputation as a distinguished orator on the anti-slavery lecture circuit. While Randolph did intend to ameliorate the plight of his congregants, he had no intention of using the church to preserve southern ways. In his autobiography, Randolph painfully recalled one of his early services at Ebenezer: "[T]he meeting carried on till a late hour, the groaning and shouting, the getting happy, and falling over benches" (Randolph 1893:107).

It seems that Randolph, in accepting the pastorate at Ebenezer, had in mind an objective somewhat at odds with his church: to reform "emotional" Black religion as part of a larger crusade to acclimate southern Blacks to life in the cold, industrial North. Although he had originated in Virginia, Randolph had been weaned in Boston's first Black religious stronghold, the First African Baptist Church, where services lacked the vigor of Baptist worship in the South. He was ordained at the Twelfth Baptist Church, known as the home of an especially staid liturgy. Thus, due to its choice of pastor, this earliest of southern particularistic churches ironically became the site of yet another clash between native and migrant sensibilities.

As Ebenezer grew into a veritable migrant magnet, attracting people not only from Virginia but from other states in the South as well, Randolph was compelled to add another mission to his crusade. In addition to extinguishing religious emotionalism, which he feared would exclude Southerners from the mainstream of northern Black life, Randolph hoped to squash the seeds of difference among Southerners themselves. Of migrant religion, Randolph observed that

> those who came from Virginia had their ideas as to how a church should be conducted, and likewise, those who came from North Carolina, Alabama, Georgia, or Florida, had theirs also. Each different set wanted their kind of a preacher, and the majority usually carried the day . . . the remedy for this babel state of affairs will come through the intelligent, educated ministry, which shall enlighten the people, and bring them up to the correct standard, and not appeal to their ignorant methods inherited from slavery. (1893:114)

If not suppressed, such differences threatened to produce an even more refined religious particularism wherein dozens of churches would materialize, each appealing to the religious tastes of people from particular southern states.

Especially during and after the Second World War, dozens of churches did indeed materialize, although not appealing solely to the believer's state of origin. Unlike Ebenezer, though, few of these congregations sought out pastors ordained in existing northern churches. It was more common for a church to "import" its pastor from the South or for religious leadership to emerge directly from a congregation that had recently split off of some other church. Also, many of the new churches permanently inhabited nontraditional spaces. Ebenezer viewed its rented hall as temporary quarters, which would suffice only until a "real" church building could be secured for the swelling congregation. But as the great migration progressed, available religious edifices grew rare. The edifices left by Whites in exodus from the core city were too few and far between to accommodate the number and variety of Black churches waiting to be born. Many of these structures had been purchased around the turn of the century as Black people first began to infiltrate the South End and Roxbury. Meanwhile, building costs were high. It soon became normal to hold church in unconventional spaces, including houses, rented halls, and especially commercial storefronts. Churches became permanent fixtures between drugstores and restaurants along commercial strips in the South End and Roxbury.

Although the first southern particularistic churches were Baptist, these were soon outpaced by churches belonging to the Holiness-Pentecostal-Apostolic family of faiths: a family often referred to as "sanctified." As Cheryl J. Sanders explains, the sanctified church emerged

> as a segment of the black church that arose in the late nineteenth and early twentieth centuries, beginning at the end of Reconstruction, in response to and largely in conflict with postbellum changes in worship traditions of oral music and ecstatic praise associated with slave religion. The label "Sanctified church" emerged within the black community to distinguish congregations of "the saints" from those of other black Christians, especially the black Baptists and Methodists who assimilated and imitated the cultural and organizational models of European-American patriarchy. (1996:3–4)

All sanctified churches emphasize the Biblical call to holiness and the experience of Spirit baptism. A common misconception is that all sanctified churches believe in glossolalia, or the gift of speaking in tongues. In fact, only Pentecostals and Apostolics attach doctrinal significance to glossolalia. It is, they believe, proof of Spirit baptism. Holiness adherents, by contrast, either reject glossolalia outright or practice "tongue-talking" without assigning any doctrinal valence to it.

Most important for the elaboration of religious particularism in Boston, though, is the tendency of sanctified churches to inculcate in the faithful an acute awareness of their uniqueness as holy people. "The saints," Sanders continues,

> follow the holiness mandate in worship, in personal morality, and in society, based on a dialectical identity characteristic of the tradition: "in the world, but

not of it." This dialectical identity reflects the social aspect of exilic consciousness, as manifested in the saints' awareness of alienation or separation from the
dominant culture, based on racial differences and religious practices. (5–6)

Given the centrality of exilic themes to sanctified religion, it is not surprising
that southern migrants gravitated toward the Holiness, Pentecostal, and
Apostolic storefront churches in the South End and Roxbury. Certain Baptist
and Methodist churches clearly accommodated the exilic experience of migrants. Still, only the sanctified church placed the experience of exile at the
heart of its religious expression.

The first sanctified church to appear in Boston was the Church of the Living God (also known as the Christian Workers for Fellowship), a southern-
based denomination founded in 1889 by a man uncannily named William
Christian. Christian taught that Jesus and all Biblical saints were Black, and
he promoted an early version of Christian Black nationalism. In doing so,
he stretched the sanctified exilic consciousness to validate the ancient, sacred, and glorious, if besieged, peoplehood of Blacks. According to the 1900
Boston City Directory, the Boston Church of the Living God worshiped initially at 33 Union Park in the South End. Also among the early sanctified
churches was the Church of God in Christ (COGIC). The COGIC, a Memphis-
based Pentecostal denomination founded in 1895, has since become one
of the fastest growing Christian bodies on the planet. Boston's first COGIC
church appeared in the South End circa 1920 at 45 Camden Street. By 1935,
two more COGIC storefronts had materialized not far from the first. Rev.
Marcus Neville, Jamaican immigrant and pastor of the COGIC congregation in Four Corners, joined the Camden Street congregation upon arriving
in Boston in 1951. He remembers the congregation as one of "poor Black
people who were coming up from the South. We [the church] used to help
them get on their feet when they came up. We helped them get jobs in the
hotels." Neville, a trained carpenter, had himself used church networks to
break into hotel work after failing to find a job in his original trade.

Other migrant churches belonging to sanctified denominations included
the First Pentecostal Church of the United Holy Church of America (established 1886 in Method, N.C.), the Church of God (1904, Sharon, Pa.), and
the Fire Baptized Holiness Mission Church (1895, Lincoln, Nebr.). Of
course, many sanctified churches in the burgeoning religious district lacked
affiliation with any denomination but still styled themselves as Pentecostal,
Holiness, or Apostolic.

Still other migrant churches did not fit neatly into any religious tradition
other than the euphemistic "sect" or "cult." Interestingly, one of the first non-
Baptist storefront migrant churches in Boston was known as a "cult" then as

today. This church, known alternately as the Church of God and Saints of Christ (CGSC) and the Black Jews, opened its doors on the corner of Shawmut Avenue and Woodbury Street in 1904, already having established twenty branches nationwide and a flagship church in Philadelphia. The theology of the church envisioned Blacks as the authentic Biblical Hebrews, an identification that Blacks previously had used to distill eschatological hope from, and assign cosmic significance to, their plight during the great absurdity of slavery. Church founder William Crowdy, who had himself escaped a Maryland slave plantation in 1863, surmised that the Emancipation Proclamation had not completely freed the chosen people. The true Hebrews, then, were called fully to liberate themselves and the world from the tenacious scourge of poverty and racial subordination through self-determination, purity of lifestyle, global evangelism, and assistance from a sympathetic Black Supreme Being.

The CGSC did not represent the theological bent of most migrants; most newcomers were partial to Baptist and Holiness-Pentecostal religion. Nonetheless, the CGSC radically embodied three traits present to varying degrees within the numerous storefronts that popped up along Black commercial thoroughfares during the great migration. These traits were vivacious worship, institutional completeness, and a critical stance vis-à-vis mainline northern Black religion and society. The Boston CGSC was highly "emotionalistic" according to Daniels's (1914) description of a service where he witnessed much ecstatic dancing, forceful singing, and passionate, lengthy testifying. The sermon, he reported, was without "reasoned order, being a hodge-podge of laudation of the prophet [William Crowdy] and exposition of his teachings. Every other sentence contained a quotation from the Bible, located with extraordinary accuracy by chapter and verse" (247). The service apparently went on for more than two hours, as Daniels arrived at the church in the morning and left at 1:00 P.M., long before the foreseeable end of the exercises.

At the same time, the congregation was institutionally complete to an extreme, or "communistic" in Daniels's language, in that much of members' lives revolved around the church, their incomes were supplemented by church enterprises, and much of this income in turn went into church upkeep. In addition, the church ran a grocery store (above which the congregation worshiped), a dry goods shop, and a restaurant, all of which furnished employment for church members. Such instrumental functions as employment often were ignored by scholarly and journalistic treatments of the CGSC and other early "storefronts."

Finally, the church was implicitly critical of the state of mainstream Black religion and, like other "storefront" churches, offered a religious alternative that spoke to the plight of Black migrants. The force of this critique is captured in Crowdy's first prophetic vision, which left him with little option other than to found a religion. On September 13, 1893, while clearing ground for a new crop, Crowdy fell unconscious and dreamt that he was in a large room. Several tables descended from above, each labeled with the name of an established church and each covered with filthy, foul vomit. The Baptist table, of which Crowdy theretofore had been a "member," was the biggest and also contained the most vomit. Then descended a small, clean, white table upon which the name Church of God and Saints of Christ appeared. Once grounded, the table expanded until it had displaced all of the vomit-laden tables. Crowdy then received a set of church tenets, which he etched onto tablets, and was presented with a Bible, which he promptly ate (Wynia 1994:21).

Crowdy's jarring vision of the mainline churches as tables dripping with vomit articulates a certain disgust with mainstream northern Black churches, especially the large Baptist ones, and a desire for spiritually liberating, yet immediately relevant religion. It anticipated the fashioning of a new "table," headed not only by an ethic of racial uplift but by a Black identity free of class and cultural conflict. It validated the small "table" as a good place—indeed, the only place—at which to worship God, thereby shifting the normative emphasis of northern organized religion from church size to social cohesiveness. Such messages must have resonated with many of Boston's Black newcomers, intimidated by the large, comparatively prim congregations and the legends of Black Brahminhood they met upon arrival. Far from being "otherworldly," apolitical, or otherwise irrelevant to the broader debate over the future of the race, the CGSC and other migrant churches presented a counterpublic (Fraser 1997) to a dominant Black public based in churches such as St Mark's Congregational and Charles Street A. M. E. They embodied a critique of mainstream northern Black social life and perhaps a rejection of mainstream Black politics, obsessed as it was with the binary opposition between protest and accommodation.

West Indian Churches

Among the temples of the native Black elite, the tenuously mixed congregations of Northerners and Southerners, and the migrant religious refuges, there appeared several West Indian churches. If southern migrants tended toward institutional completeness, so did immigrants from the West Indies. In fact, although Pleck artfully applied the term to southern migrants in Boston, "institutional completeness" originally referred to tightly knit patterns of sociability among immigrant populations (Breton 1964). At any rate, both Cromwell and Daniels refer to West Indians of the period as "clannish": a quality born of a taste for familiar ways, an inability to identify with the tastes and preoccupations of Black Americans, and the exclusionary "clannishness" of Black Americans themselves.

If West Indians found it difficult to relate to Black Americans, the latter also tended to exclude the former from its elite social circles. This is evident in Cromwell's reportage of her interview with "Mrs. X," a well-off Jamaican woman who resided "on a busy street in the heart of the Boston Black Belt":

> She said most West Indians, because of rebuffs from Boston Negroes, tried to hide their place of origin. She said further that West Indians were not welcomed into and did not participate in most Negro civic organizations. She herself had been denied the presidency of a local civic organization because she was West Indian. Mrs. X said conditions were not like this in New York, where West Indians have made a lot of money and nobody asks where you came from. (1994:226)

As soon as West Indians had formed a critical mass in Boston, they established St. Cyprian's Episcopal Church. In 1913, the congregation held its first services in the Lower Roxbury home of Miss Ida Gross. Members of the congregation previously were disappointed to learn that the only "colored" church in Boston was "high Episcopal," meaning that worship there adhered to strict, staid Anglican ritual standards. They might also have found it difficult to relate to the poor American Blacks who attended St. Augustine's, which began as a West End mission house. St. Cyprian's actually facilitated chain immigration, as church members arranged for more West Indians to come to Boston. Victor Bynoe, a native of Barbados and St. Cyprian's member since 1928, remembers,

> When I came to Boston this Church is where most West Indians were—people of your own culture . . . It was a cultural thing. We dressed differently, wearing silk shirts, straw hats and white flannel pants of the English tradition in Barbados . . . this was strange to the Boston Negro. And so we faced some ridicule. (Hayden 1983:50)

In the spirit of institutional completeness, the church also established an employment bureau, for even those West Indians skilled in the trades found it difficult to secure even the most menial employment in Boston. The necessity of such church-based services challenges Daniels's (1914) previously cited assumption that West Indians were easily employable and mostly middle-class.

According to Cromwell (1994), West Indians also congregated in numerous Holiness/Pentecostal churches. Some, like Marcus Neville, attended migrant Holiness churches. But many West Indians given to this brand of

Christianity undoubtedly formed their own congregations in tiny storefronts, as did their migrant counterparts. It is impossible to distinguish West Indian and migrant churches using Boston City Directory records. One may reasonably speculate, nonetheless, that West Indians dominated some of the Church of God (based in Cleveland, Tenn.) congregations that sprang up along Tremont and Shawmut Streets, as this denomination had established missionary outposts in the West Indies early in the twentieth century.

CONCLUSION

The period of the great migration thus witnessed the establishment of dozens of churches in Boston that functioned as havens, particularly for Southerners and West Indians, and that joined preexisting havens of northern religious sociability. These churches were particularistic spaces that offered distinctive worship and hand-tailored social and material opportunities for congregants. The resulting religious environment was dense and diverse, not unlike a contemporary shopping mall, where one finds twenty stores that sell pants. From a distance, it appears that they are all selling the same product, and that the mall is "overpantsed," as some observers concluded that Blacks were "overchurched." Upon closer inspection, though, it becomes clear that each store appeals to a certain kind of shopper with a peculiar taste in pants and a fixed pocketbook. The same applied to churches in the historic religious district, with their complex bundles of religious goods. But most significant about the rise of the historic religious district is the fact that it responded to the shifting contours of the urban social milieu itself. The great migration diversified and spatially consolidated the Black population in such a way that made the religious district possible and likely.

The story of Boston's historic religious district and, indeed, that of those appearing in other northern cities during the early twentieth century, has some important theoretical implications. R. Stephen Warner (1993: 1058) argues that "from the beginning, religion in the United States has been associated with societal differentiation, and pluralism has tended in this society to take on a religious expression." He further suggests, although without much elaboration, that the urban setting itself may thrust religion into this expressive role. Warner cites Claude Fischer's (1982) work on association in urban settings by way of asserting that "larger communities facilitate cobelievers' spending time with each other, so that urbanism can promote religious communalism rather than homogenization. Locations with high rates of in-migration thus offer attractive markets for aggressive religious organizations" (1064).

This chapter is a case in point of that assertion and indicates an important point of contact between theories in urban sociology and the sociology of religion. In a number of writings, Fischer (1975, 1981, 1982) has developed the idea that city life is characterized not by anomie or social isolation but by voluntary, selective participation in urban subcultures. The higher the density, diversity, and sheer size of the urban population, the more intense subcultural life will be, as evinced by high participation in, and reliance on, homogeneous social institutions. What this argument implies is that urban life is itself constitutively particularistic in that people, thrust together in dense and heterogeneous settings, can and will choose to associate with people of like origin or mind. The Black religious district emerged not out of an independent macroreligious transformation but as a religious expression of a more generic urban particularism. In doing so, the religious district challenged not only the idea of a single "Black church" but also the idea that all Blacks constituted, or constitute, a single urban subculture—a single tile in the urban "mosaic of social worlds" (Park 1969 [1916]).

THREE

Four Corners

BIRTH OF A CONTEMPORARY
RELIGIOUS DISTRICT

The religious district in old Black Boston responded to the density and diversity of the Black population. The contemporary district emerged in pockets of intense economic depression created in the late 1960s, when racial turnover spurred commercial disinvestment. Uneven community development exacerbated the problem by leaving some of these areas to fester, even as nearby locales began to regenerate. In inner-city contexts, a symptom of economic depression is an abundance of vacant storefronts; these storefronts become available for churches to rent or purchase relatively cheaply. Thus, the contemporary religious district, like the old, is made possible by aspects of the urban environment itself.

This chapter will trace the historical process that sent Four Corners into its spiral of economic decline. It also explains how exclusion from other revitalization projects spurred activists in Four Corners to develop a self-awareness distinct from other neighborhoods. I then describe the growth of the Four Corners religious district. Crucial to this growth, besides the availability of commercial spaces to rent, was the fact that churches were particularistic niches—that is, they served specific populations that mostly did not live in Four Corners but were willing to commute to the neighborhood to worship.

RACIAL CHANGE AND NEIGHBORHOOD DECLINE

Just prior to the 1960s, the area of Dorchester containing Four Corners was predominantly White and Jewish. Jews lived on the west side of Washington Street, and Whites, largely of Scottish and Irish ancestry, lived to the east in an area known as Mt. Bowdoin. The Four Corners segment of Washington Street was a vibrant commercial district featuring a pharmacy, a tailor, several delis and bakeries, an A&P supermarket, a bank, and a very popular movie theater. Four religious institutions served the area: St. Bridget's (Roman Catholic), Grace Methodist, Temple Beth El, and Central Congregational.

In 1966, the federally funded urban renewal bulldozers, which in the 1950s had famously razed the West End (Gans 1962), arrived at the South

End and Lower Roxbury, where the great majority of Boston Blacks still lived. As thousands of units of housing were demolished to make way for high-priced apartments and townhouses, some 22,000 Blacks were displaced (Mollenkopf 1983:166). Initially, exiled families had little choice but to settle in Jewish Dorchester, the only affordable area where Blacks would not face intolerable hostility. Newcomers indeed did not face overt hostility but were not entirely welcome, either. Ms. Bidwell, now in her 70s, was one of the first Blacks to move into the western part of Four Corners. She recalled how residents living in the brick apartments across the street had welcomed her, yet were clearly uneasy about her presence. Upon meeting her, one male resident said, smiling: "I see we have new neighbors!" Then, with utmost gravity, he continued, "This is a nice neighborhood. We hope it *stays* that way." "I like nice things, too," Bidwell replied.

As these first Black families trickled in, the Jewish section of Four Corners began its hasty "tip" toward Black predominance. Moved by the racist scare-tactics of "blockbusting" real estate agents (Levine and Harmon 1992) and lacking parishlike religious attachments to the neighborhood (Gamm 1999), Jews hurriedly left Four Corners and Temple Beth El for the suburbs. By 1970, the western portion of Four Corners was almost entirely Black.

It was not long before east Four Corners followed suit, as blockbusters began to guide moderate-income Black families to Mt. Bowdoin. Among the first was the Warner family, who moved in after their Roxbury home was taken by imminent domain for urban renewal. Within months of their arrival, recalls Ellen Warner, White families whom they had just met began moving out:

> We got to know the neighbors, and they'd come over [and say,] "We're not moving because you moved in." I'd say, "Well, that's wonderful." One guy came over and said to me—he used live in the house right across the street—that he wasn't going to move. "You people are good people." I say, "Wonderful." I think he moved out the next day!

Among the last Whites to leave the area were Beth Walker and her sister, both in their 80s. The sisters had lived in the neighborhood and attended Grace Church since 1923, when their family moved to Boston from Nova Scotia. They moved to Jamaica Plain in the mid 1970s after multiple thefts convinced them that they could not be safe in the new, Black Four Corners:

> Well, it [the neighborhood] was beginning to change, and it was mixed. And then gradually it became almost all Black. We lived in a big ten-room house. And it was finally just me and my sister living there alone, and it was too much for us, so we moved . . . The *house* was too much for us to take care of, and

work. And, um, we had had several break-ins. We saw a great deal of [racial conflict] when we lived there on Merlin Street. It was nerve-wracking. They broke in—and not only that, but I had my pocketbook stolen—grabbed from me—about four times, *right near my house.* So it was becoming very uneasy. So we came over here to live.

As the racial composition of the neighborhood changed, population and income levels plummeted, according to data compiled by the Boston Public Facilities Department (1997) on four core central tracts in the neighborhood. The population across these tracts dropped from 18,382 in 1960 to 13,127 in 1980—a 29 percent loss. During the same period, the city lost 20 percent of its population, as White Bostonians moved to various suburbs. In 1950, median incomes in Four Corners were actually $458 to $748 *higher* than the city median of $2,643. But earnings declined precipitously from 1950 to 1970, when individual tracts reported median incomes $1,322 to $3,928 below the city median of $9,133. Since 1960, Four Corners tracts have never posted median income levels meeting or surpassing city levels.

Aside from population shifts, the economy and overall feel of the neighborhood changed drastically. Municipal services, such as trash pickup and street cleaning, became irregular, and rat infestations followed. White and Jewish shopkeepers evacuated the commercial spaces along Washington Street; some reopened in newly built suburban malls. Among the first large establishments to leave were the movie theater and the A&P supermarket. Even the local branch of the Boston Public Library shut down. Meanwhile, discriminatory lending practices known as "redlining" discouraged new businesses from locating in the area.

This pattern of neighborhood decline was hardly unique at the time. Four Corners represented a single episode in a serial drama playing in urban theaters across the northern United States. During this period Black "ghettoes" were not only disbanding, with better-off Blacks putting as much distance between themselves and the urban core as possible (Wilson 1987), but *expanding* as many Blacks found it difficult to get very far (Massey and Denton 1993). The Warners, mentioned above, wanted to move from Roxbury to an inner-ring suburb, but a disparaging real estate agent guided them instead to Four Corners and other areas on the edge of the expanding Black Belt.

What chroniclers of the drama almost entirely miss, however, is the way the expansion of the ghetto led to competition *among* ghetto neighborhoods for resources—a competition that would inevitably result in some locales, like Four Corners, falling between the cracks. They also neglect a major character in the drama: churches. The next section will explain how Four Corners fell through the cracks and gained a new self-awareness in the process. The subsequent section shows how the neglect of Four Corners made way for the show-stopping appearance of a contemporary religious district.

FOUR CORNERS BECOMES A SELF-AWARE LOCALITY BY EXCLUSION

> Why create a development plan? Because the need exists.
> While the communities around the Four Corners (Codman Square, Bowdoin-Geneva, Fields Corner, Grove Hall, and Blue Hill Avenue) have realized economic resurgence and new housing initiatives, the same cannot be said of the Four Corners. Every other community has MainStreets money but Four Corners. A map of the [Enterprise Community] reveals how the parameters include Four Corners neighbors but not the Four Corners.
> —The Reverend Dennis Paul, former pastor of the Grace Methodist Church

The Rev. Paul's remark suggests that Four Corners was distinguished not only by its churches and depressed state but by an inability to keep up with the economic revitalization occurring in neighborhoods all around it. Four Corners was a casualty of a fundamentally competitive and often adversarial urban political and economic process. As in numerous other cities (Henig 1982; Mollenkopf 1983; Rieder 1985), the politics of land use, economic development, municipal services, education, and housing in Boston have often revolved around neighborhoods and their respective ability to either compete for limited resources or to defend territorial integrity. Such politics have privileged neighborhoods that are internally organized in ways conducive to mobilization around spatially defined interests. In 1957 this logic of resource distribution was institutionalized with the creation of the Boston Redevelopment Authority, the state-authorized agency responsible for the planning, development, and administration of neighborhood programs. The resurgence of community-based antipoverty strategies since the War on Poverty, including a host of public and private community development grants, has further raised the premium on neighborhood collective action (Halpern 1995). Thus, at various historical junctures, Boston neighborhoods have mobilized against urban renewal (Gans 1962), public school desegregation and busing (Formisano 1991), and more recently, in favor of community-controlled development (King 1981; Medoff and Sklar 1994). Meanwhile, Boston mayoral politics frequently appeal to the neighborhood basis of resource allocation. Raymond Flynn, mayor of Boston from 1983 to 1993, went as far as to refer to himself as "the neighborhood mayor."

While Four Corners was still caught in its downward spiral, nearby locales were, in various ways, exploiting the neighborhood-based system of resource distribution and interest politics. In the late 1960s, Dorchester Fair Share organized for increased police presence in Uphams Corner. Codman Square organized a Not in My Backyard–style campaign to stop the local transit authority from storing large amounts of rolling stock in its midst. In the late 1970s and early 1980s these locales were awarded community development block grants to start community development corporations (CDCs) and community health center funds to establish neighborhood health centers. Unlike Four Corners, though, Bostonians have for many generations recognized these areas *as distinct neighborhoods.* They continue to contain important historic landmarks, such as the old Public Library in Codman Square and the historic Strand Theater in Uphams Corner. These neighborhoods also contain secular organizations that serve those neighborhoods exclusively, such as the Codman Square Health Center.

Codman Square and other adjacent neighborhoods continued to mobilize for community revitalization well into the 1990s. Notable winnings during this period included Massachusetts Mainstreets and Enterprise Community moneys, both of which were geared toward the revival of commercial districts. At the center of these mobilization efforts were health centers, CDCs, and neighborhood councils—all organizations expressly founded to serve the needs of people in those neighborhoods. They, more than any other institutions, pulled residents together in face-to-face settings to discuss the welfare of the neighborhood. They established ties with outside agencies and perpetually milked these ties for human and material resources. Churches, block groups, social clubs, businesses, and other neighborhood organizations clustered around the efforts of these core institutions, lending an air of legitimacy and unified diversity to the revitalization process.

The initial success of revitalization in these neighborhoods threw into relief the relative destitution of Four Corners and put even more pressure on the latter to mobilize. Unlike nearby neighborhoods, however, Four Corners lacked self-awareness as such. Four Corners had never even appeared on an official city map; only maps circulated among Four Corners activists took for granted its existence as a cartographic entity. To be certain, references to the "Five Corners" appear as early as 1901 in documents chronicling the origins of the Grace Methodist Church. But "Five Corners" was merely an odd-looking intersection which later became a bustling streetcar junction. At times this intersection was associated with the Victorian Mt. Bowdoin enclave lying to the northeast. At other times it was considered a northern extension of Codman Square, which was known as "historic" even at the beginning of the twentieth century.

It was, nonetheless, the decisive *exclusion* of Four Corners from development in Codman Square and other abutting locales that sparked self-awareness within the former. When Codman Square acquired a CDC in 1981, Four Corners was included in the service boundary, yet the preponderance of the corporation's development projects carried on south of Park Street, now considered the southern boundary of Four Corners. This act of exclusion spurred residents to form Neighborhood Housing Services (NHS), the first secular organization founded to revitalize Four Corners. In an attempt to replicate in Four Corners the work of the Codman Square CDC, NHS partnered with area banks to provide rehabilitation loans for inhabitants of dilapidated housing. NHS was quickly sidetracked, nonetheless, by complaints of violent crime and illicit drug sales, a symptom of the exploding crack epidemic that was ravaging inner-city neighborhoods all over the country. People avoided evening NHS meetings for fear of being victimized in the streets. NHS responded by pressing police to provide better coverage of the area, the kind of coverage Codman Square had successfully won for its merchants. The distraction, however, proved fatal to the organization. As NHS devoted more and more time to public safety concerns, it began to neglect its portfolio of loans. Homeowners, afraid of coming out for evening training and support sessions, began defaulting on these loans, and NHS fell into a state of financial crisis. As a result, NHS died as suddenly as it was born.

Since it lacked sentience until it was excluded from something else, Four Corners might be considered as less than a "real neighborhood." Urban sociologist Gerald Suttles (1972), however, might have recognized Four Corners not as a fluke but as something resembling the norm:

> Most likely, local communities and neighborhoods, like other groups, acquire a corporate identity because they are held jointly responsible by other communities and external organizations. Thus, I suggest, it is in their "foreign relations" that communities come into existence and have to settle on an identity and a set of boundaries which oversimplify their reality. (12–13)

Four Corners came into existence because foreign relations demanded so; this makes it a "real" neighborhood and, perhaps, even an ordinary one.

Still, if foreign relations sparked neighborhood self-awareness, the death of NHS left Four Corners without an ambassador. It contained no CDC or neighborhood health center around which to organize. Aside from two church-based community development organizations, the only corporate entity containing the name of the neighborhood in its title was Four Corners Beepers. The neighborhood hosted three public elementary schools, one social service agency, and four secular voluntary associations, but none of these was concerned with Four Corners as such. The public schools served three separate districts that just happened to cut into Four Corners. The social service agency served all of Dorchester without regard to its numerous subneighborhoods. The voluntary associations included two labor union posts, a social club for immigrants from the Caribbean island of Montserrat, and a club for motorcycle enthusiasts. Rather than addressing neighborhood issues, these associations appealed to particular occupational, ethnic, and recreational interests. Moreover, they drew few or none of their members from the neighborhood.

The absence of secular neighborhood-oriented institutions placed the onus on churches to "make noise" on behalf of the neighborhood and develop the kind of interpersonal and interinstitutional networks that have supported mobilization in other locales. But these churches drew few of their members from the neighborhood, either. As I will now show, a critical consequence of unchecked economic decline in the neighborhood was a veritable explosion of religious life there. As a result of this explosion, the original religious ecology of four quaint neighborhood congregations gave way to a religious district in which dozens of churches coexisted by *not* competing for the same local membership pool.

CHURCHES MOVE, CHANGE, AND PROLIFERATE

The racial and economic shift that hit Four Corners in the 1960s presented challenges and opportunities for religious organizations. The racial turnover put considerable pressure on preexisting churches. As the face of the neighborhood changed, these old institutions faced firsthand the four options outlined in the classic religious ecology studies: move, adapt, become a "niche" or metropolitan church, or fade away altogether. The Central Congregational Church pulled up stakes and moved elsewhere, leaving the building to a Wesleyan Holiness congregation. Jewish families abandoned Temple Beth El, which remained a rotting hull until 1998, when the structure was razed and cleared. When I left Four Corners in late 1999, the vacant property was still fronted by an old black iron fence into which stars of David had been wrought. This haunting relic alone bore witness to what the space once was.

Grace Methodist and St. Bridget's became metropolitan niches, each focusing on a particular population. Although the neighborhood was becoming African American, St. Bridget's became a Haitian niche after being assigned a Haitian pastor. Traditionally, Catholic churches demarcated geographic parishes and claimed all of the residents within them (Gamm 1999; McGreevy 1996). Instead of relinquishing their hold on local neighborhoods, Catholic churches tended to respond to neighborhood racial and ethnic change by assimilating incoming populations. In this case, the incoming population was composed of African Americans, among whom there are relatively few Catholics. St. Bridget's thus became one of an increasing number of "ethnic parishes" in Boston. Ethnic parishes usually serve immigrant Catholic populations that may be dispersed throughout the city rather than concentrated in a few contiguous neighborhoods. The ethnic parish is thus a *niche* form. Until its closing in 1999, St. Bridget's Church served as a major center of Haitian life in Boston.[1]

Like St. Bridget's, Grace was unable to attract many Black Americans into its fold. The great majority of African American Methodists belong not to the United Methodist Church but to the various African Methodist Episcopal denominations. The United Methodist Church therefore assigned a series of Caribbean pastors to Grace in the hope of attracting immigrants from former British colonies in the West Indies and Africa, where British Methodism had laid deep roots. The strategy proved effective: Grace is now a solidly West Indian church with a sizeable West African minority.

If racial change sent older churches into identity crises, economic decline created opportunities for entrepreneurial churches, as it freed up dozens of cheaply acquirable spaces on Washington and Harvard Streets. These thoroughfares were not only well traveled but were accessible to other neighborhoods in Roxbury and Dorchester. The combination of access, visibility, and affordability proved irresistible to churches, if not businesses. Almost immediately, observers began to notice churches moving into vacated storefronts along Washington, Harvard, and Bowdoin Streets (Kyper 1975). A Jehovah's Witnesses congregation moved into the old theater. An Apostolic church moved into the empty public library building.

As revitalization ensued in surrounding areas, the relative cheapness of storefronts in Four Corners was thrown into relief. In 1998, merchants and pastors reported paying between $300 and $500 a month for commercial spaces in the neighborhood. Rents in Codman Square, by contrast, reportedly were twice as high. As the owner of the sole dry cleaning business in Four Corners averred, "It's much more expensive there [in Codman Square] because they have a lot going on there. But there's nothing *going on* here. There are hardly any other businesses." Ironically, at least one Four Corners church, the Haitian Maison d'Esprit, was displaced from Codman Square as that neighborhood began to realize its development plans. As compensation, the Codman Square Community Development Corporation found a new space for Maison d'Esprit: the abandoned bank building in Four Corners.

Thus, while surrounding neighborhoods came to contain many congregations, none surpassed Four Corners in density of congregations. In 1999,

Four Corners hosted a total of 29 congregations (table 3) in twenty build-ings. As table 4 indicates, Four Corners weighed in at 47.54 congrega-tions per square mile—14 more congregations per square mile than the next densest neighborhood.[2] This was so despite the fact that Four Corners had lost thousands of residents since 1960.

The availability of commercial spaces, nevertheless, does not fully ex-plain how so many churches could coexist in the same neighborhood. The rest of the explanation lies in the template for urban religious coexistence etched during the great migration. This normative religious template takes for granted that churches will locate quite near each other but assumes also that these churches will not compete with each other for spatial territory. Rather, they will compete for the attention of specific populations. Thus, in the language of religious ecology, churches could coexist in Four Corners because they were basically all niche churches, competing not for neigh-borhood residents but for certain kinds of people who might or might not live nearby.[3] The fact that churches, like residents, were highly mobile further promoted this metropolitan orientation.

In the language of religious voluntarism, churches in Four Corners, like the dozens of storefronts that sprang up in old Black Boston, were *particu-laristic* in their outreach to constituencies of color, which by the 1980s were more widely distributed over the residential cityscape than they were during the great migration. Where physical distances between churches are negli-gible, social distances compensate. Below I explain, in turn, the significance of niche status, physical transience, and particularism among churches in the Four Corners religious district.

Niche Status

If St. Bridget's and Grace became niches in order to cope with neighborhood change, the churches that poured into the neighborhood *after* it changed were niches by design. Four Corners was a grand place to start a niche church because of its ideal location at the intersection of two major thoroughfares: Washington and Harvard Streets. This religious locational logic was some-what similar to that which allows retailers and restaurateurs to locate in shopping districts, often quite near competing businesses. In a society made mobile by paved roads, public transportation, and automobiles, people from many parts of the metropolis can fairly easily get to downtown shopping cen-ters and commercial districts in ethnic enclaves (i.e., Chinatown, Little Italy). People of faith can just as easily travel to religious districts to worship at niche churches.

Faith Baptist, for example, served about one hundred American-born middle-class Blacks, many of whom were first-generation southern migrants.

Table 3 Churches in Four Corners

Church	Tradition	Attendance	Ethnicity/Origin	Class	Year Founded	In FC Since	Building Type
Anointed Church	Apostolic	70	Southern Black	Working/Middle	1998	1998	Storefront
Azusa	Pentecostal	20	Southern Black	Middle: Intellectual	1988	1995	House
Christ Church	Holiness	175	Southern Black	Middle: Professional	1968	1968	House
Church of God	Pentecostal	100	Caribbean, Mixed	Middle: Professional	1981	1981/1999	Freestanding
Church of God in Christ	Pentecostal	25	Caribbean, Mixed	Working	1970	1980	Freestanding
Church of the Holy Ghost	Pentecostal	10	Southern Black	Working	1976	1981	House
Divine Peace	Pentecostal	25	Caribbean, Antigua	Working	1981	1994	Storefront
Fellowship Apostolic	Apostolic	40	Caribbean	Working	1969	1974	Storefront
Good Tidings	Pentecostal	500	Northern Black	Middle: Professional	1979	1990	Storefront
Grace Methodist	Methodist	200	Caribbean	Middle/Working	1903	1903	Freestanding
Holy Fullness Church	Pentecostal	40	Southern Black	Working/Middle	1992	1996	Storefront
Holy Road	Pentecostal	50	Northern Black	Working/Some Professional	1980	1996	Storefront
Iglesia Christo El Rey	Pentecostal	15	Latino, Mixed	Working	1993	1992	Storefront
Iglesia de Santos	Pentecostal	50	Latino, Mixed	Working	1982	1998	Storefront
Jude Church	Apostolic	20	Northern Black	Working	1975	1975	Storefront
Kingdom Hall	Jehovah's Witness						Freestanding
3 English-speaking congregations		150	Northern Black	Mixed			
3 Spanish-speaking congregations		150	Latino, Mixed	Mixed		1994	
Maison d'Esprit	Pentecostal	50	Haitian	Working	1975	1994	Storefront
Faith Baptist	Baptist	70	Southern Black	Middle: Professional	1970	1984	Storefront
Mt. Nebo Apostolic	Apostolic	30	Southern Black	Working/Middle	1976	1976	Storefront
New Jerusalem	Apostolic	10	Caribbean, Jamaica	Working	1997	1997	Storefront
Remembrance	Pentecostal	15	Southern Black	Working	1975	1987	Storefront
Seventh Day Adventist	Adventist	100	Haitian	Working	1989	1993	Storefront
St. Bridget's English-speaking congregation	Roman Catholic	20	Northern Black	Working/Middle	1902	1902	Storefront
Haitian Creole-speaking congregation		150	Haitian	Working/Middle			Freestanding

Table 4 Four Corners and Adjacent Neighborhoods

Neighborhood	Square Miles	Population	Congregations	Population per Square Mile	Congregations per Square Mile	Population per Congregations
Four Corners	.61	14,519	29	23,723.64	47.54	500.66
Grove Hall	.87	20,170	29	23,183.91	33.33	695.52
Codman Square	1.50	26,929	38	18,195.27	25.33	708.65
Bowdoin/Geneva	.17	3,827	4	22,511.77	23.53	956.75
Fields Corner	.74	13,252	6	17,908.11	8.11	2,208.67

Note: Figures on neighborhood size and population are aggregated from 1990 U.S. Census block level data. "Number of Churches" in adjacent neighborhoods was tabulated by geocoding church addresses in the *Boston Church Directory* (Mitchell and Bass 1995). Rudy Mitchell kindly provided the contents of this publication in electronic format.

Most members commuted to church from as far away as the suburbs, and none lived in Four Corners. The church purchased a storefront in the neighborhood in 1984 after its original storefront in Codman Square was destroyed in a fire. Holy Road Christian Center, by contrast, was a Pentecostal church serving about fifty people, mostly Boston-born and mostly working-class, who lived in Roxbury, Dorchester, and Jamaica Plain. This church contained a small number of college-educated young adults, whom the pastor, the Rev. Powell, brought into the church "off the street" when they were teens. Holy Road originated in Roxbury and moved to a Four Corners storefront in 1994.

Maison d'Esprit, to which I referred above, was located in a corner storefront that used to be a bank. The Maison space actually housed multiple congregations: one Haitian and one Latina/o (Iglesia de Santos). Both congregations were Pentecostal and largely working-class. Also, like the native-born religious communities, both congregations tended to draw membership from outside the neighborhood—even from the suburbs. Most of the Maison congregation commuted from Mattapan, which contained the largest Haitian residential community. Iglesia de Santos drew primarily from Jamaica Plain and Roxbury, where Latinas/os resided in highest concentration.

Bouncing Churches

When sociologists speak of neighborhood transience, they usually are referring to the rate at which individuals change their place of residence. Urban sociologists point to this kind of transience as a primary impediment to social cohesion in neighborhoods (Sampson 1991; Kasarda and Janowitz 1974). In Four Corners, churches as well as people were highly mobile; this fact fortified their niche status as much as their auspicious location on major thoroughfares. Many of the congregations had worshiped in two or more previous locations before settling in the neighborhood. In addition, many churches were recent arrivals—in 1997, twelve had been in the neighborhood for ten years or less. Two churches *returned* to Four Corners after lengthy hiatuses elsewhere. One of these, the Church of God, was forced into exile in Codman Square when its building, a small house, collapsed in the middle of major renovations. It took six years for the church to raise enough money to build a new structure on the old property. Meanwhile, the old site remained a vacant lot, distinguished from other vacant lots only by a wooden sign protruding from the rubble and knee-high weeds that read Coming Soon: Church of God.

This instance aside, most churches move because they can no longer afford the rent, they get evicted or bought out, or they simply find a more suitable space elsewhere. When a church moves, however, it does not necessarily lose its membership. As long as the church retains its unique identity and does not move too far away, it will keep some original members and attract new ones as the church moves from place to place. Transient churches, then, widen their geographic horizons by "bouncing." As they bounce from neighborhood to neighborhood, they gather new members, become increasingly metropolitan in scope, and abandon parishlike attachment to particular neighborhoods.

The Remembrance Church typified the bouncing pattern. Remembrance was a Pentecostal faith community composed of poor and working-class American-born Blacks, most hailing from southern states. The Rev. Pride began this ministry in the 1980s as an assistant pastor at another church. When the pastor of that church moved his ministry to another city, Pride decided to start her own congregation. To attract followers, she held street services in Dudley Station, Roxbury's central business district. She eventually opened a church in a rented storefront on Blue Hill Avenue, still in Roxbury. The church regularly attracted sixty-five worshipers. After renting for a year, the asthmatic man who owned the building decided to leave Boston for the dry plains of Arizona. He sold Pride half a block of commercial space. She rented space to a variety store and another church, and opened her own restaurant in the remaining storefront.

In 1985, Pastor Pride sold her property and moved to Brockton, a Boston suburb, in the hope of establishing a larger ministry. Most of her followers did not follow her to Brockton, and she had trouble attracting new ones. She remained in the suburb for two years, then moved to her current Washington Street location in Four Corners. She purchased this space from a cleric who had decided to move his ministry to Providence, R.I. (this church has since returned to Boston and now rents its former space from Pastor Pride). Prides's church never surpassed the Sunday service attendance rates it had in Roxbury. Nevertheless, the church attracted several Dorchester (albeit not Four Corners) residents simply by virtue of its location on a major Dorchester thoroughfare. The church's mobility, then, expanded its geographic scope if not its membership roll.

The bouncing path to metropolitan church status is undocumented in the literature on congregational ecology. According to this literature, congregations adopt metropolitan orientations because they can no longer rely on immediately surrounding neighborhoods for members. The bouncing concept, however, adds the impact of church mobility to the process. In neighborhoods like Four Corners, where most congregations worship in spaces other than freestanding church structures, frequent church relocation is a fact of religious life. Such movement intensifies the metropolitan orientation of niche congregations and makes it difficult for churches to attach themselves to particular neighborhoods.

Even churches that intend to remain indefinitely in the same place face the perpetual *threat* of being involuntarily "bounced" out of the neighborhood by urban renewal or rising rents. This threat, which is salient particularly for storefront churches, may render clergy reluctant to develop mission attachments to the neighborhoods in which they settle. Indeed, the fact that some churches own worship spaces while others rent, some occupy cramped storefronts while others kick back in more spacious quarters, and some may be asked, or forced, to leave a neighborhood more readily than others, means that churches, like individuals, are divided along property interest lines. Storefront churches, then, may be thought of as an interest group whose vulnerability to being bounced gives it a unique perspective on organizational survival. For such churches, property interests may dwarf any concern for the neighborhood, especially if that neighborhood appears to be on the verge of economic development.[4]

This predicament is further complicated by the fact that storefront churches are a *transgressive*[5] form of religious presence. They are ubiquitous yet out of place. They break tacit societal norms about where and how people should worship. They emerge from the depression of the neighborhood and bluntly remind people of that depression by occupying otherwise vacant commercial spaces. The churchly norms that permit a congregation to exist comfortably near many others in a religious district can thus be radically out of step with what neighborhood residents understand as a "normal" degree and quality of religious presence. For this reason, residents I met at community development meetings tended to be cynical about the numerous storefront churches in Four Corners. This cynicism was directed less at the actual religious groups that worshiped in storefronts and more at the fact that the churches took up valuable commercial space, did not draw members from the neighborhood, and did not appear to be concerned with neighborhood affairs. Also, because there were so many storefront churches, parking spaces became a rare commodity in the neighborhood on Sundays.

Ellen Warner was particularly outspoken about the neighborhood's numerous storefront churches. She was one of a few remaining residents who could recall how rapidly churches took over commercial storefronts as grocery stores, pharmacies, and sandwich shops escaped to suburban malls and outer-ring White neighborhoods. Warner spoke calmly, even humorously, about "White flight" from Four Corners. But when I noted that there were ten storefronts occupied by churches on Washington Street alone, she grew visibly and audibly agitated:

You ain't kiddin'! E*very* storefront down that way is a church. And I think people need to ask themselves, what is it? Like, I love this little church down here, Holy Road. I like what they do. I don't go down there as often, but I like what they do. Cause they seem to do an awful lot of things with the young people. And I like that. See, that's how—that is gonna grow. Hopefully they will get a decent church, a bigger church or something to enhance what they're trying to do. But those *other* churches—you have all these little storefronts that don't do anything but open up on Sundays and close. Open and close. You don't even know who these people are, they come from outer space some-where! So you can't even say they're part of the community.

One Sunday I was standing there on Washington Street. And I was looking to see who are these people coming out of this church? And everybody got in their cars and they *left*. They just happened to find a spot somewhere and it doesn't involve the community. And I think people have to be selective. I really think people need to look at this now. I mean, do you need somebody to open up a building that's not relevant? You look at the outside of the buildings, and they're not there all week long, and they're not kept. And it's like—it's satu-rated. It's *saturated*. And I think people really need to look at it. And they say "freedom of worship," and dada dada da. You know—you got *fifteen people!* You might as well do it in your own house.

Anyway, but I just look at it and say, "I can't believe . . ." When I go up Wash-ington Street here, and I see all these storefronts—what we *need* to do is bring a business in that can be productive and if really God's called you, you can [find someplace] better. But I think they need to put a moratorium, or what is that word?

Somewhat ironically, I heard this agitated cynicism expressed most acutely during community planning meetings held in churches, albeit not storefront churches. During one meeting a resident noted, with audible contempt, that it would be necessary to take the Reverend Pride's church to put a strip mall there. In a meeting at a different church, a recently retired pastor complained about "all those storefronts" that keep their doors closed during the week and contribute nothing to the economic welfare of the neighborhood. Vitriol aside, it is true that in order to develop the neighborhood economically, a lot of churches might have to be displaced, just as some churches in Four Cor-ners were displaced from adjacent developing neighborhoods.

Some Dimensions of Particularism

I have argued that the religious district is made possible not only by the avail-ability of vacant commercial spaces but by the fact that churches are not all competing for neighborhood people. That is, churches are niches. But in the

parlance of religious voluntarism, which focuses not on the spatial but social aspects of interchurch competition, these churches are particularistic.
Implicit in the idea of religious particularism is the recognition that congregations can be meaningfully different in a *multitude* of ways, so that people
are able to sort themselves into religious communities according to complex bundles of preferences. Sociologists of religion have well documented
how race, national origin, socioeconomic class, lifestyle, level of strictness,
size, and internal organization—not to mention religious tradition and denomination—can serve to distinguish institutions in the multicongregational
field (see Warner 1988, 1993; Ammerman 1997a; Iannoccone 1994; Eiesland
1999). When people choose one church or another, they are locating themselves along some or all of these dimensions. There are also those whose religious needs cannot be met in any one church. These are the perpetual shoppers: they are committed to churchgoing but not to any one church.[6]

As particularism goes, one might easily have lumped Four Corners
churches into two groups—"African American" and "immigrant"—but these
designations would hardly capture the range of choices found in this religious district. As I hinted in the previous section, particularisms in Four Corners varied by ethnicity, regional and national origin, social class, and more.
As such, what appeared from afar as "African American" churches were actually congregations of southern migrants or native Northerners. Likewise,
"immigrant" churches includeed Haitian, Latina/o, West Indian, and mixed
congregations.

Also cutting across the two gross categories were no less than eight religious traditions. Black American congregations were Baptist, Pentecostal,
Apostolic, Holiness, Jehovah's Witnesses, and Roman Catholic. Immigrant
congregations were Pentecostal, Jehovah's Witnesses, Seventh-day Adventist,
and Catholic. Class differences were salient as well. The Church of God and
the Divine Peace churches were both West Indian and Pentecostal. Yet, the
former was composed almost entirely of upwardly mobile immigrants from
several islands, while the latter attracted working-class laborers from Antigua. But even these traits do not exhaust the dimensions of difference
among churches in Four Corners.

The following three chapters do not attempt an exhaustive cross-
classification of all twenty-nine churches. For the purpose of this discussion,
table 3 (above) will need to suffice. Instead, I consider three underexplored
yet critical ways in which churches were meaningfully different. In addition
to the dimensions enumerated above, churches differed in their application
of ubiquitous religious ideas, in modes of interaction with the immediate
environment, and in their approaches to activism, or social change. In each
chapter I will consider how the dimension in question is impacted by other

church traits, such as congregation size, religious tradition, and denominational affiliation. These considerations offer insight into the ways in which church traits interact unpredictably, posing dilemmas, constraints, and opportunities for clergy and congregants as they cultivate distinctive religious communities.

FOUR

"In the world, but not of it"
PARTICULARISM AND EXILIC CONSCIOUSNESS

The Church of the Holy Ghost was one of two religious communities actually housed in a *house*—a two-family flat, actually. Upon entering the church for the first time, I thought something was burning. The worship space, formerly a living room, smelled slightly of smoke and felt very warm. There were only eight people present, including the pastor and myself. The attendees included a young girl and boy. There were also two teenaged boys and one man who wore a beige suit with blue pinstripes and appeared to be in his thirties. No women were present when I arrived. Pastor Robert Jameson was directing the testimonial portion of the service in a distinctly southern accent. Nearly everyone stood and stated what they were thankful for. The teens stood in turn and proclaimed, as if hurrying through a book report in class, their blessings: "I'd like to thank the Lord for waking me up this morning and for giving me such a supportive family." The little boy, eager to participate, jumped up excitedly and shouted, "I'd like to thank the Lord for waking me up this morning!"

The walls of the sanctuary were covered with faded faux pine paneling, and the windows were covered with gauzy white cloth just sheer enough to let in some sunlight, yet opaque enough to prevent anyone seeing in or out. There were ten or so wooden benches on either side of the room—they were quite old and resembled the kind of benches ordinarily used outdoors. Before the pulpit, centered in the middle of the vestibule, sat a small table holding a metal collection dish and a bottle of olive oil for anointing the faithful. A sign was taped to a pillar on the right side of the room just in front of my bench. The sign depicted what looked like a vast fiery pit. It read "Hell! Is hell a real place? Are most people going to hell?" As I pondered these questions, I noticed the rattle of the two floor fans located near the front of the warm room but could not feel their breezes.

When the testimonies were exhausted, the pastor led the church in a hymn containing the refrain, "Let's go back to the good old way; we need to go way back to the good old way." The refrain actually foreshadowed the pastor's sermon, which recounted how the exigencies of life had brought him not only to holiness, but to Boston. In light of the sermon, the "good old way"

61

could be taken either as the way of holiness, which imposes spiritual exile on the faithful, or as a southern way of having church, the enactment of which could sustain migrants exiled in the urban North. During the sermon, Jameson repeatedly connected the abstract theme of holiness-as-exile to his lived experiences as a Southerner and migrant. In his discourse on the "narrow," or exclusive, path of salvation, he invoked tactile memories of the rural South, testified to the protective power of holiness as manifested during his travails in the North, and related the Church of the Holy Ghost to the intimate Holiness church he knew in South Carolina. Rather than simply preaching the distinction between worldliness and holiness, Jameson began to *extend* that exilic theme by weaving in his own migrant narrative.

Jameson began holding forth in calm, even tones. He started by describing the binary nature of humanity. The minority of people who claimed the "holiness" faith were destined to everlasting glory. The vast majority— "worldly people"—were doomed to an eternity in hell. "'Narrow is the way,'" he quoted from Scripture,

> and if you don't have the Holy Ghost, you won't make it into heaven . . . I used to fast and pray a lot when I was young, before I started ministering. But it looks like God was blessing me even more than those around me [including the ordained ministers], because I was praying and fasting more than anybody else. You have to pay the price to get into heaven, and the price is fasting and prayer . . .

He then began to reminisce about his first experience with the Holy Ghost. His account was thickly padded with images of life in the rural South: a device that effectively linked holiness with Southernness. He had first visited a Holiness church at the age of 27, when he still lived in South Carolina. He had not gone to hear the preaching, though. Rather, he was drawn to the style of "Christian singing" popularized by the great Mahalia Jackson. So,

> when the preacher came out I was hoping he would hurry and shut his mouth so they would bring forth the singing again . . . There was guitar playing— whoo! He just *played* that guitar [an instrument more common in southern than in northern Black churches], and people started shouting, jumping up and down. Later I joked with some of my friends, how they looked like those Africans jumping up and down with spears. But a few weeks later I was doing the same thing!

Then Jameson likened the sensation of being infused with the Spirit to walking on cotton—an experience available *only* to rural Southerners, just as the experience of the Holy Ghost is available only to those on the narrow path. "I was jumping up and down just like those little Africans . . . It felt like I was walking on clouds, or like there was cotton on the floor. Many people who are not from the South don't know about cotton on the ground." At this reference, an elderly woman, who had joined the service at the beginning of the sermon, nodded in solemn remembrance and said, "Yes, oh, yes." The younger worshipers, all Boston-born relatives of the pastor, listened attentively.

Once infused with the Spirit, Jameson found himself easily able to bounce back from the tribulations and temptations ordinarily faced by Black migrants in Boston. Before getting saved, he had belonged to the world of sin, which made him a "devil." "When I was a devil," he recalled, "I thought like a devil, and I acted like a devil. I smoked, I drank, I was a good diceman." Indeed, he had once made a decent living as a diceman in the South. He flirted with such temptations well into his Boston sojourn. But eventually he learned to rely on God for material needs. After he began preaching in 1969, "I never even *thought* about going back into the world. Instead, I've asked God for the things I need. A car, children, my church. God blessed me to be able to pay for most of the things in here. When you're working for God, things come up the way they're supposed to come up for you." God had also healed injuries he had sustained as a laborer. At one point he worked at a laundry, "where you have to lift the large tub of clothes and put the clothes in the extractor." While lifting clothes one day, he ruptured a disk in his spine. Wary of invasive surgery, he left the hospital after receiving the diagnosis. He prayed for healing. Over a period of weeks, God healed his back, and he returned to work. The narrow way of holiness, taught to him in the South, had won him special protection in the North.

In order to offer others that protection, however, Jameson would need to recreate the setting in which it was first introduced to him. He would also need to distinguish his own authentic Holiness church from the poseurs abounding in Boston. He posited that most northern Holiness churches, with their massive congregations, were not *genuine* because they lacked down-home intimacy. No pastor, in his view, could grow a church to gigantic proportions by preaching the steep price of salvation.

> The thing about the Holiness church is you only find a few people in a Holiness church. And I mean *real* holiness—not those places where they work roots. Those churches have *lots* of people . . . But you don't get rich in a Holiness church. Churches that need money will only preach things that people like to hear. They preach sweetwater. But if you preach about sinning and going to hell, they don't like that . . . In [the old] days, there was *power* in the

church. Sometimes you have revivals, and the Holiness church attracts a lot of people. But something is *wrong* if a Holiness church is too large on an ordinary Sunday.

At the close of the service, Jameson asked if anyone had anything to say. The elderly woman stood and began to heap praise on the pastor. She lambasted the "new style of church" that dominated the Boston worship scene and lauded "the bishop" for teaching "the old way."

The "good old way" and other exilic themes at the heart of Jameson's sermon were not at all unique to the Church of the Holy Ghost. Nearly every congregation I spent time in entertained the idea of being "in but not of the world" as a subject for discussion, preaching, or meditation. Further, nine of the churches I studied connected the theme of religious exile with the lived experiences of a particular group of people: migrants or immigrants. To borrow the language of social commentator William Leach (1999:29), these churches proffered unique ways of "standing ground against the placeless and learning how to marshal the power of centering against the landscape of the temporary." Thus, rather than uniting diverse peoples around the call to religious piety, exilic themes permitted the differentiation of churches by regional and national affinity. In this chapter, I explain how this single, simple religious notion contributed to the flowering of religious particularism in Four Corners.

The literature on religious particularism speaks little of the role of religious ideas in the proliferation of socially distinct faith communities. Yet part of what distinguishes churches from each other is the way clergy variously apply doctrines and interpretations of the Biblical text to speak directly to the lives of congregants. Previously I argued that in the first half of the twentieth century, sanctified churches promoted the refinement of religious particularism by elevating the exilic experiences of migrants and immigrants to Biblical proportions. Sanctified religious teachings that cast the life of holiness as a fundamentally exilic life, a life "in the world but not of the world," closely paralleled and deeply validated the existential realities of migrants and immigrants struggling to navigate a strange social terrain.

In the present chapter, the setting is the religious district in contemporary Four Corners. Rather than appearing solely in sanctified churches or to churches belonging to the Holiness-Pentecostal-Apostolic family, the "in but not of" theme appeared, almost uncannily, among most of the churches regardless of religious tradition. The popularity of the theme reflected not only the persistence of conversionist or "born again" religion in general, but also the arrival in Boston of new tides of southern migrants and immigrants. As I have noted, migrants still hail disproportionately from the Carolinas and Virginia. The immigrant church population now includes Latina/os and Haitians as well as West Indians.

But not all of the churches parlay this theme into direct calls to specific social groups. Indeed, the nine churches that do so stand apart from the others by virtue of their willingness and ability to work inherited religious ideas in this way. In thinking about the ways these churches work religious ideas to speak to the lives of congregants, I have found useful Erving Goffman's concept of "framing" and the related concept of "frame extension."

The term "frame" refers to "'schemata of interpretation' that enable individuals 'to locate, perceive, identify, and label' occurrences within their life space and the world at large. By rendering events or occurrences meaningful, frames function to organize experience and guide action, whether individual or collective" (Snow et al. 1986:464, citing Goffman 1974). The exilic "in but not of" theme is itself a frame that renders meaningful the irony of faith in an apparently faithless world. By invoking the words of Jesus ("Ye are from beneath; I am from above: ye are of this world; I am not of this world" John 8:23; "My kingdom is not of this world . . ." John 18:36) and Biblical images of exile (the sojourn of the Hebrews in Babylon), the "in but not of" frame moves beyond the common belief that religious adherence ensures one's place in the hereafter and addresses the earthly isolation one must endure in the meantime.

In itself, the exilic frame does not directly speak to the experiences of migrants and immigrants. Clergy and believers must do additional hermeneutical work on the frame in order to reach these target audiences. David Snow et al. (1986) have devised the term "frame alignment" to capture the multiple ways social movement organizations match their own ideological framings with the lived experiences of potential recruits. One type of alignment, what the authors call "frame extension," best describes the cognitive handiwork being done with the "in but not of" tradition in Four Corners.

> The programs and values that some SMOs [social movement organizations] promote may not be rooted in existing sentiment or adherent pools, or may appear to have little if any bearing on the life situations and interests of potential adherents. When such is the case, an SMO may have to extend the boundaries of its primary framework so as to encompass interests or points of view that are incidental to its primary objectives but of considerable salience to potential adherents. In effect, the movement is attempting to enlarge its adherent pool by portraying its objectives or activities as attending to or being congruent with the values or interests of potential adherents (472).

In Four Corners, it was not unusual for clergy to inject migrant narratives or recollections of the "old country" into conversionist talk about being "in but not of the world." On these occasions, clergy extended the religious exilic frame so that it spoke directly to people enduring nonreligious forms of exile. Through the act of frame extension, they assigned religious meaning to particular experiences of being culturally and/or geographically out of place. In this way, frame extension distinguished one church from another in the broader religious field, whether clergy intended to do so or not. The theme of exile thus became cognitive fuel for the creation of particularistic religious spaces for people who felt "out of place" in similar ways.

Below I describe how frame extension proceeded in migrant and immigrant churches. Each kind of church extended the exilic frame in two ways, both of which addressed the fundamental experience of "out of placeness."

SOUTHERN MIGRANT CHURCHES: EXILED IN THE NORTH

Migrant churches in Four Corners extended the "in but not of" frame in one of two ways, both of which spoke to migrant experiences and perpetuated aspects of southern life in the northern city. One strategy emphasized preserving an "old way" of southern worship, characterized by social intimacy, ritual "blessings," and/or lively music ministries. The other strategy sought to reconstitute in its entirety a lost, "southern" way of being and behaving. These divergent strategies were another source of variation within a group of churches easily lumped together as "migrant."

Perpetuating the "Good Old Way" of Southern Worship

The Church of the Holy Ghost introduced above typified the first kind of frame extension. In his sermon, the Rev. Jameson struck an initial parallel between his spiritual and cross-regional movements mainly to illustrate how southern-style, or "old way," holiness had protected and enriched his life in the urban North. He then extended a spiritual exilic frame, the interpretation of holiness as a "narrow way" incomprehensible to the hell-bound majority, to justify maintaining a small, family church. Here he transmitted Christian survival lessons directly to his northern-born descendants while ministering to those, such as the elderly woman, who could appreciate "the old way."

Four other migrant churches were similarly given to "old ways" of having church and extended the exilic frame accordingly. Like the Rev. Jameson, each pastor readily distinguished his or her church from inauthentic ones that offered little real spiritual satisfaction. But while Jameson emphasized intimacy almost exclusively, these churches accentuated charismatic praise, preaching, and healing as alternative or additional components of authentic worship.

Worship at Remembrance, another independent Pentecostal church, used frame extension to emphasize ritual "blessing" as the main component of authentic southern worship. The modest wooden plaque nailed beside the door of the storefront hinted at this emphasis; it read, '. . . Where everybody is somebody. Come expecting a miracle!" Blessings, which occupied a lengthy portion of every service, consisted of Pastor Pride praying on behalf of a believer and "laying hands" on her or him. During the blessing period, those seeking a miracle approached the front one by one and whispered a worry into the minister's ear. The minister, eyes clenched shut, then prayed loudly over the person, beseeching God to send the Spirit to accomplish the believer's uttered need. Inevitably her fevered prayers escalated into glossolalia.

Blessings were very physical occasions. Sometimes Pride extended both arms over the supplicant's shoulders; at other times, she placed a hand on one shoulder and extended the other as if calling divine power out of the air and channeling it directly into the supplicant's body. This particular kind of physicality was reserved especially for the few men who not only attended services but also approached the front for a blessing.[1] With women, who made up the overwhelming majority of worshipers, the pastor was much more physical. Often she used her hands to feel various parts of the woman's body: the head, the heart, the hands. Occasionally she tightly hugged the woman while praying. The entire ritual gave Pride the appearance of a meticulous, loving doctor who examines, diagnoses, and treats the ill patient. After these intensely physical blessing services, Pride was always sweaty, out of breath, and hoarse.

On rare occasions she called a person out of the audience for a blessing. "The Lord is telling me you are in need of special healing today," she might say, beckoning with arms extended toward the person. The person being blessed usually stood with head bowed, arms raised in praise, repeating "Yes, Lord!" or "Thank you, Lord Jesus!"; both of these chants are common in the world of Black Pentecostalism. The person might get the Holy Ghost and begin to shake, stomp, or dance under its animating power. After the blessing Pride would send the person off with a solid affirmation, an expression of certainty that the Holy Spirit was working for and through them. She assured one man that God was working to heal his marriage. As a woman walked back to her pew, Pride shouted, "And you're gonna *get* that house you wanted!"

Like Jameson, both the Reverend Pride and her congregants were aware that their church had to compete with other, usually larger and more lavishly appointed churches. They felt, nevertheless, that Remembrance, with its emphasis on spiritual blessing, was closer to the true path of holiness than were its competitors. Mother Sarah, a member of the church for ten years, especially resented the way these "rich-cratic" churches lured members away from humbler, more authentic churches like hers. Big churches, with "all the jewelry and the nice robes, where your feet sink all down in the carpet," had attracted many people from Remembrance, many of them women allegedly looking for husbands. "There ain't nothing here [at Remembrance] for *me*," said longtime member Mother Caren, mimicking the younger women who had left the church. Sarah added that some of the defectors "made good money, $400, $500 a week," but did not want to support a struggling church. Rather, she speculated, they preferred to go to bigger churches and "pay the pastor's salary." Pastor Pride, who personally maintained the church with income made by taking in foster children, knew that she had lost many members to "rich-cratic" churches. "But they come running right back *here* when they want a blessing!" Thus, at Remembrance, protecting religious authenticity in exile meant remaining true to intensely personal forms of worship that helped the believer to *metabolize* suffering and need—to burn them like mere calories in the fallen fire of the Holy Ghost. Here, the individual's confessed woes and wants were offered to God, who consumed them and faithfully returned the principal byproduct: peace of mind.

If ritual blessings served to distinguish Remembrance Church from its inauthentic competitors, high-powered music ministries were considered the main ingredient of authentic southern worship at the remaining three "old way" migrant churches: Mt. Nebo Apostolic, Holy Fullness Apostolic, and the Anointed Church. The Anointed Church was the flagship congregation of a new denomination founded by Bishop Apostle Dubose. The denomination consisted of several congregations scattered up and down the East Coast from Rhode Island to Florida. Dubose, a North Carolinian, broke off from the Apostolic Church of God in Christ in an attempt to better preserve the "old style" (his terminology) of worship characteristic of the southern church and because he believed in baptism in Jesus' name rather than baptism in the Father, Son, and Holy Ghost. This church was so serious about music that roughly half of the hundred-member congregation were choir members or musicians. Dubose himself led the choir. When the choir assembled, the pews were heavily depleted, and the sound of high-energy gospel singing accompanied by funky drum, bass guitar, and electric keyboard playing could be heard a block away.

Holy Fullness Apostolic lacked Anointed's massive choir but was decidedly old southern in vocal arrangement and instrumentation. The church had about one hundred members representing a mix of working-class and professional people. The Rev. French, the eighty-year-old associate minister and Sunday school superintendent, found it amusing that so many nearby churches were composed mainly of migrants. He noted, reflecting on his own ethnographic explorations, that "If you go to most of the churches around here (points to three storefronts within eyeshot) it seems like there are more southern folks than northern! [*Laughs.*] There's a whole lot of churches around here. They come up from the South and start a little storefront, and then maybe move to a bigger place . . . But," he added, "people go to church more in the South . . . And in the South they have quartets," he said, motioning toward the Holy Fullness main entrance, from which poured the tight vocal harmonies of quartet gospel music and upbeat drum, guitar, and Hammond B-3 organ accompaniment.[2]

These migrant churches began with the common "in but not of" spiritual theme but extended it to relate directly to the migrant experience of being "in but not of" the urban North. They extended the theme by associating holiness with aspects of southern charismatic worship. These aspects include southern-style music ministries, ritual blessings, and congregational intimacy. By posing these "old ways" of worship as part of the path of true holiness, migrants simultaneously aimed to resist the world of sin and protect familiar cultural practices from extinction in the northern city-world.

Transplanting Southern Society

In none of the above churches did I encounter the belief that the southern context itself was more conducive to Christian living than the urban North. Even the Rev. Jameson admitted to having spells as a "devil" in both regions. According to the "old way" frame extension, then, it was not the South itself that cultivated personal holiness but a way of "having church" that was *native* to the South. Two migrant churches took the extension a step further by identifying not just the southern Black church but the South itself with the exclusive path of holiness. The Christ Church, established in 1968 in an old wood frame structure formerly owned by Beth El Hebrew School, was one such religious community. The Christ Church belonged to a Holiness denomination, the Church of Christ. It was not Pentecostal, however, for it explicitly denounced charismatic worship and speaking in tongues. The Christ Church congregation had 225 members, and Sunday services regularly attracted 175 to 200 people, many of whom were professionals, including educators, lawyers, business people, and doctors.

Given the professional composition of his flock, Pastor David Fadden, known simply as "the minister," sometimes took up the theme of worldly accomplishment while preaching about holiness. He described the faithful in common exilic terms: as people "at war with the world," "chosen people," and "more than just human beings" chasing after material boons in the big city. In doing so, he extended the "in but not of" frame to orient the relatively affluent congregation toward spiritual concerns. But he also frequently extended this frame to speak to the migratory experiences of his congregants.

Most congregants were either born in the southern United States or were second-generation Northerners. In either case, the congregation had its roots in Alabama, Georgia, Tennessee, Mississippi, Florida, and the Carolinas. This diversity was especially evident during the lively social periods before and after Sunday services and between Bible study and formal worship. At these times people circulated freely between pews to exchange handshakes and hugs and words of comfort, congratulations, or caring. Amidst the tightly swirling crowd, I beheld a striking aural kaleidoscope of southern accents.

Nearly all of the church leaders hailed from southern states. Pastor Fadden was from Tennessee via rural Buffalo, New York. His wife was from South Carolina. Only Phillip Turner, the twenty-nine-year-old associate pastor (he preferred the title Brother), stood apart in this regard, and even he described himself as a "Virginia boy." Raised in Detroit, Brother Turner served as associate minister in several Church of Christ congregations in Virginia before arriving in Boston. Having been "spoiled" in Virginia, he was pleased to find a northern outpost that preserved southern ways, beginning with

> the fact that everyone cooks the same [laughs]—there are a lot of good southern cooks in here! There is a lot of reminiscing, a lot of talk about the South, a lot of talk about the past. People still keep their gardens, people still take care of things like they used to . . . I think they keep a good down-home feel to it, to not get so caught up in the Boston city life.

This "down-home feel" partly explained why Alicia, a Georgia native now in her sixties, had attended the church for more than thirty years. Alicia moved to Roxbury to live with her elder sister in 1952. She recalled her early disappointment with the racial and economic situation in Boston. Expressions of racism were rampant in the racially transitioning neighborhood around her Sherman Street home ("Although it is worse now," she added). Also to her disappointment, "employment was the pits, even in the department stores," which for Black women constituted the primary, and usually preferable, alternative to domestic service. During her teenage years in Georgia, she had been a faithful member of a congregation in the Christ Church denomination. Subsequently, although she lived near Roxbury's exploding religious district, Felicia was unable to find a religious home. Only in 1968, when the Dorchester Christ Church was organized, did she find a religious community that combined southern sociability with solemn worship and an insistence upon "going especially by the Bible."

But more than simply maintaining a "good down-home feel," which the Church of the Holy Ghost and other migrant churches emphasized exclusively, Christ Church members and clergy spoke of life in the South, and especially the old rural South, as being uniquely conducive of authentic Christian living. Remembering and recovering the southern lifestyle might help one resist sinful northern habits, such as slothfulness and random acts of meanness. Thus the minister taught from the pulpit that prior to entering the sacred pact of marriage, every young man should work on a farm for at least a year in order to learn the true meaning of hard work and self-sufficiency. "We do share things like that," Brother Turner commented,

> especially recently with the things that went on in Atlanta [the bombing during the 1996 Olympics]. It's not so much the city, it's just the mindset of the people, how God's not in the world anymore. Even in the South. That's why they always go back to the past. It's not current South, its always *past* South. Back when everything closed down on Sundays. They go back to things like that to get people to understand where God's place used to be in the world, and now it's not there anymore. They try to get young people to realize how it was, because if you don't, then young people will be like the children of Israel, where all the elders had died and the children had no knowledge of God and all the things he did for Israel.

Note how Turner compared young people in the contemporary North with the Biblical Israelites. This was no accident. It typified the way people in this church extended the Biblical "in but not of" frame to speak to the vicissitudes of regional exile. Turner continued:

> There was a time when you could pray in school, there was a time when you could go out and not be tempted to work on Sunday. They do that in explicit fashion—they just talk about the city, they talk about the dangers, and how things were different in the South . . .
>
> We joked with people—when we came up from north Virginia—how you *have* to be nice to people in the South. If you're not, that's considered to be rude. And if you're not nice to people, you know, it's normal around here. And we came up here and we were nice to people, and people say, "Oh, you're not from around here!" And that's something you have to get people to understand, that you should be nice to people all the time, *especially* if you're Christian. You shouldn't get so caught up in driving crazy, being mean, honking your horn, and all those kind of things.

The South was remembered, then, not only to preserve old ways of having church but also to invoke a dying way of life that permitted, demanded, celebrated, the blurring of sacred and secular. Remembrance of the South was therefore a social *and* religious imperative as it was when the exiled Biblical Hebrews remembered the prophets of old.

At another migrant church, Faith Baptist, the recently installed pastor thought about the South in ways similar to members of the Christ Church. The Rev. Winspeare, who had pastored the church for only four years when I began visiting, longed for the southern *social context,* where the church was the center of social life. He blamed the secular northern city, which he had endured for only six years, for diluting the church's taken-for-grantedness in society. He also alluded to the influence of Roman Catholicism and the racial and ethnic diversity in Boston by way of explaining the lack of uniform religious commitment in Boston. While acknowledging the existence of large Black churches, he wondered whether people "were going just to go" rather than going because the church truly was central to their social lives. Bewildered, he told me, "I'm not from Boston, I'm from Tennessee. And it's quite different from Memphis." "How so?" I asked him. He replied,

> The church setting, to me, in Memphis is more of an embedded place just for church, for worship, just for churches themselves. It's a place of embedded— seems like a place *for* churches, and it's definitely a worshiping *place.*
>
> People look forward to coming to church. Not just Sunday but whatever the case may be, whether there's a revival going on or just during the weeknights. People come out and support just being in church. Here I find out people don't really go, maybe 'cause this is a Catholic state? To me it seems like it's more people out of the church than in the church . . . I'm saying that there is a sense of worship [yet] to be in this area, a sense of God [yet] to really be in this area.

Importantly, Winspeare was not explicitly concerned with distinguishing his church from others that lacked the "old way" of in-church worship. Instead, he decried a public that did not esteem church enough, that attended church too rarely and for the wrong reasons. He implied that the overarching "sense of God" in Memphis made it normal to have church and for people to want to spend a good deal of time in church. Boston, as Winspeare told it, did not legitimize organized religion in this way. Boston did not strike him as "a place *for* churches." His strategy for creating such a place was to "fellowship" with other clergy in New England, especially Baptist ones. He believed that clerical unity would make the region more hospitable for churches, like his, that were serious about restoring the church's vital role in society.

The previous discussion illustrates how churches easily lumped together as "migrant" could in fact be distinguished according to the extending work they did on the exilic frame. In one kind of extension, the exilic frame spoke to the migrant's nostalgia for expressive and/or intimate styles of "having church" assumed to be more common in the South than in the North. Simultaneously, it presented this authentic religious practice as a kind of armor, which the migrant could don as protection against the assaults of life in the northern city. In the other variety, the exilic frame was used to validate the migrant's nostalgia for southern society and the privileged role that organized religion played in that society. Rather than envisioning religious practice as individual protection *against* society, these churches saw religion as part of a broader system of southern social norms: a system worth reproducing whole cloth in the North.

The theoretical work of sociologist Peter Berger helps to clarify the distinction between these two forms of frame extension. Brother Turner and Pastor Winspeare were nostalgic for an *overarching moral order* that in the "old South" legitimized the church's influence on society. At the same time, the church helped to uphold and legitimize that moral order. As such, one's children could pray in school during the week, and adults could devote Sundays to worship rather than to work. People were nice to each other outside church walls because it was "Christian" to behave civilly in nominally secular settings. People made church the center of their social lives. This social world bears striking resemblance to the "sacred canopy" that Berger eulogized in his 1967 treatise. According to Berger, the "demonopolization" of religion in Western societies has led to the flowering of religious pluralism, which, in turn, has hampered the ability of organized religions to uphold a unitary social order—a sacred canopy beneath which individuals enjoy a seamless, taken-for-granted sense of reality. "Religion," Berger writes,

> no longer legitimates the world. Rather, different religious groups seek, by different means, to maintain their particular subworlds in the face of a plurality of competing subworlds. Concomitantly, this plurality of religious legitimations is internalized in consciousness as a plurality of possibilities between which one may choose. Ipso facto, any particular choice is relativized and less than certain. (152)

Demoralized, as it were, by the collapse of the sacred canopy and the subsequent need to compete with a confusing array of alternative worldviews, religious institutions face two options:

> They can either accommodate themselves to the situation, play the pluralistic game of religious free enterprise, and come to terms as best they can in accordance with consumer demands. Or they can refuse to accommodate themselves, entrench themselves behind whatever socio-religious structures they can maintain or construct, and continue to profess the old objectives as much as possible as if nothing had happened. (153)

By using the "in but not of" frame to romanticize southern society as such, the Christ Church and Pastor Winspeare invoked real or exaggerated socio-religious structures that they felt had been eroded by secularization or abandoned through migration. The Church of the Holy Ghost and other churches, on the other hand, did not lament the relentless puncturing of the sacred canopy. They sought instead to distinguish themselves from the many inauthentic churches that shared the religious landscape. They agreed to "play the pluralistic game": they extended the "in but not of" frame only enough to preserve authentic "good old ways" of worship for the spiritual edification of migrants.

It is interesting, also, that the five "old way of worship" clergy were Pentecostal and the remaining two, who waxed nostalgic about the overall place of religion in southern society, were Holiness and Baptist. I attribute this difference not to the latter's more vivid memory of the South but to the former's deeper emphasis on the tangible immanence of the Holy Spirit. Like a cellular phone, the Spirit and its charismatic signs constituted a highly portable link not only to God but to ways of having church that are native to the South. It was not necessary for these churches to reconstruct an entire social milieu to feel legitimate or authentic. Consider also that Pentecostal churches dwelled, until recently, at the margins of religious culture even in the South. The South may have been "a place for churches," but this was not necessarily the case for Pentecostal churches. Rather than waxing nostalgic about the entire southern social world, then, Pentecostal churches needed only "dial up" the Spirit, if you will, and artfully distinguish themselves from churches who, because of their size, staid worship, or inability to bestow blessings, lacked authentic spirituality. Clergy who did not envision such a cellular link yet who clung to memories of religion's central status in southern society were perhaps more likely to idealize the old South itself more than isolated aspects of southern Black worship.

IMMIGRANT CONGREGATIONS: EXILED IN THE UNITED STATES

Sociologist R. Stephen Warner (1998:3) observes that "people migrating to the United States bring their religions with them, and gathering religiously is one of the ways they make a life here. Their religious identities often (but not always) mean more to them away from home, in their diaspora, than they did before, and those identities undergo more or less modification as the years pass." In the host country, church participation becomes a way to ensure cultural continuity and to encourage adjustment to the host country, although specific congregations may lean toward one or the other. Of interest here are the ways in which religious ideas themselves were mobilized in the service of adjustment and continuity, assimilation and cultural preservation.

As it turned out, the extended exilic frame figured prominently in only two of Four Corners' immigrant congregations. Clergy worked the "in but not of" tradition in ways that allowed worshipers, while having church, to confront the dilemmas of continuity and adjustment. Like the migrant churches, these religious communities used the same frame to achieve different ends.

The Church of God was founded in 1978 when the small West Indian contingent of a predominantly Haitian church broke away to form its own congregation. The new congregation, which initially met in Mattapan, quickly swelled to 118 members but then dwindled nearly as quickly because so many members had to work on Sundays. No hour of services—not even 8:30 A.M.—was convenient enough to pull together this congregation of hospital workers and laborers. The congregation soon split, with some following the founding pastor, others founding a new Church of God under a new pastor, and the remainder falling away altogether. The Reverend Mary Livingston, originally from Jamaica, joined the new Church of God upon arriving in the United States from England in 1979. She had left England following the death of her husband; Boston was an attractive destination since two of her children already lived there. Livingston found work as a nurse's assistant at Boston Hospital and served as assistant minister at the four-member Church of God congregation.

In 1981, the pastor returned to Jamaica and left the church in Livingston's hands. She immediately secured a mortgage on the Washington Street house where the congregation had been meeting and bought a church van. The next move would be cosmetic. The house/church formerly had been a funeral home—a macabre fact that repelled some would-be recruits. Pastor Livingston decided that major renovations were in order. She hired a contractor to build a church front on the house, but "the contractor rob us up." After botching the renovation and causing the house to collapse on its foundation, the contractor filed bankruptcy and disappeared. Some said he was in prison—others said he was dead. In either case, the congregation was forced into exile in Codman Square, where it rented space from the Haitian Church of God from which it had split only three years earlier. It took six years for the church to raise enough money to build a new structure on the old property.

During its long homeless stint, the church grew to some two hundred members. It became a mostly professional congregation composed of nurses, journalists, carpenters, teachers, plumbers, and computer scientists. Members were from Jamaica, Trinidad and Tobago, and Barbados. The new church was a spacious white structure that resembled an airplane hangar from the outside. A banner hung above the outside door warned, "Do Not Touch God's Anointed!" The interior, decidedly unhangarlike was luxuriously decorated with a red carpet and red cushioned chairs. Central air condition-ing ducts ran along the floors. I was grateful for these when I visited the church for the first time on a very warm Mother's Day.

The pastor's adult daughter, who delivered the sermon, used the oppor-tunity to talk about raising West Indian children in the United States. The sermon was typical for this church in the way it extended exilic notions of holiness to address existential dilemmas faced by immigrants. That morning, the preacher would propel the frame extension by likening children to or-anges. Beginning with the classic spiritual exilic frame, she reminded us that oranges have a number of layers, each of which needs to be intact in order for the child-soul, the seed, to resist a sinful world and grow to her full poten-tial. The peel is God: "You got to pass *God* before you come to *me!*" she said, reminding me of the prohibitive banner draped outside the church. The in-ner rind, she explained, is the Holy Spirit. The juice is the Word of God, with-out which the seed will grow up to be irresponsible and indistinguishable from sinners. By way of frame extension, she moved on to note that oranges need space to grow in their gardens. The garden was the United States, and "giving space" meant conforming to North American child rearing conven-tions and resisting the urge to impose West Indian culture on children:

> As West Indies parents, we feel we can live here but *abide* in Jamaica. We fail to realize that we live in *this* society. Children sometimes want to think of them-selves as Jamaican. You come here, want beef patty, rice and peas, jerk chicken, and so on. But it's not yours, that's *mine*—that's *my* homeland. But if your kids come here and want to be like Yankee-dem, we worry they will forget where they from. But they can fall through the cracks . . . Mothers, especially West Indies parents, think only the rod can discipline the child. Bible say, "Don't spare the rod and spoil the child." But it's *conditional*. It's only a temporary mes-sage. If you put the word of God in the child early, you don't need force. I am talking *brass tack* today!

The "brass tack," she further explained, was that the U.S. government, which she called "the system," could take children away from parents who used cor-poral punishment.

As Pastor Livingston later told me, this sermon was no outlier. Indeed, part of the church's mission was to teach West Indians how to negotiate life in the United States, or how to adjust. Part of that negotiation involved a com-mitment to being in but not of the world: "In a mixed-up world, you only need to know that you are in the *church*. So whatever you do, do it honestly. Even if you are an attorney, put the Lord in *front* of you." But negotiation also involved attention to brass tacks. Many church members needed to decide whether to become U.S. citizens or whether to vote. It was common for congregants to keep homes in England, Jamaica, or elsewhere, with the intention of returning home in the future. "But usually they don't," the Rev. Livingston said. Congregants therefore needed to plan, anticipate, however reluctantly, a life in the United States. Livingston communicated this point while remaining close to the theme of spiritual exile, quoting me the practical, protective injunction that Titus gave to early Christian communities in Rome: "The Word of God says, Obey laws and magistrate."[3]

In the Divine Peace Pentecostal Church I witnessed the exilic frame extended to radically different effect. To be certain, church members dutifully obeyed the laws and magistrates of their new home. But instead of extolling the virtues of citizenship and cultural assimilation, the pastor of this church highlighted the morally corrosive aspects of American culture. Divine Peace began in the early 1980s as a prayer meeting of Antiguan-born immigrants in Mattapan. The prayer meeting became a formal church only after sending for the Rev. Lucas, who promptly came up from Antigua to pastor the tiny flock. When I began visiting Four Corners, the congregation had been meeting there for six years.

On an average Sunday, the eighteen-pew storefront attracted roughly twenty-five individuals, most of whom were middle-aged women and their teenaged daughters. Services always warmed up with hymns sung to the accompaniment of organ, drum, and electric bass. Then came the testimonials. Pastor Lucas, standing at the pulpit, would listen very intently to each person's prayers. He and many of the other attendants would respond to parts of the prayers with "Yes!" and "Amen." When someone started to quote a Bible passage, the congregation finished it in unison, nodding in deep recognition of the illuminated point of contact between Scripture and present predicament. This Sunday, a woman prays for the children going to and coming from school. The pastor says, "Oh, yes. Yes, lord." She prays for the strength to keep a positive attitude in the midst of tribulation, and he punctuates her words with "Look up!" A middle-aged woman plays organ and leads the congregation in song. There are five males present, including the pastor and myself. A pre-teenaged boy sits at the trap set, his head barely visible behind the cymbals. Nearby, a seated elderly man casually but skillfully plucks the electric bass resting on his knee. There is one young boy in the congregation: he squirms on the hard wooden pew and tugs gently on his grandmother's sparkling earrings. The pastor appears to be in his sixties. As the singing starts again he stands, just barely swaying to the music, and deftly handles his tambourine. Others have tambourines, too, and work them into hypnotic, limping syncopation. They sing, "When we all get to heaven, what a day of rejoicing that will be!"

After making a few announcements, the pastor invites a woman in the pews to give a blessing. She talks, among other things, about her daughter's impending wedding. The ceremony and reception have exceeded her budget, but she trusts God will find a way to cover all expenses. The pastor now begins his sermon. With the aid of a hefty magnifying glass, he begins reading from Luke a chapter containing several parables of faith lost and found. A woman strategically seated in a rear pew brings me a Bible so that I can follow along. Lucas reads:

> Either what woman having ten pieces of silver, if she lose one piece, doth not light a candle, and sweep the house, and seek diligently till she find it? And when she hath found it, she calleth her friends and her neighbors together, saying, Rejoice with me; for I have found the piece which I had lost. Likewise, I say unto you, there is joy in the presence of the angels of God over one sinner that repenteth. (Luke 15:8–10)

He ties this passage to the marital theme of the woman's blessing by comparing the lost piece of silver with an engagement ring. "Women always make sure you see their hand with the engagement ring on it. They want to show off their ring."

Then, in what seems at first like a wide digression, he begins to talk about rampant materialism, which has led to "the Americanization of other countries," and to the corruption of many who immigrate to the United States. "Don't get caught up in the nice things of the U.S.," he warns. "If you follow certain things in the U.S., you will drop out. Be very particular, and follow the leader, who is Jesus Christ. Engagement is a joyful time. But with the same joy of marital engagement you should be joyful of your engagement with Christ. Christ is the groom who will take us as his bride and present us to his father!" he shouted. "Amen!"

Lucas then tells the story of a woman who is engaged to a man who went abroad for seven years. In her groom's absence, another man approached her. "I'll give you a house, servants, gold, silver," says the suitor. The woman retorts, "I'm engaged! He's coming back!" The man tells her that her groom has drowned at sea. The woman replies, "If he died, I hope he's resting. If he lives, I still love him." The man then goes and "cleans himself up"—it turns out that he is the groom in disguise. "And you could imagine what happened," the pastor says, laying loud, amorous smooches onto the microphone. The congregation erupts in laughter. He continues:

> We belong to Jesus Christ. He engaged us. We belong to him, and he is ours. If you lose your ring, you lose the engagement. You would be embarrassed, after making an announcement, to have lost the ring. The man comes back, upset that she lost her ring. He thinks she lost it out in the world, to some other

man. But it turns out that she lost it in the house, not outside. The church is the bride—we are the bride of Christ! There were ten virgins, and five lost their engagement. When the bridegroom was at hand, he could only take five [from Matt. 25:1–13].

Don't wait 'til after the bridegroom come and gone! Rocks and mountains will come over the people who lose their engagement. There will be weeping, wailing, moaning, and gnashing of teeth. But too late will be our cry!

The congregation eagerly recites the well-worn "too late" passage along with the pastor.

In an apparent digression, the pastor has extended the "in but not of" frame to warn his flock of the corrupting influence of North American materialism and to present cultural loyalty as a partner of religious loyalty. The woman in Lucas's story rejected the world's temptations, knowing that she was not *of* that world—she was engaged to something paradoxically absent yet immanent. Yet that "something" could be either Jesus Christ and His World to come or the Caribbean cultural universe that the congregation left behind en route to the United States. In the same breath, the sermon teaches faithfulness to Christ and loyalty to home, family, and tradition.

Thus, like the migrant churches, churches easily collapsed into an "immigrant" category were differentiated in part by their use of frame extension. The middle-class Church of God extended the exilic frame in ways that privileged adjustment over cultural continuity. This rhetorical bias promoted what Warner (1998) calls "transmutation," or the process through which "a new religious identity survives the demise of regional, national, and linguistic identities" (17). By contrast, clergy and laypersons in the working-class Divine Peace Church did not use frame extension to cast adjustment as a religiously meaningful duty. Instead, they related the call to spiritual exile to the call to cultural continuity. Rather than pushing religious identity as an alternative to national identity, they associated holiness with *resistance* to cultural assimilation.

The way these churches diverged in their use of the exilic theme is relevant to a wider discussion of class and ethnic identity among West Indian immigrants. Most recently, in her extensive study of West Indians in New York city, Mary Waters (1999:330) found that "ethnically rooted" churches played central roles in the lives of her West Indian interviewees. Churches protected West Indian children from "the worst aspects of American city life," and clergy "often [cajole] parents into accepting some aspects of the 'Americanization' of their teens, while basically upholding the overall values of the parents, which stressed hard work, stability, education, and striving for upward mobility" (202). She even noted how some churches were confronting the disjuncture between West Indian and U.S. norms regarding the corporal punishment of children and were "trying to change behaviors through education and social support" (241).

Waters's observations about West Indian churches fit the middle-class Church of God uncannily well but not the working-class Divine Peace Church. The pastor of the latter church spoke out *against* Americanization, preaching instead survival through cultural loyalty. This divergence points to the possibility of considerable difference among West Indian churches on the issue of cultural assimilation. The divergence is also significant given one of Waters's more general arguments: that middle-class West Indians maintain "sharper cultural boundaries," while working-class and poor West Indians are considerably less resistant to becoming generic Black Americans. My cases do not disprove this argument but do establish the empirical possibility of its inverse.

More generally, these churches stood out from the majority of immigrant churches in the district, which did not extend the "in but not of" tradition or any other religious frame to open up rhetorical space for issues of adjustment and continuity. It is not that these churches avoided addressing immigrant concerns; rather, such concerns were voiced without Biblical trappings. For some of these churches, denominational pressures and the desire to recruit nonimmigrant populations limited the range of available, or useful, hermeneutical gymnastics. Other immigrant churches did not face such constraints but were cautious not to pollute universal doctrines with particularistic appeals. In either case, as I will discuss further in chapter 6, the lack of explicit frame extension did not necessarily render churches blind to the practical needs of recent immigrants.

SUMMARY

This chapter has shown how clergy variously use the theme of exile to speak to specific groups of people and thus to promote the role of churches as particularistic spaces of sociability. In describing these multiple usages, I have provided examples of how religious ideas can affect church functioning not via some linear causal mechanism but through a messier process of clerical work on the idea in question (for other cases in point, see McRoberts 1999). Such work renders fairly ubiquitous ideas, like the notion of being "in the world but not of the world" glutinous enough to be used to varying effects in different churches, depending on how exactly the target population feels out of place.

FIVE

"The Street"

CLERGY CONFRONT THE IMMEDIATE ENVIRONMENT

Religion is always, among other things, a matter of necessary places, sites
where the humans and their deities, ancestors, or spirits may most intimately
communicate; religious practice in city and countryside alike engages the
vicissitudes of the environments that humans find themselves thrown into and
makes meaningful places out of contingent spaces.
—Robert Orsi, *Gods of the City*

The word "church" often conjures up an image of a structure somehow set
apart. We imagine a regal architecture, its spires towering above the roofs of
quaint single-family dwellings or competing nobly with secular temples of
downtown commerce. In our imaginations, the church may be set apart from
its surroundings by some physical buffer, such as a neatly kept lawn, or a
wrought iron fence. Rarely do we think of churches as being an integral part
of street life. In neighborhoods like Four Corners, where most congregations
worship in storefronts along busy thoroughfares, church and street, sacred
space and public space, religious space and vacant space, form a tight patchwork with one kind of space directly abutting and affecting the other. During
the workweek, this tight juxtaposition exaggerated the neighborhood's depressed appearance. Storefront churches, most of which were closed most of
the week, were barely distinguishable from neighboring vacant commercial
spaces.

On Sundays, a sonic battle ensued between church and street. In the
street, I heard the sound of tambourines, singing, preaching, and clapping—
the sound of vigorous, ecstatic praise—pouring out of the churches. Inside
church I noticed the sounds of the street: the rumbling bass of car stereos
pumping out hip-hop and Dominican merengue, the screech of car tires, the
piercing screams of fire engines, ambulances, and police cars, and the occasional shouted curse from an agitated passerby.

Even those who worshipped in traditional church structures were acutely
aware that no material buffer separated the sanctuary from the immediate
environment. In Four Corners, worshipers did not have the luxury of con-
sidering their churches as places physically set apart. About every other
week the press reported a shooting or stabbing in or near the neighborhood.
Pastors often complained of drug and alcohol addicts wandering into their

81

churches and disrupting services. At least two churches were outfitted with burglar alarms. I was caught unexpectedly by a church alarm one afternoon when I visited the Fellowship Apostolic Church for an interview with the pastor. When I arrived the doors were closed, and there were no signs of activity around the church. I tried the door—it was locked. I pressed both doorbells and waited. As it dawned on me that the pastor had stood me up, a very loud alarm, located just above the door, went off. Several passers-by eyed me suspiciously. I walked away, contemplating the ironic possibility of being hassled by police for trying to get into a church on a Saturday afternoon.

Although most of the churches in Four Corners lacked awareness of the neighborhood as such, they were intensely aware of the spaces immediately surrounding them and did not lack convictions about what to do, or not do, in those spaces. Four Corners churches conceived of the street in three ways: as an evil other to be avoided at all cost, as a recruitment ground to be trod and sacralized, and as a point of contact with persons at risk who are to be served. In addition, two churches combined "recruitment ground" and "point of contact" orientations. In each case, the street was more than just a physical place—it was a trope[1] embodying religiously assigned meanings. The meanings that church people, especially clergy, assigned to the street, in turn, helped them define what it meant to be religious in that particular church. By making sense of the immediate urban space, religious people made sense of themselves. And through their divergent sense-making, churches were further distinguished from one another in the religious district.

At first glance, this brand of religious sense-making evokes Durkheim's (1915) classic distinction between "sacred" and "profane." The subtle difference, however, is that churches in Four Corners unanimously viewed behaviors associated with the street as a problem if not as an evil, while Durkheim envisioned the profane as merely the domain of everyday, mundane life. In Durkheim's formulation, humans set the sacred apart from the profane as wholly (holy) other but did not try to annihilate, avoid, or alter the profane world. Humans lived in the profane world as a matter of necessity but held up the sacred as a reminder of society's most precious values and morals. In a sense, the sacred existed to invest the profane world with a grander purpose and meaning than would ordinarily be apparent. At the same time, the ordinariness of the profane was absolutely necessary in order for the nonordinary sacred to have meaning. Sacred and profane relied on each other for existence.

The sociological observer might project the sacred/profane framework onto urban churches, but this certainly was not how religious people in Four

Corners made sense of their own church/street dichotomies. Churches defined themselves over and against the street, but they did not take the problems of the street as ordinary workaday aspects of human life. Rather, the street threatened both ordinary life and the values to which ordinary life might be consecrated. The street was the profane gone tragically wrong.

In the following, I describe the dominant religious interpretations of the street. I then discuss the significance of these street concepts for our understanding of churches in the religious district and for the urban sociological literature. Specifically, I explain the often ambiguous roles that class and religious traditions played in pulling churches toward one orientation or another. I then explain how this taxonomy contributes to the ongoing urban sociological discussion about social interaction in Black urban contexts.

AVOIDING "ROOT WORKERS": THE STREET AS EVIL OTHER

Church of God in Christ	Church of the Holy Ghost	Maison d'Esprit
Holy Fullness	Church of God	Remembrance
Iglesia de Santos	Anointed Church	Iglesia Christo El Rey
Mt. Nebo	Divine Peace	New Jerusalem
	Fellowship Apostolic	

The thirteen churches listed above drew a thick line between themselves and the street and avoided all superfluous contact with the latter. Ministers did not preach on street corners or go door-to-door seeking recruits. After services, even on the loveliest spring afternoons, congregants moved quickly to cars and church vans to avoid exposure to danger. The "evil other" perspective, however, was not just about fear of danger. It took fear a step further, posing the street as the cosmic nemesis of the church.

Sociologist Timothy Nelson (1997:184; see also Williams 1974:158) captures the church-based "evil other" sentiment in his insightful ethnography of Eastside Chapel, a Black church located in a "ghetto" of Charleston, South Carolina:

> Because of its ghetto environment with its many dangers and temptations, services at Eastside Chapel often had the emotionally charged atmosphere of a besieged military outpost struggling to survive behind enemy lines while preventing defection from within the ranks. Indeed, members used this metaphor of the church as an army encamped in hostile territory to characterize their relationship to the world just beyond their doors.

Frequent thefts of congregants' cars and the regular disruption of services by crowds of "unruly" men outside the church further entrenched "[t]he image of the congregation as a tiny piece of God's Kingdom, isolated in the midst of hostile territory" (184).

The Rev. Robert Jameson, pastor of the Church of the Holy Ghost and one of four clergy who actually lived in Four Corners, had similar run-ins with "unruly" people. Jameson religiously kept his two used station wagons (which "don't give me any trouble, except that they drink gasoline") directly in front of his house, "'cause I don't want any dope dealers and root workers hanging around in front of my place. They used to hang out right in front of here. Once they were even selling [drugs] right over the cars. If you let them do it, people think you are involved, too." Jameson began taking pictures of the dealers. The dealers would scatter each time they noticed his camera trained on them from the second-floor window. Eventually, Jameson's next-door neighbor, an elderly woman whom he called "a great ally," began to call the police when the dealers arrived. The dealers gradually stopped selling in front of his house/church and moved their business further down the street.

During one conversation, Jameson frequently spoke of "root workers," which in the rural South refers to practitioners of hoodoo, a system of African American folk magic.[2] In his usage, "root workers" was a catch-all term for worldly people and "street people." Furthermore, root workers were consistently evil, whether discovered in the street or in the church. When discovered in the church, unrepentant root workers were to be expelled. Otherwise, as Jameson was quoted as saying in chapter 4, root workers would promote moneymaking and congregational growth over authentic spirituality, thus derailing the church's mission to save souls. Root workers may also corrupt church music with street-associated idioms, as when "people [such as the popular gospel artist Kirk Franklin] try to make gospel music sound like hip-hop."[3] Unlike the church, though, the street was a natural place for root workers and the absolute worst place for holy people. One could resist the street's chaotic power only by staying out of it, calling the police, or taking pictures. One could not save those given to the street unless they came into the church seeking salvation.

Albert Toussaint, assistant minister at the Haitian Maison d'Esprit, echoed Jameson's view when I asked him how he felt about the church's location in a high-crime, depressed area. "This is a rough area," he reflected. "Maybe God sent us to this area. God wants evil people to come to him—he wants them to get his messages. We have to be there to help the drug addicts, the evil people, people who make others' lives miserable, with no family values." The church did not send missionaries into the street to help "the evil people"— they had to come into the church. Toussaint told me that during seven years at the present location, two drug addicts, both Americans, had wandered into the church during services. He reported that both had been saved, although neither currently belongs to the congregation. Then he paused, embarrassed but not recalcitrant at the way he had been talking about the area, and added, "I hope you don't live around here!"

In churches like Maison and the Church of the Holy Ghost, the street was presented as more than merely a dangerous place. It was a place where people encountered forces operating directly against the work of salvation and holiness. Thus clergy in both churches instructed young people to avoid "running around in the street." Such advice was half-literal, half-figurative. If one literally lingered in the street, one might encounter drug dealers, prostitutes, and other tempters. But the street also symbolized sin in general; thus one need not literally hang out on the street in order to be guilty of street behavior—recall that the Rev. Jameson had encountered "root work" both in the street and in the church. In short, church people worshiped near the street by necessity, but they were decidedly not of the street, just as holy people are "in but not of the world." In these churches, the street was the world urbanized, and the world was not only "profane" but full of evil.

On that note, it is significant that all of the churches holding the "evil other" perspective were composed of immigrants or migrants. For the migrant churches, whose religiously colored awareness of being "out of place" I discussed in the previous chapter, the streets around them represented the worst the urban north had to offer. This understanding of the street was validated when church members or their children became victims of violence. Pastor Pride (Remembrance), for instance, lost her son in a drive-by shooting near a public housing project. One of the "Mothers" in Pride's church literally lost her son to the street when he was run over by a speeding car on a busy thoroughfare. As migrants realized their vulnerability to such brutality, churches became "safe spaces" (Griffin 1995), shielding members spiritually, if not physically, from an environment that appeared as evil incarnate.

Not unlike the religious communities observed by sociologist Mary Waters (1999), immigrant churches in Four Corners "allow[ed] [families] to protect their children from the worst aspects of American city life" (202). Waters, nonetheless, speculates that churches, which "were ethnically and not neighborhood based" (247), offered reprieve from the depressed neighborhoods in which many of her West Indian subjects lived. Although valid, this speculation obscures immigrant sites of worship that do not remove worshippers from poor neighborhood contexts. Some nonneighborhood-based immigrant churches, by virtue of their location in religious districts like Four Corners, are still located in the more depressed parts of cities. Paradoxically, these churches protect members from the street by preaching against its ills, even while bringing the faithful into physical proximity with "the drug addicts, the evil people, people who make other's lives miserable, with no family values."

THE STREET AS RECRUITING GROUND

Kingdom Hall   Christ Church   Faith Baptist   Grace Methodist

If the majority of churches constructed cognitive barricades between their sacred spaces and the profane space of the street, a smaller number of churches attempted, often in fits and starts, to sacralize the street through outdoor preaching and door-to-door proselytization. These churches, aware that the street is "the world" rendered in inner-city dialect, felt it was their duty as people in possession of Truth to transfigure that space by carrying the Good News into it. In this way, people in the street encountered not only evil but ultimate good. Failure to proselytize in the street could be taken as evidence that one did not really possess the Truth or that one was selfish about salvation and therefore not truly saved.

Roozen et al. (1988) identify a similar "evangelistic" orientation according to which religious people "believe that God has given them a message that must be shared with their friends and neighbors, and the message itself—the need to respond to God's saving action in Jesus Christ—is at the center of congregational life." They do not, however, describe this as an orientation toward the environment immediately surrounding churches—as a way of viewing "the street." And since the evangelical churches in their study were not located in depressed areas, the authors did not notice how fear could make evangelical orientations difficult to act on.

To Be "Better Doormats": Fear of Abuse and Rejection

In Four Corners the Jehovah's Witnesses, given as they are to systematic "publishing," were by far most adept at the recruitment ground approach to the street. Their theology was also the only one that absolutely required all believers to do public evangelization. The Witnesses have divided Boston, and every other city, into discrete geographic mission territories within which local congregations do their door-to-door publishing work. Although members of the Kingdom Hall congregations in Four Corners came from all of Roxbury, Dorchester, Mattapan, and multiple suburbs, its publishing territories formed only a one-mile radius around the church. This area overlapped part of Four Corners, although neither of my informants, Brothers Eldridge and Grimes, had heard of such a place.

Most city dwellers in the United States have at some point been approached by Witnesses on the street if not at their front doors. Few, however, are aware of the extensive training that each publisher must undergo before tackling the recruitment ground. Each week, Witnesses attend the Theocratic Ministry School, at which publishers are taught how to conduct fieldwork.[4] According to Brother Grimes, this training, along with the rigorous Scriptural study undertaken by all Witnesses, equips publishers with Biblical virtuosity, an ability to speak clearly and convincingly (and to read, in the case of the occasional illiterate Witness), interact comfortably with people from all walks of life, and last but certainly not least, endure inevitable abuse in the field. Even for seasoned publishers, the act of street proselytization is accompanied by fear of verbal insult and rejection.

At one Sunday service, or "discourse," the speaker directly addressed the psychological hardship involved with publishing the Kingdom. The service began promptly at noon with exactly ninety-five people present (according to an official count rendered in the middle of the service). The officiating minister asked us to rise for the first song and prayer. He referred us to "Forward You Ministers of the Kingdom" in the hymnal *Sing Praises to Jehovah*. Recorded piano music swelled over the PA system, and the congregation began to sing. Some of the older women produced operatic vibratos. The song was simple, even puritan. The chorus went: "Forward going, preaching the Kingdom message ever far and wide. Forward moving, keeping ever loyal on Jehovah's side." Hearing the song, I imagined the Witnesses marching proudly out into their respective mission areas to publish the Kingdom in the streets.

The officiator then introduced the day's speaker, a minister visiting from a nearby Witness Hall. The minister began by observing how diligently ministers went about their witnessing, all the while maintaining "a kind and glad heart" in spite of abuse from people in "the field." He noted that Jesus himself had been like a "doormat"—he willingly took abuse from people and did so joyfully because he represented the Truth. "We go from door to door and people treat us bad, but we give good witness. And when they finally come around we're still there to give a very good witness." The minister then related a story of how people's dreadful ideas about Jehovah's Witnesses interfered with their receptiveness to the Truth. "Even though someone might recognize the truth in what a minister is saying," he said, "they ultimately reject it." The minister had once spoken with two men about the Bible for half an hour, and the men were very engrossed in the discussion. But as soon as they realized that he was a Witness, the men ended the discussion and sent him on his way. Why? Perhaps because of their "negative conditioning" regarding Witnesses. Or, he speculated, perhaps they "feared the very name of Jehovah," even though it appears in the Bible. "But [publishers] understand that Jehovah has blessed them with this privilege. Ministers must ultimately learn to become better doormats, to better take the pressure. And when the end comes, it will be OK, because we are preaching. We are doing what we are supposed to do."

Fear of Violence

The Witnesses were not alone in their fear as they attempted to sacralize the street. In two churches, clerics were torn between complete avoidance of the street and full immersion in it. They felt it was their religious duty to treat the street as a recruiting ground. Nevertheless, fear of violence prevented these middle-class churches from fully adopting an interactive stance vis-à-vis the world immediately beyond church walls.

The Christ Church was one of these religious communities. Here, the middle-class status of the church played a major role in its reluctance to do street ministry. Brother Turner and church members regularly canvassed the immediate area to advertise special Gospel meetings. They normally covered the main streets near the church, but "we never ventured into the area across Harvard Street," said Turner. This area was considered especially dangerous. Turner tried, with little success, to get members to expand their mission radius. He explained that members "are all within five minutes driving [of the church], yet this is a different world than those that members come from." Church members, including Turner, came from relatively stable, middle-class parts of the metropolis. They were not used to walking around in neighborhoods like Four Corners.

Still, people of the Truth had to spread the word where they worshipped, if only to dispel the "falsehood" aggressively being spread by other churches. As Christians, they had to do this work, even at risk of death. Turner continued:

> If they're [other churches] already doing something for the community, and they may not have the Truth, if we have the Truth, we should be doing it. We shouldn't sit back and say somebody else is doing it, let them do it. No. If we have the truth, we should be doing it. It's our responsibility. And a lot of folks will disagree with that.
>
> McRoberts: Not everybody in the church agrees with that?
>
> Turner: Aw, no! That's what I think. I think we have a great responsibility. Because once you understand what Jesus has given to you and what he wants you to do with it, you have a responsibility to make sure other people know about it.
>
> McRoberts: What has gotten in the way of this church doing more outreach?
>
> Turner: Probably fear. I think that's the biggest obstacle to overcome, even for

me. When I was entertaining coming back up here [to Boston]—I got spoiled by Parkersburg [Virginia]. I lived in an area where I had forgot to lock my door. And I went home and everything was still in my house. I worry a lot about my wife; I don't like city areas. So it's fear, on my part and on a lot of other members' parts. Because you can't turn on the television at night and not hear about somebody getting killed—in this area! There are some rough people that walk up and down the street, and there are some people that come in the church building demanding certain things.

McRoberts: What kinds of things do they want?

Turner: Well you know, "I need some money to get home," and you know, they've been drinking and they want somebody to give them attention. And they figure, "Oh, a church building, they'll give you money." Well when they don't get it, you know, you have to handle it delicately so you don't have a situation. It scares people. It's kind of a paradox because when you're a Christian you say, OK, as long as I'm living right I know if somebody takes my life then I already know I'm going to heaven. But it's hard to get that in your mind when you're out there trying to do what you know you need to do. Even though you know it, it's hard to overcome that fear. And I think that's just something that the devil uses to keep us in check.

Note that while the Witnesses believed one had to endure abuse from people in the mission field in order to enter paradise, Turner felt it necessary to overcome the fear of death, knowing that death in the field assured one a place in heaven. The street, in this worldview, was thus imbued with the power to make martyrs as well as sinners.

The Faith Baptist Church was similar to the Christ Church in class makeup. Most members were professionals: nurses, lawyers, doctors, educators, and tradespersons. Unlike the Christ Church, however, Faith Baptist lacked leaders like Brother Turner, who insisted on a more intensive street presence. Pastor Winspeare, an insurance investor who commuted to the church from the Black suburb of Brockton, believed Christians were called to take the Gospel into the street. He theorized that by doing so, Christians could make people in the street feel more comfortable about coming to church. But the Rev. Winspeare was afraid of the street; he felt unsafe even inside the church when he worked there at night.

One dark winter evening I walked to the church to meet Winspeare for an interview only to find the doors locked. After a few minutes of waiting, an old brown van pulled up beside me. The driver, whom I did not know, asked, "You waiting for somebody?" I told him I was waiting for Pastor Winspeare. The man nodded slowly, as if in disbelief, and drove off. I waited for about twenty minutes on the corner, then walked home. Later that night, Winspeare and I spoke on the phone. During the course of the conversation, Winspeare observed that young people from the area were not in church. I asked if he had been walking around talking to young people. He replied, chuckling, "Mmmmm, brother, I don't do too much walking." I told him how earlier that night a man in a van had questioned me, and I had left the church after waiting for some time. "I know you did," he replied,

> because it's a very—so much goes on in this area. Like when I pulled up there tonight there were two guys standing out across at the other church on the cor- ner. And I was like, OK, what are they up to, what are they doing, this and that, you know. So I pull up, and they walk off. And I get up and go in the church and I always lock myself inside. And one of the members came, the late pas- tor's wife came, and she said, "Why you got this door locked?" And I said, "I'm being wise as a serpent and humble as a dove." And wise means to look out for yourself. I would dare not be in that area and just leave the door unlocked. I don't know who's gonna walk up in there.

In this remark, Winspeare referred to a Scriptural passage that entirely cap- tured his simultaneous fear of and evangelical call toward the street: "Behold, I send you forth as sheep in the midst of wolves: be ye therefore wise as ser- pents, and harmless as doves" (Matt. 10:16). Winspeare felt "sent forth" by God to this church and its environment. He thought it necessary to go into the street with the word of God: "Some people in the community would never come inside the church . . . Them that are walking, them that are standing on the corner doing their own thing, smoking, drinking, whatever the case may be." Yet he felt he had been set in the midst of wolves. He felt unsafe in his own church. And as of that conversation, he had yet to prose- lytize in the street.

Street proselytization is, of course, a form of recruitment as well as a part of religious identity. Thus, even in the absence of theological barriers or fear, ministers given to aggressive evangelization might nonetheless prefer mech- anisms more convenient than appealing to random pedestrians. St. Bridget's Haitian congregation and the Seventh-day Adventist church, for example, did not proselytize in the street because they recruited primarily through family and work networks. Especially via family networks, recent immigrants were integrated into church life directly upon arrival. Good Tidings, the clos- est thing to a "megachurch" in Four Corners, attracted most of its members by broadcasting high-energy worship services on AM radio stations. As its broadcasts offered access to the entire city, there was no reason to proselytize in the space immediately around the church.

THE STREET AS POINT OF CONTACT
WITH PEOPLE AT RISK

Members of one church, the Azusa Christian Community, co-opted what they felt were aspects of the street in order to reach persons at risk of being consumed by violence in the street. They took the street neither as an inherently evil space nor as a space good only for recruitment. To the contrary, the street was the place where Jesus tested the commitment of the faithful to those poor and vulnerable. Put differently, Azusa drew a perforated line between church and street across which certain norms and idioms bled both ways. It was still a line, mind you. Members still felt they had something that street people lacked: a proper relationship with God. But they also felt called to engage the street on its own apparent terms rather than proselytize or avoid it altogether. They certainly wanted to offer spiritual salvation to all, but in the meantime attempted, through preemptive and palliative social services, to treat the causes and consequences of youth violence.

The very physical culture of the Azusa sanctuary signified its attitude toward the street and indicated the place of the street in the religious identity of the church. No traditional religious symbols or artifacts marked this space as a sanctuary. Instead, upon entering, one was literally bombarded with images of the Four Corners streetscape. Lining the walls were black and white photographs of police officers, speed-blurred ambulances, littered alleyways, deserted storefronts, and the aforementioned Coming Soon: Church of God sign. Behind the simple wooden lectern hung a shot of a brick wall, upon which "RIP LARRY" had been spray-painted. This sanctuary stood out in a neighborhood where many churches tried to keep images and idioms associated with the street out of the church. Through the photographs, not to mention the actual content of sermons and prayers, worship was suffused with an acute awareness of poverty and violence and of the role of Christians in addressing those problems.

Azusa blurred the line between church and street even further by offering its Ella J. Baker House as a "gang-neutral space" and "safe space" for young people trying to avoid trouble. Throughout any given day, young people were literally walking in off the street to take advantage of the Uhuru Project's (Azusa's social services arm, a distinct 501c3 nonprofit) tutoring and job placement services, or just to hang out. Some of Uhuru's programs directly incorporated secular activities that, in many churches, would have been considered decadent. For instance, in the safe space of the Baker House basement, young men held boxing tournaments, which frequently served to settle "beefs" between individuals and rival "crews" without resorting to armed struggle. Uhuru also sponsored a music industry program for aspiring hip-hop artists. Although they deliberately exposed young people to the church and church people, and while young "clients" sometimes came to Sunday services, none of these programs involved direct proselytization.

Nor did Azusa's work in the street proper. Several days and nights a week, Pastor Rivers and a cadre of young men from the church who called themselves the "Christian Brotherhood" walked through Four Corners and Codman Square. They approached youths congregated on corners, prostitutes, and anyone else willing to stop and talk about their needs, problems, aspirations, and current events (often recent shootings, stabbings, "beefs," or shifts in intergang relations). The street patrollers often directed their "clients" to social programs available at the Ella Baker House.

One warm July night I joined the Brotherhood patrol. I arrived at Ella Baker House around 9:30 P.M. By then, five young men and one young woman were gathered in front of the building. Wilmore, who invited me out that night, introduced me to the rest of the Brotherhood. Before making the first walk through the neighborhood, we stood and talked for at least one hour, watching cars and pedestrians go by.

Often, while standing in front of Baker House, Brotherhood members would talk to young people who congregated at the rather spacious bus stop seating area just across the street. The bus stop was not only a popular mingling spot but a hot spot for illicit commerce. While we watched that night, two groups of young people met at the stop, mingled briefly, and departed. This, Wilmore pointed out, was probably a drug deal. A bit later, two white cars met in front of the stop. One car had four people inside, and the other, only one. Stephen, another patroller, noted that the people in the former car were drinking and passing a joint and that they were probably making a cocaine deal with the "Dominican" in the other car.

Wilmore then informed me that prostitutes often met customers in the small park sloping downward from the bus stop. The patrollers were not sure whether prostitutes actually delivered services in the park. I had noticed, both at night and during daylight hours, many more empty Trojan packages and spent condoms in vacant lots around Four Corners than in the park. On the other hand, municipal workers might be clearing away such evidence from the park's basketball court and simple wooden jungle gym, just as they regularly cleared away the little piles of tobacco left behind when people roll the Churchillian marijuana-cigars known as "blunts."

A Black man and a White woman approached and passed on our side of the street. "The prostitutes are out tonight," Wilmore observed. He further noted that transactions would increase all over Washington Street as the night wore on. In other words, the religious district would become something of a red light district. Eventually, police would begin to move the sex workers up and down the street—clearing them off of one corner, and the next, and the next. About twenty minutes later, the couple came back and passed us again. Wilmore speculated that, in return for the worker's favors, the John would smoke crack with her the rest of the night.

Between twenty-minute expeditions into the neighborhood, Brotherhood members stood in front of the church and brainstormed for ways to improve the immediate area. To begin, they wanted more lighting installed in the park across the street, and Drug-Free Zone signs erected near the playground, basketball court, and bus stop. Drug-free zone status would make the penalty for drug sales in and around the park a bit steeper (two years incarceration instead of one, they said), and the lighting would make illicit activities more difficult to carry out. As they talked, a police car, the only one I saw for nearly an hour, came gliding up the street. The officer slowed the car and threw a suspicious glance at us (instead of the bus stop or park) before continuing onward.

The Reverend Eugene Rivers arrived around 10:00 P.M. with his wife and daughter. They were returning from a movie. "Rev," as Brotherhood members affectionately called Rivers, emerged from the car, greeted us, and entered Baker House in search of some papers. He then returned to the sidewalk and briefly delighted the patrollers with upbeat banter. Rivers would not join the patrol tonight, but other nights I watched him engage nearly every person he encountered in the street, sometimes calling them by name. Often he knew the kids congregating or parking near the bus stop across the street. "Hey! Black man!" he would yell out, already dodging speeding automobiles to get to their side of the road. Sometimes one or two youth would quietly walk away or slouch deep into a back seat to avoid being spotted by the ever jocular, but never naïve, "Rev."

When Rev. talked to young people on the street, it was evident that he, far more than most members of the church, possessed what one *Newsweek* columnist called "street-smart charisma" (Leland 1998). He interacted with them in a way that suggested, especially through his use of colloquialisms, a willingness understand their world in their own terms, minus the linguistic trappings of evangelical Christianity. Even during one-on-one interviews, Rivers's rapid-fire discourses were peppered with metaphors and allusions that the Reverend Jameson, of the Church of the Holy Ghost, would surely associate with "root work." Drawing from the same *Godfather*-inspired lexicon that young Black self-styled "gangsters" have sometimes appropriated, Rivers has referred to himself as a *patroni* and claims to have enlisted his congregation in the Church of God in Christ denomination because it was becoming "the biggest Black crime family." Lest the reader leap to sensationalistic conclusions: Rivers did not really fancy himself a mafioso. He appropriated idioms associated with the street by way of meeting youth at risk where he felt they were cognitively situated.

A MIXED CONCEPTUALIZATION: STREET AS RECRUITMENT GROUND AND POINT OF CONTACT

Two churches, Holy Road and Jude Church, viewed the street as a point of contact with persons in need yet retained much of the "street as recruitment ground" orientation. They attempted circuitously to attract people to church by offering social services and championing abstract social causes such as violence and drug use prevention.

Holy Road, founded by the Rev. Powell in 1980, was built on the pastor's attempts to sacralize the street. Powell began the church by holding street services in Roxbury's Dudley Station. He aimed these services primarily at young people—and to this day most congregation members are less than thirty years old. By the time I started visiting Holy Road, Powell rarely preached the Gospel outdoors, but his church operated an after-school program, a summer camp, and a basketball league for area youth, many of whom he first met on the street and in local parks. Powell claimed to spend about sixty hours a week canvassing: "I'm constantly out there on the street corners with these kids, convincing people's kids to come in. Going into homes talking to families, trying to get their—so on the average, its more like an eight- or nine-hour-a-day job, really." In addition to its regular youth programs, the church also held block parties in a vacant lot across the street from the church and once sponsored a hip-hop–flavored theatrical performance for young people at a theater in the adjacent Uphams Corner neighborhood.

Powell did not camouflage his recruitment motives. His programs served in part to get children and their parents to join the church and embark on the narrow path of salvation. At the same time, Powell's brand of ministry could not be reduced to its spiritually salvific functions:

> We deal with the total person: that means the soul, the spirit and the mind and the body. First of all, before we get a person to really understand about salvation, we first must reach the needs, whether it be homes, food, clothes, job, whatever a individual person might need. That's the first need I try to meet first of all. And then a relationship comes second. And then I introduce him to salvation.

Serving the "total person" in part meant withholding condemnation of those who had chosen the "street" over the church. Instead, they were to be viewed as people with complex spiritual and secular needs. Thus, in one sermon he said, "It's so easy to condemn—it doesn't mean anything to be a crook, a crackhead, a prostitute. Our job is to lead them to the Lord. And all this beating people over the head and saying people are going to hell is not the way." In Powell's view, churches that "beat people over the head" in order to convert them lacked a "broad vision" of what Christians are called to do:

> It's a narrow vision that they have. Not a broad vision of what Christianity is all about. If they would look at the scope of Jesus, the way the twelve disciples operated—they [made] sure that the total man was taken care of, and they got involved with social problems. I don't understand how a church could say that they don't want to get involved outside their church doors and folks are getting shot around your church. To me, you shouldn't be in that community.

Thus, although the church ultimately wanted to lead people to the Lord, its strategy was not simply to sacralize the street, like the Witnesses. The street was a place where Christians had to go in order to meet the needs of the "total man." Powell tried to build relationships with young people on their own terms, using secular activities they might ordinarily be drawn to. These activities exposed youth to the church but also aimed to keep youth out of immediate trouble.

Holy Road's theatrical production nicely illustrated the way "church" and "street" idioms were blended to reach the "total person." According to Powell, the play was "about a young brother who wanted to be in the church and the world at the same time." The actual script lacked such clear "in but not of" language. The protagonist lived part of his life in the street, where he encountered the temptations of drugs, illicit moneymaking, and gang involvement and the other part in the church, where people advised him to abandon his dangerous alter ego. Although its denouement placed the young man squarely within the church world, the story did not present his dilemma as one between sin and salvation. Rather, the choice was between death or incarceration, on the one hand, and participation in a safe, life-affirming community, on the other. The use of hip-hop music throughout the play implied that not all things associated with the street were bad—just those that led young people to self-destruction. The event, which charged only a dime for admission, drew nearly eight hundred young people from several New England states, thanks in part to someone who posted the flier on the Internet.

The Reverend Barbara Calvin, pastor of the Jude Church, had a similar brand of street ministry. Every Wednesday night, in a dual effort to make converts and find clients, Pastor Calvin walked the blocks around her storefront with a bullhorn or portable PA system, preaching her unique blend of Gospel talk and antiviolence, antidrug reasoning. Often she placed a speaker outside the door of the church so that her Sunday sermons could be heard from the street. During one sermon, she took her cordless microphone outside, leaving the worshipers in the church. Inside, we could hear the disembodied voice preaching to passersby, inviting them inside, inquiring into the state of their souls.

Somewhat like the Remembrance Church, the Jude ministry focused on healing grief and emotional distress related to violence. Unlike Remembrance's Pastor Pride, though, Calvin, who holds a master's degree in counseling psychology, did much of her healing work outside the church. In the early 1980s she started an organization called Citizens Against Homicide, which she used to counsel the parents of murdered children. She also worked in the Randolph public school system (she lived in the suburb of Randolph), where she ran an in-school suspension program. In addition, she was contracted to counsel troubled children through the Department of Children and Family Services.

But more than all of these, Calvin had always been drawn to street work. "In 1981, when all the drive-bys started, I was already out here!" she proclaimed. Being "out here" was a part of Calvin's religious identity—her call to Christian ministry was also a call to address the psychic needs of strangers outside the church. After all, she reminded me, "Jesus himself was a street minister. He ran the people *out* of the temple. And he worked a lot with grief. He gave anything he had to the suffering. How you gon' have a sandwich and not give someone half of it who needs it? Some people would say, 'Uh! Why did you just give that person half of your sandwich?'"

Like the Rev. Powell, Calvin felt her street work distinguished her church from those given entirely to prayer and proselytization. It is not enough, she said,

> to have a "Jesufied" service and stop there. In this day and age, you need community activism. I mean, look at the homelessness and joblessness right here on this corner! You can't have this many churches across this city and nobody does anything about the drive-by shootings happening every other night . . . If people keep throwing trash outside your church, you can keep praying inside, but eventually you have to go out and clean it up!

Significantly, in vowing metaphorically to "clean up," Calvin encountered negative gender bias—not from potential converts and clients but from her male clerical peers. On numerous occasions, male clergy told Calvin she was not supposed to work in the street; she was not supposed to offer that psychological or material "half a sandwich" to people in public spaces. Some rejected her work on Scriptural grounds; they interpreted street ministry as public prayer, which appears as forbidden in Matthew 6:5–6.[5] Most, however, argued that she did not need to be in the street because she is a woman.

This perspective implicitly considered the street a male space: a place not fit for women and girls. The implication was that home and church were safe places, appropriate places, for females.

DISCUSSION

The taxonomy presented here raises a number of issues worthy of further explication. First of these is the way religious tradition ambiguously impacts clergy orientations toward the urban environment. Most of the Pentecostal churches in the religious district understand the street as an "evil other." This would appear to validate and augment the observations of religion scholar Robert Orsi (1999:53), who writes that "Pentecostal mappings of the city constitute a disciplinary cartography, marking out forbidden places and re-visioning places of secular entertainment as sites of evil, transgression, and damnation."

Yet, in three Pentecostal churches, clergy viewed the street either as a point of contact with people to be served or as a combination recruitment ground/point of contact. These churches highlighted the mandate set out in Luke 4:18: "to preach the gospel to the poor . . . to heal the brokenhearted, to preach deliverance to the captives, and recovering of sight to the blind, to set at liberty them that are bruised." So, although many Pentecostals may view the inner-city environment as evil, there is considerable room for variation, with some churches arriving at "mappings of the city" that require full immersion within it.

Middle-class status can operate ambiguously as well. For the commuter-based Faith Baptist and Christ Church congregations, fear of the street was the primary barrier to street evangelization. This fear, in turn, was rooted in the fact that members resided in far less dangerous parts of the metropolis— suburbs and enclaves that happen to be middle class. Worship in Four Corners only highlighted the differences in lifestyle and privilege that separated congregants from those they feared. For the Azusa Christian Community, by contrast, middle-class status was considered a barrier to be overcome for the sake of depressed Black neighborhoods like Four Corners. The willingness to face the street, to become vulnerable to it, and to sacrifice upward class trajectories for it, was a central component of Azusa's mission. In a sense, by worshiping and circulating in Four Corners, members redeemed their middle-class status. Rather than underscoring differences between middle class and poor, this form of religious presence saw "spiritual significance in crossing the border that has separated the 'inner city' from the middle-class domains" (Orsi 1999:9).

More generally, this taxonomy of church conceptions of the street contributes to the urban sociological discourse on the interaction of social groups in Black neighborhoods, as recently advanced by ethnographers Elijah Anderson and Mary Pattillo-McCoy. Specifically, the taxonomy makes explicit some ways that churches, through their various interpretations of "the street," mediated between their members and others in the immediate locale.

In one study, Anderson (1990) explains the fragile, teetering coexistence of middle-class gentrifiers, including Blacks and Whites, and the poor Black majority in a core Philadelphia neighborhood. He describes the emergence of an informal public etiquette—"street wisdom"—that has allowed middle-class residents to "[negotiate] day-to-day actions and interactions with minimum risk and maximum mutual respect in a world full of uncertainty and danger" (253). In a later ethnography, Anderson (1999) is concerned with interactions of Blacks in a uniformly poor neighborhood. Not unlike the churches in Four Corners that viewed the street as "evil other," Anderson's interviewees see their neighbors as falling into two camps: "decent people" and "street people." Decent people are characterized by civility and dedication to work and family, while street people are associated with violence, public lewdness, personal and familial irresponsibility, joblessness, illicit activity, and nihilism. Importantly, though, most people saw themselves as "decent." Moreover, "decent" people frequently found it necessary to "code-switch"—that is, affect certain street-associated behaviors for the sake of self-protection. Still, some of the subjects in both of Anderson's studies were religious, he did not study religious institutions as such.[6] He therefore does not discuss whether or how churches proffer a religious version of "street wisdom" or of the street/decent dichotomy.

In her illuminating study of a "middle-class" Black neighborhood in Chicago, Pattillo-McCoy (1999) complicates Anderson's street/decent distinction by showing how "decent" young people, through overlapping social networks and powerful cultural messages, often veer into "street" social groups and behaviors. She also depicts the eleven neighborhood churches in a number of pivotal roles, each serving to defend "decent" lifestyles. These churches are antidrug and crime crusaders, inspirational fonts of spiritual strength and optimism and agents of social control, as some parents use church involvement to keep their children out of "street" networks and activities. This last function suggests that neighborhood residents use churches as institutional buffers between street and decent groups.

What remains unstated, however, is whether the churches have actively defined that which they buffer against and whether these definitions are invested with religious meaning. Also unstated is how encroachments of the "street" into the church world are taken by religious persons. For instance,

Pattillo-McCoy described how discussions in a church youth group revealed the young people's enthrallment with "the rebellious possibilities of ghetto styles" (132). I wondered if such expressions constituted a youthful subversion of churchly intentions or a controlled incursion of "street" into "church," such as the boxing matches orchestrated by the Azusa Christian Community.

Building on these studies, I have described three ways that churches made sense of the street and of the people and activities associated with the street. Out of this sense-making came prescriptions for how church people, as religious variants of "decent people," were to interact with "street people." Street people were seen as worthy of careful avoidance, conversion to decent churchly lifestyles, attentive service, or some combination of the latter two. Only those churches attaching religious significance to serving street people welcomed street idioms into the church, albeit under controlled circumstances. They devised a religious variety of street wisdom, or better yet, a "street-smart charisma," which defined the terms of interaction.

Importantly, these prescriptions were taken by nonresidents, since the churches in the religious district tended to draw members from outside of Four Corners. Clergy, therefore, were not telling their congregants how to interact with their neighbors; much to the contrary, they were telling outsiders how to interpret the environment in which they happened to worship. Churches in Four Corners thus underscored the fact that not all consequential interactions in Black neighborhoods take place between co-residents. The bulk of a neighborhood's institutions may in fact serve outsiders. Those outsiders' impressions of and behaviors in the host neighborhood may be shaped not so much by "public interaction, the give and take of street life" (Anderson 1990:5), as is Anderson's "street wisdom," but by the normative prescriptions of the institutions themselves.

As churches are concerned, these prescriptions constituted yet another dimension of particularism in the religious district. How a church conceived of and acted in its immediate environment was part of the great bundle of traits that distinguished it from other religious institutions in the multicongregational field. Black Pentecostal churches, for instance, might easily be considered as having cornered a single niche in the metaphorical religious market. But in fact, those that view the street as evil are distinct from those that view it as a mission ground or as a social service arena. They attract different people, interested in different flavors of worship, fellowship, and ministry.

SIX

Changing the World
CHURCH-BASED "ACTIVISM"

The term "church-based activism" usually refers to very extroverted forms of religious presence—forms that somehow benefit not only congregation members but people who do not belong to the church. Churches with food pantries and shelters for survivors of domestic abuse, or that build homes and run welfare-to-work programs, or whose leaders organize marches and protests, are considered "activist." This understanding of religious activism is partly the legacy of the civil rights movement, during which African American churches transmitted a powerful normative message about the ability and necessity of religious institutions to work in some way for social change. By contrast, churches that do apparently little for nonmembers are called "nonactivist."

It is tempting to call one group "worldly," and the other, "otherworldly," as so many observers have done. Related and equally tempting polarities are church and sect (Weber 1993; Troelsch 1931; Iannoccone 1988; Johnson 1963), instrumental and expressive (Drake 1940), and resistance and accommodation (Baer and Singer 1992; Lincoln and Mamiya 1990). Indeed, when I began this research I thought it might be sufficient to divide churches along those lines and explain why so many clearly fell into the otherworldly/sect/expressive/accommodative/nonactivist category. Only the most extroverted churches would be counted as authentically activist. The rest would fall into some variant of pie-in-the-sky retreatism. As I looked more deeply, though, it became clear that these binary understandings of church work did not capture what churches in Four Corners thought they were doing in and for the world. Nearly all of the clergy felt their churches had to leave an indelibly positive imprint on the world and could therefore be called "activist." In Four Corners, only the Kingdom Hall congregations approximated "otherworldliness," insofar as they viewed all attempts to change the world as futile; they preferred instead to inform as many individuals as possible about the Truth and await the time when Jehovah would establish His earthly kingdom. In short, the question became not whether but how churches saw themselves as agents for world betterment.

While searching for ways to classify these self-understandings, I flirted with a number of nonbinary typologies that attempted to capture various aspects of religious presence (Roozen, et al. 1988; Becker 1998; Dudley and Johnson 1991). The problem with these typologies, though, was their tendency to collapse multiple dimensions of difference into a few catchall categories. Typologies often tempt us to squeeze empirical cases into one category or another, meanwhile disregarding the staggering potential for variation among churches. This diverts our attention from the social processes always percolating just beneath the outward forms—the molten lava coursing just beneath the deceptively cool, solid crust. These processes can lead churches to move across types or to embody entirely new forms of religious presence.

Davidson and Koch (1998) offer an alternative to binary and catchall approaches to classifying church activisms. They point out that churches and other voluntary associations vary along two continua. On the first continuum, churches may serve members more or less exclusively (priestly), a mixture of members and nonmembers ("pastoral"), or mostly nonmembers (prophetic). On the second continuum, churches vary in the extent to which they advocate individual change (personal) or broad social change (social). To this continuum I add a middle point—"socialization"—which applies to activities that prepare individuals for participation in broader social worlds. This two-dimensional perspective not only permits a more subtle appreciation of how churches vary in their attempts to "make a difference" but allows us better to describe change, as churches deliberately or accidentally adopt new modes of making marks on the world.

Table 5 maps the churches in Four Corners along the member-nonmember and individual-social continua and indicates how certain churches are changing within this "activist space." The following discussion begins by focusing on two clusters of churches in the space: 1) churches that focus entirely on members but socialize them in ways that impart the strength and mindset necessary for life outside the church, and 2) churches that have some focus on nonmembers and aim to attack social problems, such as poverty, violence, and economic underdevelopment. The first cluster is composed entirely of migrant and immigrant churches. Within the second cluster are as many Pentecostal churches as "mainline" ones.

The discussion then shifts to the ways churches were changing within the activist space. While Davidson and Koch identify broad societal trends and shifts in denominational funding patterns as key sources of church change, I identify four microsources of change, two of which involve inadvertent "drift" and three of which involve congregational growth. Importantly, only

Table 5   Activist Orientations of Four Corners Churches

	Personal Transformation	Socialization	Social Transformation
Priestly		Remembrance, Missionary, Christ Church, Holy Fullness, Church of the Holy Ghost, Anointed, New Jerusalem, Fellowship, Seventh Day, Maison, Iglesia del Santos, Iglesia Christo, Mt. Nebo, Divine Peace, Church of God, Church of God in Christ	↑
Pastoral		Good Tidings →	← Grace, Holy Road, St. Bridget's, Jude
Prophetic	Kingdom Hall		← Azusa

one church moved toward the extroverted, socially transformative kind of involvement commonly associated with church-based activism—and this change was more the result of drift than design.

PRIESTLY/SOCIALIZATION CHURCHES OF MIGRANTS AND IMMIGRANTS

The fact that so many churches in Four Corners were "priestly," or geared entirely toward member needs, would seem to imply that the religious district had little or no impact on the wider society. One might conclude that these churches operated as alternative social worlds, as isolated "sanctuaries" (Roozen et al. 1988), within which individuals diligently pursued their own salvation while enjoying a modicum of respect and social status (Paris 1982; Williams 1974). That conclusion would not be invalid. It would, nevertheless, be grossly out of sync with what the churches themselves believed they were doing.

This cluster of churches, almost entirely Holiness and Pentecostal by tradition and containing all of the migrant and most of the immigrant congregations, was priestly but not "otherworldly." The migrant churches used ritual interaction to equip members to function in and perhaps transform social worlds beyond church walls. The immigrant churches, especially the Spanish- and Haitian Creole-speaking ones, used their priestly enclaves to render some very practical social services to recent arrivals—services that prepared them for survival in the host country. Like parents who attempt to make a mark on the world by raising sane children, these churches tried to change the world by injecting well-adjusted individuals into it.

MIGRANT CHURCHES AND "TRICKLE-DOWN"
SPIRITUAL ACTIVISM

The clergy in this group did not condemn all direct attempts at social transformation, as did the Witnesses. Social transformation was considered necessary to meet widespread needs and right large-scale injustices. Nor did
these clergy eschew individual activism in the secular world: most encouraged congregants to vote, at least. Yet they believed that unjust systems were
the strange fruits of a societal spiritual crisis, a crisis that had to be resolved
through spiritual means, one prodigal soul at a time, at least until that time
when God returned. Churches, therefore, should avoid prophetic varieties of
struggle, such as political mobilization, protest, and large-scale social service
provision, lest they forget the privileged role of the church: to be an incuba-
tor of saved souls and sane psyches, ready to face the world. Churches were
thought to catalyze social change by creating communities that instilled in individuals the virtues of equanimity, confidence, and determination. Once
empowered by these qualities, individuals from the South were not only able
to handle the trials and indignities of life in the northern city but also were
better able to resist and challenge oppressive systems.

In migrant churches it was not unusual for preachers to make pronouncements such as this: "The same God in Jesus is in you . . . 'I gave man
power over all the earth. Nothing shall hurt you. I gave you the power to
speak to beast, the sun, and moon.'" This affirmation, delivered by Pastor
Pride (of Remembrance Church), is not otherworldly—it aims, in fact, to
connect the believer with cosmic, divine forces that might enable him or her
to function in the world with a sense of power and agency. This is another implied meaning of Pride's church motto, Where everybody is somebody.

In the charismatic migrant churches (this would exclude only the Christ
Church, which was not charismatic), affirmations of power were internal-
ized, experienced firsthand, during periods of "ritual antistructure" (Turner
1977; see also Ammerman 1997a). According to anthropologist Victor
Turner, certain aspects of ritual are designed to thrust participants into a liminal state "betwixt and between" conventional roles and statuses in the social
structure. Once roles and statuses are dissolved, a *communitas* emerges, characterized by shared feelings "of lowliness and sacredness, of homogeneity
and comradeship" (96). Turner recognized the socially subversive potential
of *communitas* when he wrote:

> My view is briefly that from the perspectival viewpoint of those concerned with
> the maintenance of "structure,'" all sustained manifestations of communitas
> must appear as dangerous and anarchical, and have to be hedged around with
> prescriptions, prohibitions, and conditions. (109)

Victor Turner's *communitas* is a glimpse of radical equality—a vision that can be carried into the world of structures, statuses, and hierarchies to effect social transformation. Scholars of African American religion have followed suit, noting the *communitas*-generating, hierarchy-subverting potential of ecstatic worship (Sanders 1996; Alexander 1991; Kostarelos 1996).[1]

Ritual antistructure begins with the descent of the Holy Ghost, which is manifested in glossolalia, ecstatic shouting, and dancing. At such times it appears that the entire structure of the service, with all its assigned roles, has irreparably broken down. Men and women alike weep and "fall out" under the Holy Ghost. Church leaders become nearly indistinguishable from common congregants in the emotional outpouring. After this liminal period, while individuals are still drying tears and riding out the last shudders of the Spirit, congregations often sing in unison a slow hymn of thanks, as if to solidify the *communitas* generated during the liminal period. During these parts of religious services, the "cosmic power" referred to above reveals itself to believers as more than a feel-good rhetorical device; that power actually descends into the room and demonstrates its ability to level social distinctions. Migrant churches used this ritual leveling not to separate members from the world but to affirm their ability to operate, however cautiously and selectively, in the world.

Pastors of migrant churches agreed that people "built up" in the church community were uniquely suited to push for social transformation outside the church. Pastor Winspeare summed up the attitude this way: "If the people in the church are being built up spiritually they must be spiritually fed, spiritually built up in order to go into the community to be able to feed the people that need to be fed." He called this a "trickle-down" approach to social transformation, since spiritual power metaphorically came from "above."[2]

Pastor Pride shared the trickle-down perspective. In one sermon she used the example of Jesse Jackson to illustrate the connection between in-church socialization and social change. According to Pride, Jackson delivered a speech in Roxbury in which he likened his childhood experiences to those of today's youth at risk. He allegedly credited his positive attitude, acquired in the nurturing social world of the church, for his ability to escape the "ghetto," pursue advanced education, and struggle for social justice. Pride implied that the church community had saved Jackson so that he could engage in socially transformative work.

Pride and other pastors of migrant churches ultimately assumed a kind of division of labor among churches and secular organizations. Prophetic activism was the work of secular entities. Churches, by contrast, were best suited to employ spiritual means, the effects of which would "trickle down" to change social arrangements. In short, they attempted to change the world by "orient[ing] worship toward redeeming the worlds in which members live" (Davidson and Koch 1998:299).

Immigrant Congregations as "Complete Institutions"

In the early part of the twentieth century, Black migrant churches often served as employment and social service referral agencies, literacy schools, and travel coordinators (recall that churches facilitated "chain migration"), as well as spaces of sociability and emotional release. Migrant churches were institutionally complete (Breton 1964) in that they gave members the information and resources needed to make the most of grim northern urban realities.

In contemporary Four Corners, only the immigrant congregations achieved similar levels of completeness. Although these churches served members exclusively, the very practical nature of that service made them resemble social service agencies that relied on referrals from satisfied clients. Recently arrived immigrants learned of these churches through friends and relatives who were members and were usually drawn into congregational life directly upon arriving in the United States. These newcomers knew that membership carried tangible benefits, such as information on jobs, medical care, educational opportunities, naturalization services, and so on. Thus, the priestly/personal orientation served two purposes. On the one hand, it saved souls; on the other hand, it helped members settle into the host country, not unlike a secular immigration agency. In fact, the social quality of their priestly activity made these churches appear quite worldly.

The presence of multiple immigration "cohorts" (Warner 1999:26) in priestly churches further facilitated the flow of information and resources, especially when pastors and other church leaders had lived in the country for some time. For instance, the pastor and assistant pastor of the Maison d'Esprit had lived in the United States for more than ten years—long enough to achieve prominent management positions in area hospitals. On numerous occasions they used their positions to find jobs for church members in the hospitals where they worked. They also routinely encouraged unemployed, nonnaturalized members to secure citizenship and apply for welfare.

Another case in point was the Seventh-day Adventist church, which was second only to the (now defunct) Haitian congregation of St. Bridget's in institutional completeness. The Adventist church had been in Four Corners since 1994 in a storefront that used to house an African American Pentecostal church. Lucknor Dessalines, a church elder and professional engineer who had lived in the United States for more than twenty years, described the congregation as "a family, where everybody knows everybody else." Moreover, it was a family where long-settled members assisted unsettled recent arrivals. "When you are a religious minority and an ethnic minority," he told me, "you have to pull all of your resources together."

The church, Dessalines noted, did not have social outreach programs. "If someone came knocking at the door, of course we would help," he said. "But we are a poor church—we don't have the luxury of going out and starting programs like that." Instead, the church did do a good deal of what Dessalines called social "inreach." Most of this inreach took place in the spacious church basement, which Dessalines was renovating himself. The basement contained a large baptismal tank, a kitchen, several communal areas, and a children's room already decorated with their delightful crafts. In this space, usually over traditionally prepared Haitian meals, church members socialized informally and in the process shared a great deal of information and made known a host of personal needs. Some needs frequently voiced and met included shelter, especially for illegal immigrants; money for rent or medical care in the absence of health insurance; immigration and legalization services; help with children experiencing adjustment problems in school; help translating important documents; and general emotional healing for members who were "nostalgic" or missed home.

The West Indian churches were far less institutionally complete than the Latino/a and Haitian Creole–speaking ones. Since West Indian immigrants confronted lower language barriers than their Spanish and Haitian Creole–speaking counterparts, they could more readily take advantage of secular programs and services. This language-based differentiation calls to mind one of Raymond Breton's (1964:204) key observations about the nature of institutional completeness: "The more different the people of a certain ethnicity are from the members of the native community, the easier it will be for them to develop their own institutions to satisfy their needs." Breton found language difference, in particular, to be associated with a high degree of institutional completeness.

At most, West Indian churches posted job opportunities on church bulletin boards (Divine Peace) or operated youth ministries (Church of God and Church of God in Christ) that informally counseled young people about educational advancement (for similar observations, see Waters 1999:202). Otherwise, their strategies for socializing members closely resembled those in use at the migrant churches. Here the goal was not to meet as many concrete needs as possible but to instill in members the values and dispositions they would need to meet their own needs, protect themselves from calamity and exploitation, and perhaps work for social change outside the church.

Rather than being entirely "otherworldly," then, the priestly churches socialized members to make it in the world (although not necessarily in the immediate streetscape, as chapter 5 illustrated). It is significant that all of the priestly churches were composed of migrants or immigrants. Their commitment to serving members rather than outsiders reflected a heightened sense of being fundamentally different from outsiders in nonreligious ways and a subsequent need for in-group sociability. In the priestly context, people were able to build communities whose nurture enabled them to operate outside the priestly context. But important differences emerged even among these "homes away from home." Southern migrant and West Indian churches focused on the cultivation of psychic fortitude, while Spanish- and Creole-speaking churches provided more tangible forms of assistance.

THEOLOGICAL CONSERVATISM
IN PROPHETIC AND PASTORAL CHURCHES

A host of sociological studies have found conservative theology—with its Biblical literalism and individualist, conversionist views of salvation—to inhibit ecumenism (Boldon 1985; Myers and Davidson 1984; Kanagy 1992) and social activism (Guest and Lee 1987; Hoge and Faue 1973; Kanagy 1992; Stark and Glock 1969; Hoge et al 1978:122). Ethnographic studies of Black Pentecostal congregations also reveal a tendency for conservative theology to suppress social activism (Paris 1982; Williams 1974). Meanwhile, studies of ecumenical activist coalitions and recent dispatches from major sponsors of such coalitions report that few, if any, participating churches represent theologically conservative traditions (Scheie, et al. 1994; Davidson 1985; Rogers 1990; Rooney 1995; Warren 1995, 2001). Scholars have taken this scarcity as further evidence of the "other-worldly" inclinations of theologically conservative people (Davidson 1985; Johnson 1967; Tamney and Johnson 1990; Johnson and Tamney 1986). The implication is that conservative clergy will join or establish efforts that fight only for traditional moral concerns, such as those championed by New Religious Right organizations. Otherwise, these clergy will gravitate toward in-church activities that promote individual spiritual salvation.

Three churches, all with northern-born congregations, challenged the negative association between theological conservatism and social activism. Azusa, Holy Road, and the Jude Church were all Pentecostal or Apostolic—two very conservative theological traditions—yet engaged to various degrees in prophetic, socially transformative activism. These churches did not assume carte blanche—like other religious organizations, they still faced theological constraints. Even so, they were a testament to the inherent flexibility of conservative religious traditions.

Elsewhere I have presented a three-part explanation of the emergence of politically and socially activist Black Pentecostal clergy (McRoberts 1999).

I argued that the apparent increase in Black Pentecostal clergy activism nationwide reflects historical forces and organizational pressures. Specifically, the highly visible church presence in the civil rights/Black power movements of the 1960s and 1970s inspired some members of the latest generation of Black Pentecostal clergy to develop activist interpretations of that faith. In the meantime, Pentecostalism has become a major faith community.[3] Within this constantly expanding community, religious strictness is no longer such a distinctive trait for individual congregations. This development has forced individual clergy to develop original ministries, including socially activist ones. In the hands of these entrepreneurial and innovative clergy, basic Pentecostal ideas are surprisingly supple.

This argument holds for the three churches now in question (two of these churches appeared in the 1999 study). All of the pastors came of age during the civil rights/Black power era and were influenced by the norms of church engagement that crystallized in that era. Likewise, all of the pastors built their congregations by reaching out to populations previously "untapped" by Pentecostalism. Their congregations were socially particularistic in some very nontraditional ways. Rivers (Azusa) built a church of Black intellectuals. Calvin (Jude Church) was trying to create a space within Black Pentecostalism where women enjoyed more positions of authority and power. Pastor Powell (Holy Road) worked to attract youth at risk to the Pentecostal fold.

The clergy also did considerable theological work in order to justify their pastoral and prophetic stances. Their ability to do such work supports the view that theology is not a rigid predictor variable but rather a cultural resource that believers can use to justify both activism and retreatism (Mock 1992; Roberts 1990; Dudley and Johnson 1991; Wood 1994). Pentecostal theology and practice, in particular, contain elements that may restrict engagement in extroverted social activism (as I illustrated in chapter 5); but they also contain elements that can facilitate and complement, rather than obstruct, social engagement (Silva 1984; Alexander 1991; Warner 1995).

Saving the "Whole Person"

For the three clergy just mentioned, the most powerful enabling element was an understanding of "salvation" that involved the satisfaction of the entire spectrum of human needs, including physical and social, as well as spiritual ones. This understanding is part and parcel of Pentecostal theology, which is distinguished in part by its emphasis on the tangible, or "radically embodied" (Cox 1995), presence of God's power in the believer's life and by its experience-oriented hermeneutic, or method of Scriptural interpretation. Theologian Mathew Clark (1983:102) writes that the Pentecostal emphasis on tangibility contributes a sense of expectation that truth will not only be held in remembrance, or objectively proclaimed as "pure" doctrine—but that truth will be realized in the midst of the people. Liturgy, preaching and missions are all conducted in this expectation—that sins will be forgiven, bodies and psyches will be healed, spirits will be uplifted, relationships will be restored, believers will be endued with spiritual power, etc. Truth is both personal (i.e., Jesus is the Truth) and empirically realizable, as opposed to merely conceptual.

Simultaneously, the Pentecostal hermeneutic permits the reader of Scripture to

> identify with the writer by virtue of common spiritual experience . . . [T]he Bible is associated with activity and experience rather than viewed as a textbook of doctrine. Experience after the Biblical pattern takes precedence over confession according to the supposed theological content of Scripture. (101)

This understanding of Scripture encourages believers to apply Biblical insights to the exigencies of daily life.

In pastoral accounts, the idea of radical embodiment was manifested as an uncanny agreement about the Biblical mandate to serve the "whole person" in all his/her social and spiritual complexity. The following remark, made by the Rev. Powell, referred to this mandate. Note his Scriptural justification for social concern:

> When you look at the Bible—right?—from Genesis to Revelations— there's always been a Christian man who could lead the nation . . . Christians always got involved with politics. And I think it's really sad when the church say, I'm not gon' get involved with that stuff. That's our problem. We get involved with the spirit too much and not dealing with the total man. How do I reach this guy and get him into a job, into a house and into some kind of structure, and let him know he has a reason to live?

This statement reflects an experiential interpretation of the Bible. Such interpretations were also evident when ministers expressed the conviction that Christians are called to fight against sin in all its forms, especially social injustice and inequality.

The clergy's application of "whole person" theology supports the findings of previous studies that show that theological conservatives tend to justify their views and activities in strictly religious terms (Tamney and Johnson 1990; Johnson 1967). It also contributes to scholarly evidence that charismatic/ evangelical religion, with its heavy reliance on the Holy Spirit and Biblical insight, can be used as "fuel" for liberatory struggle and community development work as well as priestly, personal functions.

Community Building and Conversionism

As it turned out, these activist clergy had subverted even the theologically conservative disdain for "the world." Because of this disdain, Pentecostals have tended to build exclusive, priestly communities that stand at high tension with the social and cultural environment—even if individual members were allowed or encouraged to support social change work outside of the church. The clerics in question extended this communal ethic to help build communities of clergy and laypersons committed to social transformation. The Rev. Rivers was a founding member of the citywide ecumenical Ten Point Coalition and the central organizer of Operation 2006, an antiviolence collaboration of police, clergy, and social workers. Pastor Calvin convened several regional conferences of Black clergywomen concerned with violence and drug abuse. The Rev. Powell began organizing "small churches" like his own that wanted to balance organizational growth with demonstrations of social concern. For each minister, the idea of the highly committed community served as a kind of mediator between Pentecostal practice and social activism.

This connection became clear during discussions about the effectiveness of structural- and individual-level strategies for social change. All of the pastors agreed that both societal and personal transformations were necessary to improve life in poor neighborhoods. They also favored the development of independent activist structures to meet the social, political, and economic needs of Black people. This sentiment did not conflict in any way with the pastors' commitment to Pentecostal practice. In fact, their advocacy of do-for-self social and political empowerment tended to jibe with statements stressing the traditional conversionist values of "reborn social identity, personal dignity, and newfound community" (Baer and Singer 1992:172). The unifying theme, however, was the value of the highly committed community within which moral consistency, trust, and equality would provide a basis for unity against a perceived adversary—whether that adversary was global capitalism, racist members of the U.S. Congress, or city regimes that ignore the needs of people in poor neighborhoods.

Religious and Ideological Constraints on Socially Transformative Work

Although conservative theology provided "fuel" for their activism, the clergy were constrained by elements of the same theology, sometimes in combination with nonreligious ideological tendencies. They avoided forms of activism that might make them sublimate their faith or compromise the spiritual integrity of their churches. Like their priestly, personalistic counterparts, these pastors were still committed to the spiritual person as much as to the social, political, and economic person. In fact, they used the "whole person" concept as a kind of measuring stick to evaluate and compare local social programs before supporting them. Each expressed strong preferences for church-based efforts designed to propagate Christian moral standards as well as to generate life opportunities for disprivileged people. Efforts lacking a religious foundation, they felt, would ultimately leave people in the "same position" despite temporary physical, social, or economic amelioration.

Sometimes the constrictive elements of conservative theology interacted with wholly separate ideas regarding the nature of worldly politics to produce a wariness of certain kinds of activism. Pastors Calvin and Powell, for instance, told me about the conspiratorial, if not genocidal, motives of Whites and agents of the state. Although they were committed to activism in general, both avoided collaborative efforts that might make them vulnerable to these actors, thereby severely diluting the only institution in Black society committed to serving the whole person: the church.

Pastor Calvin believed that Black-on-Black violence was perpetuated in part by a White conspiracy. She argued, for example, that the White-controlled media had helped "immobilize" Black people with respect to youth violence. By assaulting the Black public with regular images of Black youth murdering each other, the media led Blacks to "hate the kids" and to don an attitude of helplessness. She also believed Black youth were getting guns from the White-dominated law enforcement community, since Blacks neither import nor manufacture military-grade assault weapons.

Her suspicion of White motives surfaced again only when she explained her refusal to join the Ten Point Coalition, a Boston-based organization of clergy concerned with youth violence. The coalition was spurred by an instance of the "street" coming into the "church": in 1992, gang violence erupted at the Morning Star Baptist Church during a funeral for a youth murdered in a drive-by shooting. In response to the now infamous "Morning Star" incident, which included a shootout and multiple stabbings, a handful of clergy gathered to devise a plan of action, resolving that: "Since we haven't brought the church into the street, the street has come into the church." Calvin avoided Ten Point because she did not trust the motives of the White clergy who instantly rallied around it. She thought the organization was a lavish expression of "White guilt," designed to further distract Black churches from the real work in the street. "You know, long before there ever was a Ten Point, I was the only 'point' around here. Ten Point," she said, "is a product of guilty White people who decided to give some money to Black churches. Even the [Roman Catholic] cardinal came to express his concern about

Morning Star. But young people were getting murdered long before that. Where were all the ministers then?"

Pastor Powell was suspicious of White politicians and other agents of the state. He was, therefore, wary of public programs like Charitable Choice that funded churches to administer social services to poor people. In one conversation, Powell worried that, despite the neighborhood revitalization efforts of churches like Azusa and Grace, the neighborhood still appeared too "disorganized" to attract public money for community development. He suspected that White people from community development corporations in Codman Square and Mt. Bowdoin, who attended community organizing meetings at both churches, were reporting to City Hall and telling officials "that Four Corners isn't ready." He feared the city would ultimately "give the neighborhood to Codman Square [CDC]."

Later I asked if he had heard about the Charitable Choice clause. Powell seemed perturbed at the mere mention of that particular piece of legislation:

> We [churches] should try to get away from the secular world's money. Because they want to come control what you do. The Feds are trying to control the churches. We used to be an institution that nobody touched, but preachers like PTL [Praise the Lord television ministries], Swaggert—the Feds want to crack down on them. The Feds are 'round about, giving churches money through organizations so they can take control. They will come and say what you can't teach and preach.

On another occasion I met the Rev. Powell at his apartment, which was located just above the church. He told me he was trying to purchase the entire building so that the church could open an educational complex there. He complained about the paucity of money available for churches to do this work. I asked if he had approached any public agencies for funding. "I can't sell out to politicians," he replied in a cynical conflation of politicians with agencies. "They'll try to put something in the neighborhood, and I'll have to support it even if it's bad for the neighborhood. Then I have to be the one who goes to the people to tell them."

The words of Pastors Calvin and Powell indicate that there are ideological constraints to prophetic activism other than those embedded in theological conservatism. To be certain, both clergy sought to protect the integrity of the Black church; their high esteem for the church partly reflected their conservative belief in the church's exclusive possession of truth. Still, their objections to certain forms of activism did not come from the same cognitive place as the "trickle-down" philosophy discussed previously. Calvin and Powell were not protecting their churches from the corrupting influence of extroverted activism. They were protecting their churches from the perceived malintentions of White people and agents of the state.

The three Pentecostal "social transformation" clergy illustrate why theological conservatism need not always lead to priestly and personal orientations. These pastors took their theology as is and sifted and kneaded it to support their extroverted, socially transformative imperatives. To be sure, religious ideas and ideological leanings limited the pastors to certain kinds of activism and collaboration. But on the whole, conservative theology was a resource rather than an obstacle.

TAXONOMIC MOBILITY: CHURCHES GRAPPLE WITH ORGANIZATIONAL CHANGE

Churches are fluid, fluctuating organizations. Like other voluntary associations, they often must change in order to remain viable. Otherwise they die, to be replaced by innovative, entrepreneurial entities. As the religious ecologists teach us, churches may change in response to shifts in the environmental demography. Churches also change with the installation of new leadership (Warner 1988) and in response to new members with novel needs and interests. When faced with environmental or internal shifts, churches may adopt new approaches to changing the world. It is important to understand how these changes take place, especially in an antipoverty policy environment that increasingly asks churches to develop new relationships with the state and with nonmembers.

Davidson and Koch (1998:300–301) emphasize the possibility of such change but identify only one trajectory among American congregations: from prophetic, socially transformative orientations to priestly, personalistic ones. They trace this movement to the rise of political and social conservatism and individualism in the 1970s and 1980s (Lasch 1979; Bellah et al. 1985) and to a decline in federal and denominational expenditures on social concerns (Phillips 1990; Dudley and Johnson 1991). These large-scale shifts, while undoubtedly consequential for religious practice, do not speak to the many microlevel pressures that can nudge churches toward new activist orientations.

I identify four directions of change, and explain the organizational impetuses behind those shifts. During the period of study, four churches in Four Corners either stood at the crossroads of eminent change or morphed into new activist forms. The organizational changes at work were not the result of environmental shifts; churches were responding neither to changes in the demography and economy of Four Corners, nor to the broader political and cultural climate. Rather, changes precipitated from leadership turnover and congregational growth. One pastoral church moved from social transformation toward the personal when the denomination installed a new pastor. A pastoral/social transformation church was pulled toward the priestly as the founder struggled to meet the priestly needs of his growing congregation. A pastoral/socialization megachurch grew to the point of inadvertently incorporating socially transformative functions. And a prophetic/social transformation church contemplated incorporating more socializing functions in order to accommodate impending congregational growth.

Grace: Toward the Personal

In 1995, when I began studying Four Corners, this "mainline" church was among the most extroverted in the neighborhood. Over a period of four years, though, it began to leave its pastoral/social transformation orientation behind for more priestly, personal roles. The changes precipitated from denominational decisions regarding church leadership (Ammerman 1997a)—a fact that highlights via contrast the relative autonomy, or "defacto congregationalism" (Warner 1993), of the other changing churches.

Grace United Methodist Church is a testament to the influence of pastoral leadership on the mission orientation of a church. Since its formation in 1901, Grace had nearly always been a pastoral, socializing church. In the early 1910s, members enjoyed more than thirty different church clubs, societies, and extraworship activities; nonmembers enjoyed the church's frequent fairs, such as the "Italian Fete," the "Puritan Fair," the "Colonial Fair," and the "Fairless Fair." As the locality's racial composition began to change in the 1960s, Grace abandoned only its parishlike neighborhood orientation in order to become a West Indian and African niche church. The United Methodist Church (UMC), Grace's denomination, responded by installing an African American pastor in 1970. Following his tenure, Grace received three more pastors of color, two of which were from the Caribbean. Then, in 1984, the United Methodist Church installed the Rev. Dennis Paul as pastor. Dennis Paul, born and raised in Jamaica, was a British Methodist, not a member of the U.S.-based United Methodist Church. According to Paul, British Methodists maintained a territorial system of evangelization organized around local "house clusters," despite Methodist founder John Wesley's assertion that "the world is our parish." The Reverend Paul brought this territorial awareness to Grace and used it in part to initiate a program of transformative activism around local violence, poverty, and unemployment.

In 1988, Paul established the Living Center, a multiservice agency that reached people in Dorchester, Mattapan, and Jamaica Plain. The Living Center administered outreach to youth at risk, English as Second Language classes, summer day camps, and after school programs. In 1991, the Rev. Paul played a leading role in establishing the Four Corners Revitalization Group, a decidedly "secular" collaboration between the Living Center, leaders of the former Neighborhood Housing Services organization, and representatives from CDCs and health centers in abutting neighborhoods. The Revitalization Group had funding from the Hyams Foundation specifically to organize Four Corners residents concerned about crime and pubic safety issues. Eventually, though, the group would turn its efforts to economic development. As such, by installing a particular pastor with a particular biography, the UMC inadvertently spurred a church long given entirely to socialization to develop a socially transformative orientation.

This development, nevertheless, proved to be an institutional blip rather than a harbinger of permanent change. When Pastor Paul retired in 1996, the denomination replaced him with Marlyne Devry, an African American woman raised in western Massachusetts. Devry's ministry prioritized those aspects of Methodism that spawned the Holiness movement at the end of the nineteenth century, such as its insistence on the perfectibility of the individual human soul. Within the church, she concerned herself primarily with building up the ministerial capacities and responsibilities of laypersons. Congregants, she felt, should not need to rely solely on the pastor for guidance and comfort. Rather, they should be empowered to minister to each other. Devry hoped this would create more time for her ministerial work outside the church. In the short run, though, she would need to spend much more time than the previous pastor providing religious education for congregants.

The work Devry did do beyond church walls had a personal, ecclesial flavor. She did not devote a large portion of her time promoting the Revitalization Group and Living Center, as had her predecessor. Instead, she organized a spirituality group for a women's drug addiction recovery program, and she gravitated toward other efforts that similarly allowed her personally to minister to individuals. Her attraction to this kind of work reflected her conviction that social, political, and economic transformation without spiritual transformation was futile. Indeed, the most radical, large-scale transformations would begin with individuals praying together:

If we want healing in our community, if we want a community where our children are not killing one other, where our children are getting adequate education, where our politicians are working for the good of the people, then prayer needs to be the heart of that, and churches need to be leading that by example, and in unity.

Reverend Devry's emphasis on the social significance of prayer and individual spiritual empowerment infused Grace's pastoral ministry with the "trickle-down" activist sensibility favored by some of the migrant churches. Like the Reverend Paul, she was committed to serving nonmembers as well as members, but in ways that took individual change as the necessary prelude to broader social change. Thus, under the UMC-appointed Devry, the Grace ministry began to adopt a more personal approach to the pastoral orientation.

Holy Road: Drift toward Priestly

In Four Corners, "pastoral" usually meant that the head of the flock divided her or his time between prophetic work and the priestly needs of the congregation. Congregations themselves were not involved in outreach—the pastors did this work on behalf of the church. Moreover, sometimes individuals with priestly needs were attracted to churches with pastors doing prophetic, socially transformative work. Such individuals participated only vicariously in this work; their real participation was limited to activities like Bible study, worship, and evangelization.[4]

The Holy Road Church exemplified how a church could originate with pastoral intentions, then slowly drift toward the priestly as a swelling congregation settles into priestly routines. At its founding, Pastor Powell wanted the church to deviate from the insularity of the priestly, personal churches he remembered attending throughout his youth in Virginia. As noted previously, he wanted to serve the "total man"—this meant the church would serve the spiritual needs of members, the secular needs of nonmembers, and the grand cause of social transformation. For a while he succeeded: in only a few years, Powell had amassed a fifty-member congregation composed largely of young people he had met "out in the street." Through a host of educational, recreational, and spiritual ministries, he shepherded the flock away from the hazards that turn youth into "youth at risk." To Powell's delight, some of the original members earned degrees from the likes of Columbia University. Others held steady jobs as accountants, secretaries, and teachers. Meanwhile, Powell was active in socially transformative efforts such as the Ten Point Coalition.

Then, twenty years into the life of the church, Powell began finding it difficult to split his time between the priestly needs of his congregation and the street outreach and antiviolence, antidrug crusading that had always been his calling. Church members, for the most part, did not participate in the church's prophetic work, although many of them came into the church because of it. Members enjoyed the effervescent worship services, which featured several "anointed," or Spirit-invoking gospel choirs backed by some very polished young musicians. In other words, the congregation thrived on the church's priestly functions.

Powell wanted his church to move back in the direction of systematic prophetic work. He wanted the whole church to become a powerful activist organization, not unlike the Azusa Christian Community, which involved practically every member in its multiheaded transformative activism. The challenge would be to accomplish this change without alienating, and possibly losing, his congregation.

Good Tidings: Drift toward Social Transformation

Good Tidings, a burgeoning megachurch with two thousand members and rising (although the average Sunday service attracts about five hundred), represented a somewhat different type of institutional drift. Like other large churches, Good Tidings functioned like a "community" (Becker 1998), whose numerous social groups, clubs, and discussion groups allowed members to socialize selectively with others in the congregation. This community feel effectively held the interest of the church's relatively young and largely professional congregation.

Since 1985, the church had been led by the Rev. Samuel Keys. Keys's father founded the institution in 1971 in an abandoned synagogue on Southern Boulevard in Codman Square. This made Good Tidings part of the first wave of Black churches to arrive when the area began turning from White and Jewish to Black. The church moved to its current location, a giant "storefront" that once housed an A&P supermarket, in 1990. As the church continued to grow, nevertheless, Keys has had to do more than find a bigger space. To accommodate the diverse needs of the congregation, the pastor appointed seven associate pastors, each charged with a different duty.

In 1997, Keys appointed thirty-two-year-old William Curry as youth pastor to more effectively evangelize the growing body of teen and young adult members. Curry practically grew up in Good Tidings. He told me Keys had been "like a father." Nevertheless, Curry differed critically from his spiritual father in that he believed the church should move toward a socially transformative orientation to address issues of youth violence. To this end, Curry subverted his role as youth pastor by directing the congregation's attention, usually during the "announcements" portion of worship services, to activist efforts outside the church. At one service he announced an event sponsored by Operation 2006, an antiviolence coalition organized by the Rev. Rivers, whose Azusa church met just two blocks down the street. Curry had been an active member of the Operation since its inception.

This drift proceeded to the senior pastor's considerable chagrin. Keys believed in "prayer war" and in opening the church to youth at risk. To emphasize the church's openness, he redubbed it the Good Tidings Church and Community Center. The church provided space for tae kwon do classes and a number of other socializing programs open to nonmembers as well as to members. Keys initially was not excited, though, about involving the church in explicitly transformative work, especially outside the church. Regardless, he inadvertently incorporated that orientation in an attempt to respond to the phenomenal growth of the church itself. In order to remain relevant to his flock, he felt he had to delegate power to new leaders. In minting new leaders, he lost some control over the trajectory of the church's social orientation.

AZUSA: TOWARD SOCIALIZATION

If Good Tidings incorporated transformative activism as a result of its growth, members of the Azusa Christian Community wondered whether their church could remain prophetic despite impending growth—the Holy Road case has already introduced this concern. Azusa was the only prophetic/ social transformation church, in the sense that it heavily involved congregation members in its extroverted attempts to address social problems. It met in the Ella J. Baker[5] House—literally a rehabilitated Victorian home that previously served as a local base for the sale and use of illicit drugs. Worship services, which rarely exceeded twenty attendees, were held in the living room/sanctuary. It was on this floor that Rivers delivered his "old-time Holiness, down-the-line" sermons, which in not so "old-time" fashion elaborated on the unique responsibilities of radical Black intellectuals of Spirit-Baptized ilk. The second and third floors were dedicated to Azusa's Uhuru Project, a distinct nonprofit organization that administered the church's impressive and ever widening slate of social efforts. These efforts included sports, job readiness, court advocacy, street outreach, and after school programs, the Four Corners Planning Committee, and the Twenty-First Century Group, which organized, among other things, a series of symposia on the AIDS crisis in Africa.

The Rev. Eugene Rivers, the founder and pastor of the community, has achieved national celebrity, not only because of his church's innovative work with youth at risk but because of his persona, which combines sanctified morality, street sensibility, intellectual agility, and a notoriously sharp tongue. In his teens, Rivers was kicked out of his church home in Philadelphia for challenging the pastor to institute aggressive social and political programs. He was impressed by the Black Panther Party's grassroots activism and, as a consequence, became a critic of apolitical Black churches:

> See, when I started pushing the issues back in 1969 and '70, the church wasn't ready . . . I didn't understand the institutional constraints of the church be-cause I was simply a kid, like you, with some books, trying to talk about being Black. And why was the Black Panther Party running a free food program and a health clinic, and the Black churches weren't?

In 1981, Rivers and a handful of Black students established the William J. Seymour Society[6] on the campus of Harvard University. Many of the students came to the fledgling Pentecostal body from mainline faiths. "I can actually show you the Harvard *Crimson* article back in 1984, sort of announcing the fact that we were laying the foundation for launching a church," Rivers told me. "And the concern then was for integrating biblically orthodox Christian theology, social theory, and policy analysis with some programmatic organizing on the ground, with the goal in mind of building a movement . . . Now that was completely atypical for Pentecostal churches."

In 1988, the young evangelists moved to Dorchester to put their politi-cized faith into practice. They located first in Grove Hall, and in 1995 moved to Four Corners. The move to Dorchester was symbolic as well as physical. By leaving Cambridge, the Azusa members intended to express solidarity with the poor and displeasure with the burgeoning Black middle and upper classes. According to their analysis, upwardly mobile Blacks, especially the academic intellectual elite, had abandoned the struggles of the poor and re-treated into smug materialism. Thus from Harvard Yard emerged a church of Black intellectuals who believed not only in the need for transformative social activism but in the literal truth of the Bible, ascetic Holiness living, and glos-solalia, the aural footprint of the Holy Spirit.

By 1999, Azusa's ministry had evolved to the point where members began to feel overwhelmed by their own activism. By growing the congregation, the church might be able to relieve some of the weight now pressing on the shoulders of core members. Yet, members wondered whether they would be able to maintain the church's intimate feel, its sense of discipline and com-mitment, with a larger congregation. They believed that the priestly functions of the community, maintained through a rigorous spiritual regimen of fasts, Bible studies, and prayer retreats, empowered them to carry out the church's transformative work. Azusa was a "family" church (Becker 1998), where mu-tual support undergirded outward activity. This fact further corroborates

Davidson and Koch (1998), who observed that "member-oriented programs in [prophetic/social transformation] churches were designed to provide members with the spiritual and social resources they needed to sustain their efforts toward social reform" (300).

In one interview, conducted in an upper room of the Baker House, Pastor Rivers summed up the problem, all the while pacing the floor and jabbing the air with a professorly index finger:

> This is the decision you have to make: as you grow a church you will never maintain the same level of intensity. See, Azusa's been a family. We're almost a Chinese restaurant, where you've got three generations of family. So it can run with a high level of efficiency—like those Korean delicatessens. If Azusa is to grow as a fellowship, as a worshiping community, in excess of two hundred it would be a very different operation . . . It's highly efficient [now] because people will work eighty hours a week. When our fellowship has a thousand members, the percentage of spectators will be much larger.

The core dilemma was what to do with these "spectators," since so much of the pastor's time was devoted to nonmembers. Would the church need to become more pastoral, like Holy Road, as new members demanded spiritual attention from the pastor? Azusa members speculated that they would have to become more of a socializing church if they were to incorporate new members while maintaining its transformative mission. They consistently referred to megachurches, which maintain participation by offering "something for everybody" in the form of clubs and small discussion groups. Some new members might be drawn into the church's transformative work if they recast the various outreach programs as opportunities for small group socialization. In short, Azusa would ultimately look more like Good Tidings, which is more of a "community" than a "family."

These profiles offer insight into the multiple reasons why churches change activist orientations. Church orientations can change in response to at least four forces, three of which involve congregational growth and two of which involve inadvertent institutional "drift": 1) changes in leadership, possibly precipitated by denominational authorities; 2) congregational growth, leading to inadvertent "drift" toward the needs of new congregants; 3) congregational growth, leading to the incorporation of new leaders, who in turn "drift" the institution toward their own social orientations; and 4) congregational growth, leading to new strategies of maintaining member involvement.

It is interesting that most of the changing churches were moving away from prophetic, socially transformative functions. This was due not to large-scale cultural, political, or denominational shifts, as Davidson and Koch (1998) might have predicted, but to the organizational dynamics of churches themselves. The Azusa and Holy Road cases underscore the plain difficulty involved with maintaining extroverted forms of social activism. The Grace case illustrates the extent to which such efforts may rely on the influence of particular leaders. Given this reliance, denominations can alter church orientations not only by changing broad funding patterns but also by deciding which pastors are to serve which congregations. That said, denominational influence was a nonissue for the majority of churches in Four Corners. Most of these were either independent, belonged to laissez faire denominations exerting minimal control over local churches, or were themselves flagship churches in emergent denominations.

SUMMARY

Nearly all of the churches in Four Corners felt they were in some sense "activist." Yet, these churches distributed social benefits and thought about social transformation in a variety of ways. Approaches to "activism" thus further distinguished churches in the particularistic religious field that was Four Corners. Churches engaging in ritual activism that "trickled down" to change the world were different from churches that distributed social services directly to members. And both of these groups were substantially different from churches committed to hands-on social transformation. Moreover, some churches changed activist orientations, thereby changing part of what made them unique. They changed not only in response to large-scale societal and denominational shifts but also in response to leadership turnover and congregational growth. Despite the current popularity of church-friendly social policies, which appear to reward extroverted religious activisms, these microlevel forces were steering extroverted churches away from socially transformative prophetic work.

SEVEN

Who Is My Neighbor?

RELIGION AND INSTITUTIONAL
INFRASTRUCTURE IN FOUR CORNERS

In the prelude to the parable of the good Samaritan (Luke 10:25), a lawyer asks Jesus, "What shall I do to inherit eternal life?" Jesus replies, "What is written in the law? How readest thou?" The lawyer recites, "Thou shalt love the Lord thy God with all thy heart, and with all thy soul, and with all thy strength, and with all thy mind; and thy neighbor as thyself." "Thou hast answered right," says Jesus. "This do, and thou shalt live." The lawyer accepts the first four conditions, but disputes the last. He asks, "And who is my neighbor?" In this final substantive chapter, I explain how the dense, diverse religious district has impacted its host neighborhood. As it turns out, the factors that allowed twenty-nine congregations to inhabit the same neighborhood—niche status and particularism—were the same factors that proved most consequential for the neighborhood itself. These factors complicated the nature of congregational identity with Four Corners, such that there was no single, parochial answer to the question, Who is my neighbor?

Churches have fundamentally ambiguous relationships with the local communities that surround them. On the one hand, they are part of a broader field of institutional agents whose actions, inactions, and interactions impact the quality of life in local communities in general, and depressed neighborhoods, in particular. This matters because "place matters"; that is, neighborhoods continue to differ in terms of race and class composition, concentration of particular health problems, and crime rates (Sampson 1999:243; Jargowsky 1997; Wilson 1996; Massey 1996). Public and nonprofit community development programs tend to target discrete neighborhoods for grantmaking, and many municipal services are administered by local district. For this reason, neighborhoods persist as social units where collective action can and often must take place in defense of spatially bounded interests (Henig 1982; Crenson 1983).

According to scholars of neighborhood social organization,[1] one way institutions such as churches foster such collective action is by building and participating in the networks that make such action possible. Neighborhood institutions are social spaces where interpersonal networks form; they are also corporate agents whose interorganizational networks can impact the collective quest for public goods (Sampson 1999). Connections among neighborhood institutions, what are called "horizontal" networks, help to coordinate and focus existing resources to address neighborhood problems (Kornhauser 1978; Pattillo 1998). Connections between neighborhood and extraneighborhood institutions (such as social service agencies, foundations, and agents of the state), or "vertical networks," draw precious resources into the neighborhood while presenting neighborhood affairs to a broader public (Bursik and Grasmick 1993). When local institutions perform these vital networking functions, they form an "infrastructure" through which neighborhood concerns can be aired and addressed.

This all assumes, of course, that institutions are somehow oriented toward the neighborhood and its affairs. As the case of Four Corners will underscore, the institutions in a given neighborhood are not necessarily attached to that neighborhood by membership or mission. Neighborhoods may well persist as important social worlds with real, geographically defined interests. Yet, like individual residents (Taub et al. 1977; Janowitz 1967; Suttles 1972), institutions may have little incentive to identify with neighborhoods. Voluntary associations in particular, as servants of urbanites who are themselves transient, widely diverse, and only partially attached to neighborhoods, are not the natural anchors of neighborhood life. Suttles (1972:59; see also Warren 1975) observes that rather than drawing members from and trying to represent entire neighborhoods, associations tend to serve fragmented "communities of limited liability."

Alternatively, an association's members may hail partly or predominantly from other neighborhoods. Suttles (1968) discussed this phenomenon in his study of a neighborhood on Chicago's Near West Side. Four out of twelve churches in the area drew most of their membership from outside the immediate area and consequently had little to do with neighborhood affairs. The point is, rather than operating entirely within and for particular neighborhoods, voluntary associations may be partially or nonattached to the neighborhood. Nonattached associations are physically located in the neighborhood yet draw members primarily from other parts of the city. These organizations may pay little attention to neighborhood affairs, preferring instead to aim resources and services at geographically dispersed target populations. Partially attached associations either draw membership from select neighborhood populations or champion fragmental neighborhood concerns.

Churches, then, are not just places where people meet to worship. They are institutional agents that can impact the trajectory and outcomes of neighborhood collective action for the acquisition and defense of public goods such as impeccable social and municipal services, access to community development resources, public safety, quality schooling, decent housing, and effective, but humane, policing. Churches, by virtue of being located somewhere in the urban space,[2] can and do affect local urban life; what remains problematic is the extent to which churches are *attached* to the neighborhoods that host them.

CHURCHES AND NEIGHBORHOOD ATTACHMENT

As attachments are concerned, churches in Four Corners were like the lawyer in the Gospel story related above: They were clear on how to love God. Yet, the definition of "neighbor" remained problematic among churches, in terms of both membership and mission. In this sense, to return to the exilic theme discussed in chapter 4, a congregation can be *in,* yet not entirely *of,* the neighborhood. Two ordinary conditions of life in the religious district constrained church attachment to Four Corners: the fact that churches were particularistic niches, drawing members from a very wide geographic area according to affinity; and frequent, or impending, church relocations, which I have called "bouncing."

Particularism and Niching

Since they did not rely on Four Corners for members, most of the churches had no reason to aim mission activities at the neighborhood. No church tried to recruit exclusively from Four Corners. Only two churches, Grace and Azusa, housed programs that specifically addressed the neighborhood's social and economic needs. Indeed, few of the pastors seemed at all concerned about the precise geographic locations of their churches. All but four of the pastors were unaware that their churches were in Four Corners. When asked what neighborhood they considered their church to be located in, most of the pastors identified the locality, after some hesitation, either as Codman Square, Fields Corner, or Grove Hall. A few pastors simply claimed "Dorchester" or "Roxbury" as their neighborhood. One church, the Church of God, even retained "Mattapan" in its official name, even though it had long been located in Dorchester. The pastor of this church was aware of the discrepancy but retained the inaccurate identifier in order to distinguish her church from the Church of God *in Christ,* located only a few blocks away. In any case, nearly all of the clergy perceived their churches to be located in a particularly troubled area, even if this area did not seem to have a name or identity of its own. As Pastor Calvin confessed: "I don't *know* what they call this area. Drug-infested? In need of AA [Alcoholics Anonymous] on every corner?"

Again, not all churches entirely lacked neighborhood awareness. Grace

Church had been nonattached ever since its transition from a Scots-Irish parish to a West Indian and Caribbean niche. But its activist ministry, developed and driven mainly by former pastor Dennis Paul, eventually *spawned* a secular organization that developed partial neighborhood attachments. As I related in the previous chapter, the Reverend Paul played a key role in the establishment of the Four Corners Action Coalition. The Hyams Foundation had awarded the Coalition funding to organize Four Corners residents around public safety issues. Paul and his collaborators, however, envisioned launching a large-scale, multineighborhood intervention program for youth at risk. They appointed as director a woman with extensive social service experience but without a background in community organizing. The director proceeded to develop a slate of multineighborhood youth programs.

Hyams eventually detected the gap between the purpose of their grant and the Action Coalition's actual work. As Rev. Paul recalled, chuckling, "Them vex up at we!" In order to ease their funder's vexation, the Coalition replaced the first director with Marvin Martin, a seasoned community organizer who focused all of his efforts on mobilizing Four Corners residents, homeowners and tenants alike. Over time, the public safety focus ballooned into "comprehensive development." For homeowners—the section of the population that responded most enthusiastically to the new door-to-door organizing approach—this meant fostering home ownership, beautifying public spaces, and attracting commercial amenities to the area, in addition to lobbying the police for more effective patrolling. Since it mainly attracted homeowners as opposed to tenants, the Action Coalition was, by default if not by design, partially attached to that neighborhood population.

Most significant for Grace's neighborhood orientation, though, was the way the Reverend Paul used the Coalition's neighborhood work to channel his congregation into transformative activism. To that end, Paul, who served as president of the Coalition's board of directors during its first five years, made sure that congregants sat on the board. He also promoted the Coalition from the pulpit and encouraged congregants to assist its labors. Thus, the activity of this immigrant niche church began to reflect more awareness of neighborhood affairs. Importantly, though, it was a private foundation that spurred the Action Coalition and the Rev. Paul to develop a single-neighborhood brand of activism.

Azusa members had expressed identity with and concern for Four Corners since the church moved there from Grove Hall in 1995. Only a few members lived in Four Corners proper, but the congregation felt called as a matter of religious, intellectual, and political conviction to serve and advocate for the neighborhood where it chose to worship. Their neighborhood efforts, referred to above, included a night patrol aimed at establishing contact with youth in the street, a number of educational programs for young people and their parents, and the Four Corners Planning Committee, whose charge was to create neighborhood jobs through the development of light industry. Azusa's mission activity, then, reflected its unique understanding of the needs of a distinct neighborhood population. This partial mission attachment, in turn, was rooted in particularistic aspects of the congregation itself.

Bouncing

Church mobility, what I call "bouncing," further complicated religious attachment to the neighborhood. Far from spurring storefront churches to take an interest in neighborhood affairs, the prospect of displacement can pit churches against the local community, thus inspiring nonattachments in mission orientation. In Four Corners, the aggressive prodevelopment stance taken by the Four Corners Action Coalition and the Four Corners Planning Committee put these efforts at odds with the pastors of some small storefront churches. Such churches were perpetually concerned about their physical foothold in the spatial environment as well as with their social alcove in the multicongregational environment.

The Rev. Powell (Holy Road) was pastor of one such church. Powell was one of four pastors in Four Corners who were aware of their churches' location in a neighborhood called Four Corners (the other three were Rivers, Keys, and Paul [Paul's successor, the Rev. Devry, was also aware of Four Corners as such]). And as I have already established, he was concerned about neighborhood youth: Holy Road sponsored basketball tournaments, a summer camp, and other programs for area youngsters. "We got a lot of activities," Powell told me, proudly. "A lot of activities we do within our little, small building." Powell was also concerned about the place of his church, and churches like his, in an economically revitalized Four Corners. Previously his church had been displaced from Roxbury, where he rented space from the youth multiservice center at which he worked. In 1996, the center acquired a new executive director, who promptly evicted Holy Road. Regarding the prospect of being displaced again, Powell said:

> We as a body aren't prepared to move, so development could hurt in the short run. In the next four years, a lot of storefronts will be out of their storefronts. They have prime space on major arteries. They will get kicked out. We won't see as many churches in the inner city.

Upon moving his church to Four Corners from Roxbury, Powell began attending meetings of both the Action Coalition and the Planning Committee. He soon realized, however, that these efforts had no plans for relocating, or otherwise compensating, churches that might be displaced for the sake of neighborhood economic development. He began attending meetings only on rare occasions. Meanwhile, his church began sponsoring events aimed at a wider geographic area. Usually these events were held in neighborhoods other than Four Corners. The point, however, is that Powell, upon realizing his precarious property status in Four Corners, began directing significantly more of the church's energy toward developing programs outside Four Corners. Meanwhile, his attention to affairs pertaining strictly to Four Corners waned considerably.

Church mobility, then, can widen the geographic scope of a congregation such that it will have little incentive to attach itself to any particular neighborhood. Meanwhile, property status renders some churches, particularly storefronts, vulnerable to forced mobility. Even if a church has no inclination toward high mobility, the threat of displacement can prompt it to develop nonattached, rather than neighborhood-focused, missions.

CHURCH ATTACHMENT AND NEIGHBORHOOD
INFRASTRUCTURE

I have explained why churches tended to lack identification with Four Corners or feel to partially attached to the neighborhood. What remains is to explain the consequence of this religious institutional reality for neighborhood social organization. Churches, I learned, *did* act as interactive social spaces and as architects of vertical and horizontal networks. Indeed, it appeared that all the requisites for neighborhood institutional infrastructure were in place. In fact, clergy and congregants even had a word for the network building that occurred within and between churches: "fellowshipping." But the problematic nature of religious attachment to the neighborhood hampered the development of such an infrastructure.

Religious services offered an opportunity for interpersonal fellowshipping, and churches fellowshipped with each other by supporting special events, planning joint functions, and swapping preachers. But fellowshipping within churches generally did not build networks among neighborhood residents, for many of the people who worshiped in Four Corners were not from Four Corners in the first place. Subsequently, vertical connections between churches and outside agencies did not immediately become resource links for neighborhood residents; rather, in nonattached fashion, these links served the geographically dispersed members of particular congregations.

Horizontal linkages were equally problematic, at least as the prospect of neighborhood collective action was concerned. Churches in Four Corners fellowshipped extensively with churches outside, as well as within, the neighborhood. Just as most individual churches had nonattached, or outward facing attachments, the emergent horizontal networks among churches were neither identified with nor bounded by Four Corners. Meanwhile, due to conflicts over voice and vision, those institutions with partial neighborhood attachments failed for some time to build working relationships with each other. These conflicts jeopardized existing and potential links with grantmaking agencies, as the latter tended to require evidence of neighborhood unity.

In-Church Fellowshipping and the Application of Vertical Ties

Congregations, by definition, bring individuals into face-to-face contact and, thus, can potentially nurture interpersonal networks in the neighborhood. Recall, however, that congregations in Four Corners were not attached to the neighborhood by membership. They were niche congregations, drawing worshipers from all over the city, if not the metropolis. Clergy and congregants were well aware that their churches did not attract many people from the area immediately surrounding their churches. One sunny Sunday afternoon I spoke with Minister French just as services were starting up at his church, Holy Fullness Apostolic. We were standing outside the church, and the eighty-year-old lay minister, dressed impeccably in a crisp black suit and tan fedora, tipped stylishly to the front, was waving to congregants as they stepped out of shiny minivans and late model sedans.

I asked him where Holy Fullness members came from in the city. He replied: "From different parts. Almost everybody comes from somewhere else— nobody comes from around here. It's funny—seems like almost every church you go to, people come from other places, and the people in that neighborhood go to other churches." Minister French's observation agreed with my own finding that churches in Four Corners generally drew members from outside the neighborhood. Consequently, these churches, for the most part, were not social spaces where neighborhood cohesion was fostered. Rather, they were places where cohesion was cultivated within specific affinity groups, such as the Black southern migrants who made up most of the Holy Fullness congregation.

In other words, these churches were communities in themselves that happened to be located within the geographic bounds of Four Corners; they were not nodes in a network of neighborhood residents. As such, whatever vertical connections churches made with outside agencies tended to benefit the members of specific congregations, not residents of Four Corners. The exceptions were the Grace and Azusa churches, discussed previously, which used money from public and nonprofit agencies to establish programs for local immigrant and poor Black populations, respectively. The vast majority of churches, however, were neither as well connected nor as concerned with channeling resources into the neighborhood as these two churches. The most common vertical connections churches established were with employment, health, and immigration services, which sent newsletters and fliers to area pastors. Pastors, in turn, posted these publications on corkboards that hung on the rear or side walls of churches.

The corkboard at the Seventh-day Adventist church, for example, featured numerous pamphlets, many in Haitian Creole, addressing health concerns. One pamphlet described the dangers of cigarette smoking. Another tried to rally support for a health care for all campaign. These postings resonated with the Adventists' theological emphasis on physical health.[3] By contrast, the corkboard at the Divine Peace Church contained several employment bulletins, including dispatches from the "Boston Pastors Job Alert," and a staffing and outsourcing employment firm.

Clergy and congregants generally did not distribute these materials outside of their churches. In order to view such information, one needed to enter a church and view its corkboard, presumably at the hour of religious services or Bible study, since few churches were open on a daily basis for walk-in visitors. As such, the information and services provided by these vertical connections, however modest, were not widely available to neighborhood residents. Churches with connections to health agencies did not become neighborhood centers for health services and information. Churches with ties to employment agencies did not become neighborhood clearing-houses where residents could learn about employment opportunities. In short, the lack of membership attachment to the neighborhood influenced the way churches applied vertical connections. Rather than serving the neighborhood, vertical connections ultimately served the members of particular congregations.

Horizontal Networks and Interchurch Fellowshipping

In a sense, the particularistic niche church, with its problematic neighborhood attachments, validates Martin Marty's (1987:213) suspicion that "social distance" is steadily replacing physical distance in the religious cityscape. At the same time, though, social proximity is replacing physical proximity among religious people. While churches need not lay exclusive claim to a particular neighborhood in order to assert their uniqueness, congregants and clergy need not limit their associations to people within their churches or neighborhoods. Most churches in Four Corners regularly invited guest preachers and held events with other churches around the city. Some laypersons actually rotated between churches in various neighborhoods in order to visit with friends and relatives in other congregations and enjoy multiple worship styles. These nonattached forms of interchurch fellowshipping linked religious institutions horizontally across neighborhoods, thus contributing to cross-neighborhood forms of community and diverting attention away from *intra*-neighborhood horizontal network building.

In one way or another, practically all of the churches in Four Corners fellowshipped with other churches in different parts of the city. Many churches held joint seasonal revivals. Pastor Pride, for example, had held revivals with preachers from all over Boston, Providence, R.I., and even Chicago. At revivals, each sponsoring pastor got a chance to preach and heal the sick. Smaller churches, like Pride's, benefited most from these joint events, for some unaffiliated attendants inevitably "got saved" and decided to join one of the sponsoring churches. Meanwhile, existing members of sponsoring churches got to meet each other and socialize, and clergy built a support network that extended throughout the city and region, if not the nation. Churches also invited guest preachers and sent their clergy to other churches to preach. According to the Reverend Winspeare, pastor of Faith Baptist, guest preaching opportunities arose when a minister or layperson casually visited another church. As an analogy, Winspeare described how he met me:

> *Winspeare:* So you met me at my church Sunday and I handed you a card. And we kinda conversate and I kinda got a sense of you then. OK, and we talked again today or tonight or whatever. That's basically how it go. You may meet someone, for whatever the case may be, at another church. You may not even be the preacher or the speaker for the evening or the morning, but somebody else may be there, and they may enjoy your speaking, and they say, "Gee I'd like you to come and worship with us," and you exchange numbers, and that's how it sort of works. And you establish a rapport, and a bond is connected there.
> *McRoberts:* Ok, so people sort of circulate between churches—
> *Winspeare:* Yeah, they network.

Through guest preaching, clergy not only witnessed (and practiced) different homiletical styles, but they learned how other clergy ran their churches. When Winspeare, a relatively young cleric, visited Pastor Lawrence's church in Codman Square, he found her to be a "sharp" leader worth emulating. He also learned about Mattapan-Dorchester Churches in Action, a church-based activist network that Lawrence led. The result of interchurch fellowshipping, then, was threefold: people met members of other churches, clergy established relationships with their peers, and churches supported each other's events. In turn, each of these effects helped to build horizontal networks, linking churches across neighborhoods according to interest and affinity.

On occasion, these networks became formalized as ministerial and activist associations, such as the Black Ministerial Alliance, the Ten Point Coalition, and the aforementioned Mattapan-Dorchester Churches in Action. Each of these groups formed around existing fellowship networks, and each grew as a result of further fellowshipping (recall that the Rev. Winspeare learned about Mattapan-Dorchester Churches in Action because he preached at the Rev. Lawrence's church). Nine pastors in Four Corners were members of such cross-neighborhood church networks. Meanwhile, only the pastors of Grace and Azusa participated in organizations aimed exclusively at revitalizing Four Corners.

At least one formalized cross-neighborhood church network originated in Four Corners. As I argued in the previous section, the vulnerable property status of some churches deflected their attention away from neighborhood concerns. The same property interest inspired some of these churches, led by the Rev. Powell (Holy Road), to develop horizontal networks with vulnerable churches in other neighborhoods. In 1997, the Rev. Powell began convening meetings of pastors from a handful of vulnerable churches located in Dorchester, Roxbury, and Mattapan. The pastors, all storefront renters, began to organize to further their property interests while doing community work as well.

The pastors promoted this nascent effort as an alternative to neighborhood revitalization campaigns that inevitably bounce little churches out of their spaces. According to the Rev. Powell, the organization of small churches hoped to pool money to buy houses, renovate them, and put congregants in them rent-free. By providing free rent, the pastors expected to get more in tithes from those congregants. The pastors also discussed forming a community credit union. The group eventually wanted to approach up to one hundred small churches in depressed neighborhoods—churches that, in Powell's words, "are doing an excellent job but need the finances to do other things." "Other things" included purchasing or building permanent church structures. Once delivered from their vulnerable property status, member churches would be expected to "do an excellent job" at addressing the social and economic needs of their neighborhoods.

So churches in Four Corners do participate in horizontal institutional networks. Yet, the churches' outward-facing orientations effectively broadened the purpose and geographic span of such networks beyond the immediate neighborhood. Rather than focusing and coordinating church efforts to address neighborhood concerns, interchurch fellowship networks extended well outside the neighborhood and served the survival and growth imperatives of congregations themselves.

Arrested Fellowshipping: Horizontal Conflict within Four Corners

I began to witness the conflictual aspect of life in the religious district when I was awakened early one morning by a phone call from an irate Reverend Rivers; he wanted to know my real intentions. For some time I had been making computer-generated maps of Four Corners for the neighborhood's two main community development organs: the Four Corners Action Coalition, located in the basement of Grace Methodist Church, and the Four Corners Planning Committee, operated by members of the Azusa Christian Community, of which Rivers was pastor. This assistance might not have been a problem in itself, except that the two groups were struggling over which should represent the neighborhood to outside agencies. Rivers had heard that a Harvard graduate student was "working" for the other group, which meant that I might have duplicitous motives for working with his group. In lending my name and, by implication, Harvard's name, to the other group's work, I was indicating my real allegiance.

I never expected to find the few neighborhood-aware churches acting of one accord. Their respective neighborhood organizations always had different strategic emphases, different understandings of what it meant to "save" Four Corners. Only outside agents, public and private, those granting money to and conferring legitimacy on community development groups expected to hear a single neighborhood voice. Naively, I did not consider how such expectations might turn legitimate differences among neighborhood advocates into bitter, protracted conflict over what *e pluribus unum* should look like in a depressed neighborhood. As a result, I, another outsider representing a powerful institution, had "worked" myself into the midst of a struggle between the two would-be voices of Four Corners.

The struggle began in 1995, when both the Action Coalition and the Planning Committee launched "comprehensive" neighborhood revitalization efforts. As I have already intimated, the Action Coalition's tactical repertoire resembled that of a traditional community organizing campaign, including door-to-door canvassing, small focus groups, and mass meetings with public officials. The goal was to pressure vertically situated operatives, such as public officials and city agencies, to provide better services and policing, and to grant the community full control over the economic development process. Meanwhile, the Planning Committee quietly raised money through its informal vertical ties to local foundations and public entities, including the mayor's office. Each of the groups, located literally across the street from one another, felt that it represented the real Four Corners. The Action Coalition felt it had tapped the full range of interests in the neighborhood through its systematic canvassing, small group forums, and mass meetings. To them, the Planning Committee appeared as a small group of Black intellectual elites claiming to represent the downtrodden yet failing to involve actual residents in their planning process. The Planning Committee claimed to serve the interests of endangered youth and the poorest of the poor. These populations, Planning Committee members speculated, could be reached not through traditional canvassing and organizing but through targeted social services and night patrols. To this body, the Action Coalition represented a privileged minority—homeowners—who felt besieged by unruly youth and thought of neighborhood stability largely in terms of home ownership and commercial conveniences.

The conflict peaked in the summer of 1996 when Massachusetts Main-Streets, a publicly funded neighborhood block grant program, announced that the following summer it would be reviewing a round of applications. MainStreets focuses on commercial development, particularly the aesthetic rehabilitation of commercial storefronts. Both the Planning Committee and the Action Coalition intended to submit applications on behalf of the neighborhood. Each felt that it best represented the neighborhood's economic development interests. Meanwhile, MainStreets officials emphatically reminded the two groups that grant applicants should speak with a single voice, representing all the residential, commercial, and institutional constituencies in the neighborhood. After a year of heated contestation, the organizations managed to submit a single application. The damage, however, had already been done. According to Marvin Martin, executive director of the Action Coalition, MainStreets declined the Four Corners application because "our organizational infrastructure wasn't strong enough."

In the fall of 1996, both organizations independently sent letters to the City of Boston requesting that special attention be paid to Four Corners' economic and social needs. Each entity represented itself as the premier neighborhood organization. The Action Coalition addressed its letter to Mayor Menino and copied to the Boston Redevelopment Authority (BRA), two city councilors, and Charles Grigsby, the director of the Boston Public Facilities Department. The Planning Committee had already established an informal dialogue with Grigsby and therefore sent its letter directly to him by way of concretizing an already amicable vertical relationship.

The letters differed in tone as well as in trajectory. The Action Coalition's letter took a somewhat adversarial pitch, noting that the state of the neighborhood could be blamed partly on the indiscriminate sale of city-owned properties for undesirable uses:

> If homes and especially businesses are allowed to be auctioned off to anyone with sufficient funds, the Four Corners Action Coalition will not be able to effectively plan the type of community-oriented services which are so desperately needed. It is not difficult to grasp that the last thing Four Corners needs is another auto body repair shop or related automotive business. However, if a lot is auctioned off to an unknown business person, that is exactly what could happen.

The letter demanded that the city place a moratorium on property transactions in Four Corners until the Action Coalition had developed a comprehensive plan of development. It also suggested that the city "revisit" a BRA-commissioned study of southern Dorchester conducted in the 1970s. According to the letter, the study had proposed

> that approximately $86.5 million dollars be spent between 1975 and 1989 for residential and industrial development for South Dorchester. If this study was ever taken beyond the planning stages, its impact was not felt in the Four Corners area. Instead, during that period of time there was a slow deterioration of the social and economic fabric in this neighborhood.

The Planning Committee's letter apparently was more conciliatory. As Lorne Alcott, then chair of the Planning Committee, recalled: "We said we wanted to work together to make change. It was a friendly letter, that's all. Getting some neighborhood studies done, doing collaborative planning and things like that."

Several weeks later, the Rev. Rivers arranged for Alcott to meet with Charles Grigsby to follow up on the letter. Alcott was surprised to find Grigsby "looking evil" at her because of the communication's "confrontational tone." According to Alcott, Grigsby had confused the two letters and was prepared for a showdown. Martin, of the Action Coalition, later told me that Grigsby thought *both* letters were from the Planning Committee, and expected a confrontation. In any case, when Alcott informed him that two letters had been sent under separate cover, Grigsby was miffed at the apparent lack of communication between the two groups. Rather than responding to the multiple missives, he insisted that the groups decide who would act as the official neighborhood representative. The double letter incident thus spawned a series of joint meetings at which the two groups debated over who should represent the neighborhood to the city's multiple development agencies. The meetings produced more pyrotechnics than pacts; the organizations therefore resolved to seek professional mediation. Eventually they agreed on a division of labor: the Planning Committee would focus on raising funds for neighborhood social services, and the Action Coalition would negotiate with the city over economic development issues.

The conflict between these groups illustrates why the mere presence of churches and other institutions with ostensible neighborhood attachments may not lead directly to the formation of an institutional infrastructure. The divergent mission orientations of such groups can frustrate horizontal fellowshipping within the neighborhood. In Four Corners, the first task facing community development organizations was not to successfully launch comprehensive revitalization efforts but to negotiate their partial neighborhood attachments and *forge* a more or less unified identity and purpose for the neighborhood.

CONCLUSION

The case of Four Corners offers insight into why particular kinds of neighborhood institutions, churches in this case, might not instinctually work to build collective agential capacities in neighborhoods. Churches clearly build networks—among congregants, with each other, and with vertically situated agencies. Yet, particularly in neighborhoods with high concentrations of churches, congregations tend to be particularistic and mobile. These factors lead churches to either disregard neighborhoods as sources of membership and objects of mission or to identify instead with distinct populations that happen to co-reside in the neighborhood. Whatever "infrastructure" emerges among such churches, then, may not immediately be brought to bear on neighborhood-level issues. Otherwise, churches and other institutions may, at least initially, fall short of producing a *harmonious* network of organizations. Clashes may be especially heated when consensus is required by an outside agent wielding the power to grant or withhold vital resources. Conflict, however, should be understood not as a moral failure but as an ordinary byproduct of any process that seeks to produce some semblance of consensus. In Four Corners, interchurch conflict resulted in a higher degree of mutual understanding and cooperation. I am reminded of Georg Simmel (1971), who once theorized that both conflict and cooperation

> are fundamentally distinguished from the mere indifference of two or more individuals or groups. Whether it implies the rejection or the termination of sociation, indifference is purely negative. In contrast to such pure negativity, conflict contains something positive. (71)

Put simply, the opposite of conflict is not consensus but indifference.

The larger point, though, is that a neighborhood full of churches will not necessarily emerge as a cohesive community, regardless of how much community is enacted within churches on certain days of the week. Ultimately, it is the purpose and quality of connections within and among churches, and between churches and secular organizations, that matters for the development of neighborhood institutional infrastructure. The latter requires that churches identify with neighborhoods in mission if not in membership and establish peaceable interinstitutional relationships that reconcile their divergent attachments to the neighborhood. Rather than indicting churches that do not emerge as neighborhood advocates, single-handedly "organizing" people and institutions, we would do better to examine closely the nature of voluntary associational life in neighborhoods like Four Corners. Neighborhood institutional infrastructure relies on the presence of institutions that are oriented toward neighborhood concerns and able to overcome their own differences. Churches, which routinely build networks for all sorts of purposes yet may or may not function as neighborhood institutions, are no more "naturally" suited for this work than any other kind of organization.

CONCLUSION

Saving Four Corners?

In 1999, after having applied twice, the Four Corners Action Coalition won a Massachusetts MainStreets grant. The modest grant was intended only to help business owners renovate store facades. Even so, MainStreets began to attract to the neighborhood the recognition it would need to win larger grants for comprehensive revitalization. The announcement of the award in area newspapers was the first positive press Four Corners had received in years. One editorialist, nonetheless, could not help but begin on a sardonic note:

> The Four Corners area of Dorchester is well-fixed for churches but little else. The area's application for MainStreets designation—a city-funded program to boost commercial activity in struggling business districts—says it all: 0 super-markets; 0 bakeries; 0 hardware stores; 0 accounting offices; 11 religious organizations; 14 vacant storefronts. (*Boston Globe,* November 8, 1999, A20)

Like the editorial, this book began with the observation that Four Corners contains many churches—far more than eleven, in fact. At the time of this writing, nearly all of the churches remained, although many undoubtedly will be displaced as plans for revitalization become a reality. By the close of the year 2001, a Walgreens had been slated for the area. The drugstore might provide the "anchor" necessary to attract smaller businesses. There were also plans to build affordable housing and a small senior citizens complex on a patch of vacant lots. Other lots were earmarked for light industry. Marvin Martin, executive director of the Four Corners Action Coalition, was collaborating with the Four Corners MainStreets administrator to lobby the Metropolitan Boston Transit Authority to reopen a long-dormant commuter rail stop in Four Corners.[1]

To help reduce the appearance of disorder and improve the overall aesthetic of the neighborhood, Four Corners community organizations collaborated with their counterparts in Codman Square and Bowdoin-Geneva to educate residents about proper trash disposal while lobbying the city for biweekly trash pickup.[2] Meanwhile, a series of shootings and armed robberies of beauty salons in summer 2001 prompted a renewed focus on public safety in the neighborhood. In response, the Ella J. Baker House, the

Four Corners Action Coalition, and the Codman Square CDC and Health Center organized a series of public safety forums attended by residents (the first drew more than one hundred) and local police captains.

Unlike the *Boston Globe* editorial this book has tried to show how so many churches could concentrate in a 0.6-square-mile neighborhood in the first place. It has explained why the blanket euphemism "storefront church" or even "religious organizations" does not reflect the diverse, particularistic forms of community being enacted in churches each week. It has also explained why so many of the churches have been largely absent from the early stages of community revitalization. In short, this book has tried to explain the religious district itself as both product and part of the urban process, mindful all the while that this spatially dense and characteristically diverse multi-congregational form is hardly unique to Four Corners or to Boston. In cities around the country, religious districts have emerged from similar patterns of Black migration, economic disinvestment, uneven urban resource distribution, and of course, religious particularism and "niching."

THE CONCEPT OF THE RELIGIOUS DISTRICT

As I pointed out in the introduction, religious particularism is a common feature of religious practice in the United States. It is not something to be found solely in religious districts or among Black and Latino/a churches. Still, the religious district relies on particularism, for it is social distance, not spatial distance, that mediates competition between congregations, thus allowing them to locate quite near each other. To be certain, religious institutions are aware of each other as competitors, but since they are "niche" churches they do not need to claim the neighborhood as territory in order to lay claim to worshippers. It is for this reason that I have compared the religious district with commercial districts, although I do not intend to push the commercial analogy too far. The religious district does not operate exactly like a commercial one. The district metaphor is meant to evoke images of a spatially dense, superficially similar (in this case, they all offer religious experience), yet necessarily diverse set of institutions.

I have also drawn comparisons with shopping malls, but there was no "anchor" congregation drawing little churches to the neighborhood the way a behemoth department store attracts smaller retailers to the newest mega–shopping center or, for that matter, the way the new Walgreens is meant to woo stores into the storefronts in Four Corners. In this sense, the religious district is more like a flea market, where vendors set up shop not to feed off of traffic generated by a major store but simply to peddle wares in the way that incurs the least possible overhead cost.[3] Flea market vendors know that shoppers will come, almost regardless of how peripheral or dusty the location. Likewise, people came from all over the metropolis to worship in Four Corners despite the condition and reputation of the neighborhood. Sometimes people passing through the neighborhood would notice and join a church, and it was not uncommon for people who already worshipped in the neighborhood to discover and visit nearby congregations. But unlike a flea market, commercial district, or mall, people do not flock to Four Corners expressly to shop for a church.

I have emphasized that the religious district is made possible by features of the broader urban environment. In the case of Four Corners, the glut of vacant commercial spaces, itself a symptom of urban economic depression, provided ample space for religious institutions looking for cheap rents. Religious organizations will happily inhabit abandoned storefronts when a once-vital commercial crossroads wanes to the point of stagnation. This helps explain why certain poor neighborhoods contain so many churches and why so many nonresidents of various socioeconomic classes descend on such neighborhoods every Sunday morning.

Apparently, though, not all religious districts appear in depressed areas. Historian R. Scott Hanson (2002) describes the remarkably dense, diverse religious environment in Flushing, Queens, as a "microcosm of world religions." Unlike Four Corners, this neighborhood positively bustles with economic activity and is not by any definition a "poverty area." Moreover, the very dense residential population of this one-square-mile neighborhood is uncommonly diverse. Literally dozens of national groups share the neighborhood, and each group supports several of the 150 religious congregations located there. Flushing's religious district is therefore not a commuter-based one but one sustained primarily by residents of the neighborhood. The point is, a variety of urban conditions may give rise to the dense, diverse religious district. This book has focused on what is probably the most common set of conditions: concentrated poverty and economic depression coupled with a proclivity of worshippers to choose and to commute to the houses of worship that suit their particular tastes and needs.

In Boston, as in other major cities such as Chicago, Detroit, and New York, the prelude to this confluence of conditions was the great migration, during which resettled Blacks established many new churches. The resulting religious environment provided an institutional matrix for the kaleidoscopic expression of Black subcultures. This urban religious history reminds us that Blacks in "ghetto" or "inner-city" neighborhoods have never constituted a singular culture with a unitary civil society and public sphere. There was never a "golden age" when all Blacks mixed seamlessly and effortlessly across class, gender, and ethnic lines (Drake and Cayton 1945; Fainstein and Nesbitt 1996; Gregory 1998). Likewise, there was never really a single "Black Church," despite a scholarly and popular tendency to assign heroic attributes to or to proclaim the tragic failure of, such an entity. Powerful mainstream institutions such as the National Baptist Convention surely served as Black counterpublics to a dominant White public (Higginbotham 1993; Dawson 1994); but these were challenged from within the Black populace by smaller, marginal, more numerous religious institutions. Recall William Crowdy (chapter 2), founder of the Church of God and Saints of Christ, who in a dream saw the Black Baptist and Methodist churches as giant tables covered with filth and vomit. In sum, the old religious district embodied "the heterogeneity and plasticity of African American social identities and the multiplicity of public spaces where they are crafted" (Gregory 1995:168).

The Four Corners religious district was similarly pluralistic in congregational makeup, although church members came not from a contiguous and compact "Black Belt" but from a much larger swath of the metropolis. We can see, then, that subcultural groups, even when not grounded in particular neighborhoods, still must convene somewhere. Social networks, even when connecting spatially diffuse populations, are usually activated in institutional nodes, like churches, that are locatable in space. It is for this reason that I would differ somewhat with sociologist Barry Wellman (1979, 1999; see also Fischer 1982), who emphasizes the "liberation" of human community from space by technologies such as the telephone, the Internet, the highway, and so on. True enough, we can be assured that human community has not been disemboweled by urbanization, as some earlier sociologists feared (Tönnies 1957 [1887]). It has persisted in the form of networks that transcend the confines of particular neighborhoods. But community has not been disembodied either, as the "liberation from space" language tempts us to think. Communities, no longer rigidly circumscribed by residential neighborhoods (if they ever were), still tend to meet in *somebody's* neighborhood. The case of Four Corners reminds us that spatially liberated communities not only continue to materialize in space but may materialize in certain places more than others, depending, for one, on where the cheapest meeting places are located. So depressed, "undesirable" neighborhoods like Four Corners ironically become perfect places to host the gatherings of numerous urban subcultures whose constituents mostly reside elsewhere in the metropolis.

DIMENSIONS OF DIFFERENCE

But what are these subcultural gatherings like? I have emphasized that there is more to particularistic religious congregations than ethnic, racial, regional, or national homogeneity. To be sure, churches in Four Corners could roughly be divided into four main groups: African American, Haitian, Latino/a, and Caribbean. Nevertheless, an ethnographic look inside these churches revealed other dimensions of difference that enhanced diversity in the religious district. The dimensions I have presented here were hardly exhaustive, but they did appear to be quite salient among clergy and worshippers. Indeed, it is plausible that they are salient in other religious districts. They include different constructions of peoplehood in exile, varying conceptions of the immediate environment, and divergent understandings of what it means to change the world for the better. In most cases, clergy used theologically conservative ideas that might be thought to unify evangelical and "sect" types but were, in fact, flexible enough to serve the particularistic aims of congregations. Peoplehood itself was constructed differently from church to church— so not all migrants would attend the same migrant church. By variously applying the theme of religious exile, clergy spoke to different migrant groups, all of whom felt "out of place" but in different ways. Similarly, clergy at immigrant churches applied the theme of exile to make some widely contrasting arguments about the value of cultural assimilation, so not all West Indians, for example, would flock to one West Indian congregation.

Religious views of the immediate environment also distinguished churches in the district. As people flocked to Four Corners to enact subcultural communities, the "streets" became part of their religious identities. I have described three ways that churches made sense of the street and of the people and activities associated with the street. As a religious trope, the street alternately embodied notions of irredeemable evil and combatable sin. Out of this sense-making came prescriptions for how church people were to deal with "street people." Street people were considered worthy of careful avoidance, conversion to "decent" churchly lifestyles, attentive service, or some combination of the latter two. Of course, since most churchgoers did not reside in Four Corners, these prescriptions were taken by nonresidents. This religious district thus reminds us that not all of the most consequential interactions in neighborhoods take place between co-residents. The bulk of a neighborhood's voluntary associations may in fact serve outsiders who, "liberated" from space, are free to meet in places like Four Corners. Those outsiders' impressions of and behaviors in the neighborhood are likely shaped more by the normative prescriptions of their associations than by actual contact with residents of that neighborhood.

Finally, churches differed in the ways they thought about changing the world. Practically all of the church people I met in Four Corners felt their institutions were in some sense "activist." Yet, the churches distributed social benefits and thought about social transformation in a variety of ways. Migrant churches engaging in charismatic ritual activism that "trickled down" to change the world were different from immigrant churches that distributed social services directly to members. The mystical proclivities of the former, nevertheless, did not necessarily betray an otherworldly orientation. Indeed, this conclusion, drawn frequently and all too hastily by scholars and laypersons alike, may have more to do with our own latent ideas about the "otherworld" than with a particular faith's irrelevance to terrestrial pursuits.

I, for one, brought to the field the vestiges of a preadolescent fascination with the paranormal. The twelve year old who placed a tape recorder in the basement to capture the melancholic whisperings of ghosts delighted in the possibility of witnessing the unworldly stirrings of the Holy Ghost in the form of miracles. Worshippers and clergy sometimes sought these, too, but never solely. What I witnessed most routinely appeared as profound events of psychological healing and subjective empowerment. To the believer, such events proved, at least as much as stupefying miracles, that God's Spirit is here, moving people and things in the most intimate way imaginable. The Spirit was not known as something on the "other side" or in some parallel dimension. It did not leave behind an iridescent ectoplasm trail. True, clergy and congregants often spoke ill of "the world" and its evils. Yet, for the believer, the Holy Ghost was not exactly otherworldly either, for nothing in all of existence could be more practical, more in the world, than God's power.

Social science should be open to the simultaneity of world and otherworld in Black religious thought and practice and in all of organized religion. This means taking religious ideas and practices as flexible cultural resources that can be used as "fuel" for a variety of earthly engagements (McRoberts 1999; see also Pattillo-McCoy 1998; Harris 1999), not as hard rules that suspend believers, inevitably and indefinitely, between clearly defined poles such as "world" and "otherworld." In other words, we must take seriously the consequences of religious belief but avoid assuming that these effect actions in a linear, causal fashion. Only in doing so will research reveal how religious institutions creatively combine worldly and otherworldly, instrumental and expressive elements to form wholly unique modes of religious presence. Only when sensitive to simultaneity as well as to linearity, will social scientists begin to appreciate the dizzying diversity of institutions that make up the "Black Church" or, for that matter, any of the religious institutions upon which we have hung convenient, deceptive, euphemisms.

THE RELIGIOUS DISTRICT AND
NEIGHBORHOOD COLLECTIVE ACTION

Regardless of the numerous ways churches engage in "activism," though, what matters for Four Corners and similar neighborhoods is the extent to which churches recognize and are willing to advocate for the locale. Neighborhood advocacy is made necessary by an urban political economy that distributes resources on a competitive, place-by-place basis. Those neighborhoods able to mobilize or at least to project the appearance of univocality win attention from the mayor, local development agencies, foundations, and other money-bearing agents that recognize geographic neighborhoods—not spatially "liberated" communities—as primary ontological units. Still, as a number of urban scholars have pointed out (Abu-Lughod 1994a, 1994b; Gregory 1995, 1998; Henig 1984; Crenson 1983), mobilization within the bounds of geographic neighborhoods is complicated by the fact that neighborhoods can be quite diverse internally. The challenge of neighborhood mobilization thus becomes one of finding unity in difference. These scholars, however, focused on neighborhoods whose residents were diverse and where institutions sprang up expressly to serve the partial interests of diverse neighborhood constituencies. Compared with these locales, Four Corners appears as a different, although by no means rare, species of neighborhood. Here, the institutions were constitutively diverse but, for the most part, were not formed to serve residents and did not try to incorporate them, either. The idea of forging unity in the neighborhood was therefore doubly daunting, for not only were institutions diversely constituted, but many did not even acknowledge the existence of the locale. The rare institutions that did claim the locale differed in their approaches to neighborhood problems and fell into conflict.

As such, the very factors that allowed twenty-nine congregations to inhabit the same neighborhood were the same factors that proved most consequential for the neighborhood. The religious district, made possible in part by the depressed state of the neighborhood, inhibited, or at least delayed, the process of neighborhood revitalization. The two "neighborhood" institutions, only one of which was formally church-affiliated, had to overcome their differences to spearhead that revitalization.

The "in but not of the world" relationship of so many churches to their host neighborhood and the local resentment that these churches incurred when they apparently lacked concern for neighborhood issues point, among other things, to the ambiguous place of African American churches in Black urban life. Many writings powerfully and accurately depict the social, economic, and political centrality of the Black church. They describe how the church has necessarily been the center of Black social, economic, and political life almost since the beginning of the African sojourn in North America (for example, Lincoln and Mamiya 1990; Billingsley 1999). I do not dispute these central roles. I do intend to complicate this vision by highlighting and explaining the peculiar absent presence of Black religious institutions in many Black neighborhoods. Organized religion may be central to many aspects of African American life yet peripheral to the most localized of Black urban struggles. It is not contradictory for African Americans to attend services regularly and testify honestly to the primacy of religious institutions in their lives yet to speak vituperatively of the "little storefront" or "rich-cratic" church down the street that does little for the neighborhood. Like other urbanites, Black city dwellers may live in one place and worship in another. As such, we should not expect Black neighborhood interests and Black religious interests to be identical or even harmonious.

My findings regarding the relationships between churches and their host neighborhood also bear on the civil society and social capital debate, which has been revitalized by Robert Putnam's (1995) seminal "Bowling Alone" article and subsequent book (2000; see also Lang and Hornburg 1998). Much of this debate has centered upon whether the formal associations that make up the infrastructure of civil society, forge human relationships of trust and reciprocity, and inculcate civic skills are in decline, on the rise, in flux, or display some combination of the latter two. My experience in Four Corners has convinced me that much of this discussion is misplaced. Rather than asking so many "how much" questions, students of human association should be asking "what for?" That is, assuming that people are still associating (especially in religious congregations, which have not dwindled, but multiplied [Ammerman 1997a; Warner 1993]), still forming social networks (Wuthnow 1998), and still acquiring a vast array of civic skills (Verba et al. 1995), for what purposes are these associations coming into being, and to what ends are the resultant networks and skills being mobilized?

In Four Corners the key issue was whether the vibrant civil society being enacted there had any "place-based" purpose. This is relevant since, as I have already emphasized, the politics of urban resource distribution often requires that neighborhoods mobilize to secure resources and defend integrity. In Four Corners, I observed a critical disjuncture between human community and place: the geographic neighborhood was the site of multiple institutions of civil society in the form of religious congregations but was not a central object of institutional concern. For this reason, the capacities and connections that churches generated had little relevance for the neighborhood.

On that note, I have described churches imparting two kinds of civic capacities: 1) "moral and spiritual capital" (Ammerman 1997a), or "trickle-down" spiritual empowerment, which enables congregants to function in society with self-confidence and an eye toward social transformation; and 2) citizenship skills, as in the case of immigrant congregations that offer very practical assistance and direction to recent arrivals. Neither of these capacities is purposively aimed at the neighborhood as such, though. Rather, they are aimed at migrant and immigrant constituents. Likewise, churches in Four Corners not only introduced congregants to interpersonal social networks but also participated in interinstitutional networks as well, such as the Ten Point Coalition, the Black Ministerial Alliance, and Mattapan-Dorchester Churches in Action. In other words, both interpersonal and interinstitutional forms of social capital were being generated in and by Four Corners churches. Yet, few of these networks were substantively geared toward the neighborhood itself. Only the Azusa Christian Community and the Four Corners Action Coalition struggled to forge such connections within the neighborhood for the purpose of addressing neighborhood concerns.

The case of Four Corners thus highlights the hydra-headed quality of civil society. Two heads are evident here: civil society can be either constituent-based or place-based (or some combination of the two). It can serve spatially diffuse subcultural groups or spatially discrete neighborhoods. As such, neighborhood civic engagement can come to overshadow subcultural ties (Abu-Lughod 1994a, 1994b). Or, as in the case of Four Corners, a neighborhood can literally host dozens of subcultural institutions of civil society yet contain little neighborhood-focused civic engagement.

Of course, some may take Azusa and, to some extent, Grace as evidence that churches can overcome the disjuncture between human community and place, patch the allegedly moth-eaten fabric of local civil society, and "save" inner-city neighborhoods. I think this interpretation, however valid, obscures a more fundamental policy question: to what extent are churches inclined to save the inner city, either on a neighborhood-by-neighborhood basis, or through direct service to low-income individuals? The most recent wave of "community development" discourse appears to take these inclinations and capacities for granted. Sociologist Robert Sampson (1999), for example, acknowledges that contemporary urban neighborhoods will never reproduce the tightly knit "urban villages" (Gans 1962) of yore. Yet, he argues, community development strategies should aim to "promote community empowerment through overlapping involvement by residents in local organizations and voluntary associations, horizontal ties among neighborhood institutions, and the vertical integration of local institutions with city hall and other extralocal resources" (Sampson 1999:276; see also Sampson et al.

1997). This proposal assumes that: 1) institutions identify with neighborhoods in the first place; 2) institutions are not already embedded in horizontal and vertical networks; 3) the likelihood of interinstitutional conflict over vision and voice is nil; and 4) increased associational participation will lead to an increased focus on neighborhood concerns. In light of my findings regarding the behavior of churches, these assumptions deserve deep interrogation.

Meanwhile, policymakers should develop revitalization strategies that account for the spatially defined aspects of urban poverty and disadvantage while recognizing the spatially diffuse propensities of neighborhood institutions, especially churches. Such balance will be especially crucial as policy increasingly turns to religious institutions to address the causes and consequences of neighborhood poverty. Numerous features in the popular press count "faith-based" neighborhood programs among the most promising local initiatives. Public officials have also joined the ranks of faith-based community development advocates. In an essay entitled "Higher Ground: Faith Communities and Community Building," Henry Cisneros (1996:4), former secretary of housing and urban development, wrote:

> There is little disagreement that the problems of inner-city neighborhoods go far beyond the simple lack of material wealth. The youth of these areas need values and moral structure to hang onto. They need reasons to believe that there are things worth living for—the understanding of value in life itself over the long term. They need nurturing. Few institutions other than the faith community and the family can provide youth this kind of support.

Such pronouncements push churches to think of themselves not only as purveyors of religious ideology but as champions of neighborhood interests, along with CDCs and secular neighborhood social service providers. But to what extent does this recent policy interest in churches implicitly and erroneously presume that churches function as traditional parishes, where congregants come from the neighborhood and religious community is coterminous with geographic community? To what extent can we expect churches to champion neighborhood concerns over the concerns of congregation members or communities of interest that transcend the neighborhood? These are questions of inclination rather than constitutionality or capacity. They encourage us to consider whether churches are likely to respond to antipoverty efforts that take neighborhoods as primary and ideal social units.

My observations in Four Corners suggest that if churches do not respond to these calls for increased neighborhood activism, it may not be because of an allergy to ecumenism or worldly activity. Rather, churches may not respond because of the general tendency of congregations to delocalize in membership and mission. As indicated by the popularity of activist groups like the Ten Point Coalition, the Black Ministerial Alliance, and Mattapan-Dorchester Churches in Action, churches may be more inclined to organize at levels that include yet transcend the local community in geographic scope. Among African American churches, the historical precedence for this type of organization includes the wide, intricate matrix of ministers and congregations that birthed the Black civil rights insurgency of the mid-twentieth century. As Aldon Morris (1984:11) stated in his pathbreaking work on that movement:

> It was (and is) common for Black ministers in a community and even in different communities to have personal relationships among themselves. They met at conventions, community gatherings, civil affairs, and the like. At times they exchanged pulpit duties and encouraged their choirs to sing at the churches of colleagues. Furthermore, Black ministers in a community were linked formally by either a city ministerial alliance or an interdenominational alliance, through which they were able to debate and confer on issues important to the Black community.

In addition to facilitating activism, such networks may also help affiliated churches achieve new levels of public visibility and organizational health. As previous studies have speculated (Gibbs and Ewer 1969; Kanagy 1992), collaborative church work can help pastors to carve out their membership "niches" by offering precious visibility and legitimacy as unique actors in the ongoing drama of urban life. Many of the churches that participated in such groups could have developed activist programs without the aid of a coalition. In fact, several of the clerics had been active for many years before any of the large coalitions were conceived. For those churches new to extroverted forms of social activism, ecumenical groups may share vital information not only on how to develop particular ministries but on how to protect and grow a religious organization. Those who organize and lead multicongregational networks often are well aware that clergy seek tools for church development as well as opportunities for activism. The Rev. Rivers, who helped organize the Ten Point Coalition, averred:

> What I'm seeing is that most of these Pentecostal churches come to me for advice about how to get money and technical assistance: "Rivers, show us a boilerplate prototype of your proposal. How did you get money from the Boston Foundation? Who are the major players?" I mean, literally, much of my time now during the day is meeting with other ministers to talk about how they can get technical assistance to put together their shops.

Rev. Lawrence, a lead organizer for Mattapan Dorchester Churches in Action (MDCIA), had a similar viewpoint:

> I tell them all the time that leadership development—you can use it anywhere. If you learn good leadership skills, that is useful on your job. It helps to build up your church . . . And the Hyams Foundation [a primary funder of MDCIA], they offer excellent training. I mean, they pay people to come out and teach fundraising, how to do an ad book, how to write proposals . . . We go on trips, so you're exposed to different cultures, see what people are doing in other cities. It builds up your church.

Such tantalizing incentives may further convince religious congregations to join cross-neighborhood coalitions instead of neighborhood-based efforts.

Even those churches and clergy who want to champion neighborhood concerns may be put off by the threat of displacement. Ironically, their efforts at local revitalization just might result in their own inability to keep up with rents or to resist the pressure to relinquish their storefronts to "higher and better uses." Community development organs should find creative ways to accommodate these would-be neighborhood actors, these viable communities-in-themselves, which almost inevitably get displaced as a result of putting stores in storefronts. In Chicago, the Target Area Development Corporation, which operates in the South Side Auburn-Gresham neighborhood, avoided displacing smaller churches by incorporating several small meeting halls into one of its first major developments. These halls, each named after a book of the Old Testament, are rented to smaller churches that might otherwise have been displaced from the neighborhood. Since they are made available to nonreligious as well as to churchly groups, these halls literally provide sorely needed "space" for neighborhood civic activity.

Still, the question remains: Who will advocate for neighborhood interests in the near-absence of secular institutions such as CDCs? A few religious institutions will undoubtedly emerge as advocates in some neighborhoods. But we cannot assume this to be normative, especially if the bulk of churches are not oriented toward neighborhoods in mission or in membership. A reasonable prediction is that many more neighborhoods will fall through the cracks, with no institutions emerging as local advocates. Policymakers and community organizers should therefore focus on the larger problem, which is that poor neighborhoods must compete for and defend resources in the first place (Abu Lughod 1994a; Warren 1975; Fainstein 1987) and that residents so often must squeeze complex, cross-neighborhood, and even regional interests and grievances into a neighborhood or "place bound" framework in order to get attention (Gregory 1998). With this arrangement, someone's neighborhood will always lose, regardless of the urgency of the problems there. As Janet Abu-Lughod (1994a:198) sagely noted in her study of social diversity and housing activism in Manhattan's Lower East Side,

> Neighborhood activists, no matter how well-intentioned and mobilized, cannot block forever the effects of economic cycles that set the parameters for the investment "climate" in local housing. Nor can local community action determine city, state, and national politics and policies that make resources differentially available, constraining the agency of some and enhancing that of others.

Instead of pushing churches to spearhead the next wave of placed-based Community Action Programs, we should reevaluate policies that "make resources differentially available" and that rely on nostalgic, inaccurate, spatially reified notions of "community" and "church."

Also, policies such as Charitable Choice must not be oversold as a way to devolve federal welfare functions to the local level. Not surprisingly, much of the debate over this legislation has centered on issues of constitutionality, namely, the separation of church and state. A much smaller portion of the discussion has focused on the inclinations and organizational capacities of churches. In a multivariate analysis of a nationally representative survey of 1,236 religious congregations in the United States, sociologist Mark Chaves (1999) found that "64 percent of predominantly African American congregations expressed a willingness to apply for government funds, compared with only 28 percent of those from predominantly white congregations" (841). The relative eagerness of Black congregations, he argues, can be explained by two factors: first, African American religion has a "lower barrier" (Pattillo-McCoy 1998) between church and state than other religious communities in the United States; second, Black clergy exercise more power than their counterparts over the programmatic trajectories of their churches (Lincoln and Mamiya 1990:405). I doubt neither the figures nor the explanations. I do, however, wonder about the hefty minority—36 percent—of Black churches that say they would refuse to accept government funds. Since Chaves groups all Black churches into a single category, it is impossible to tell which of these are likely to resist Charitable Choice. Only with an understanding of the diversity and complexity of Black religious forms will we understand why so many African American churches apparently are not interested in government money.

As inclinations are concerned, this study reveals two reasons why churches may object to government partnerships. One is that they prefer spiritual varieties of activism that change the world by changing individuals; these churches are not so much "otherworldly" but prefer to keep religious institutions out of the corrupting world of secular social change work. In his most recent work, Robert Wuthnow (1998:127) observed this rationale as well, referring to it as an avoidance of "bureaucratic entanglements." The other reason may be that clergy are wary of the state and/or White political agents, who are assumed not to have the best interests of Black people at heart. Recall pastors Calvin and Powell (chapter 6), who were interested in prophetic activism yet cynical of White and state interference in Black church affairs. Again, Wuthnow (1998:116) found similar patterns among "inner-city" residents and clergy. He concluded that

> inner-city residents cannot take lightly issues that affect their very survival, such as health, welfare, and shelter. They talk about the power of public officials to get things done—and about their unresponsiveness to inner-city needs. Public policy is disturbingly effective, in their view, but it is dictated by interest other than their own . . . Government is perceived as "them" and as very distinct from "us."

Even churches lacking such reservations may lack the capacity to carry out the social welfare programs sanctioned by Charitable Choice. Recall that two Four Corners churches were struggling to balance the priestly needs of growing congregations with aggressive social service outreach. These churches were moving away from full immersion in the latter in order to address the former. Other churches similarly may find it difficult to strike a balance between social service work and spiritual work. If forced to choose, many will likely lean toward spiritual work; it is this work, after all, that most distinguishes religious congregations from other voluntary associations.

This book thus challenges both scholarship and policy to focus more on the actual behaviors and inclinations of religious institutions in depressed urban neighborhoods. Particular attention should be paid to the urban religious districts: the dense, diverse religious ecologies that appear as symptoms of neighborhood decline yet contain richly complex forms of community. The more we appreciate the intricacy of religious practice in such settings, the better we will understand the "place" of religious institutions in urban life.

AUTHOR'S NOTE

At the start of this book, I noted the influence of St. Clair Drake's 1940 WPA manuscript, *Churches and Voluntary Associations in the Chicago Negro Community*, on my own work. Drake illustrated the impact of the great migration on Black associational life in Chicago's Black Belt but also described how those associations structured the social and political lives of Black urbanites. Similarly, my work in Four Corners set out to uncover and elucidate the relationships between a little-understood urban religious form (the religious district) and the broader urban process. My methodological approach, too, resembles Drake's. Both studies used participant observations, in-depth interviews and archival research to cobble a story about a locale and the institutions within it. This is sometimes called "triangulation": the use of multiple data sources to secure an in-depth, multiperspectival understanding of the phenomenon in question (Denzin and Lincoln 1998:4).

Even so, in seeking and presenting data this study placed more emphasis than Drake on ethnographic insight into particular churches. The idea was to balance Drake's sweeping "landscape" style of qualitative research with the more intimate "portraiture" common to single church ethnographies. *Churches and Voluntary Associations* (and other WPA reports that Drake and Cayton eventually folded into *Black Metropolis*) reflects the methodological influence of W. Lloyd Warner, the University of Chicago anthropologist who designed such classic community studies as *Yankee City* (Warner 1963) and *Deep South* (Davis et al. 1941). Warner had devised a method of "examining communities as wholes where the several interconnected social institutions are seen as functioning in the total social economy" (Drake and Cayton 1945:771). The method combined participant observation of community institutions, collection of individual "life histories," and close examination of demographic data, press records, and other archival matter. This approach ultimately produced what Robert Nisbet (1976) called the "sociological landscape," in which particular features of social life are offered as brush strokes toward a larger, unified vision. In Drake's case, the larger whole being portrayed was "the Chicago Negro community," not institutions or individual lives per se. That community, when observed from one close-up perspective, turned out to be the aggregated attributes and simultaneous functioning of a variety of churches and voluntary associations.

This study partly aspired to landscape, as I wanted to explain the religious district as a feature, an attribute of the wider urban scene and particular churches as attributes of the religious district. What the sociological landscape cannot depict, however, are the internal workings of particular attributes. Although he envisioned institutions as serving distinct functions, Drake apparently did not intend to present institutions as living, mutating entities in themselves, with complex missions and memberships and with varying degrees and kinds of *awareness* of their role in some "big picture." In other words, Drake did not conduct a study of institutions per se but, rather, studied a community by focusing on its institutional attributes. His writing therefore does not betray a sympathetic understanding of how particular institutional settings worked, what the inner logics of their beliefs and opinions were, what (if any) bigger landscape they perceived, and what they took to be their place (if any) in that landscape. This study aspired to achieve some of that understanding.

Such understanding is the strength of the single church ethnographies: they approach what Nisbet called the "sociological portrait." "It is well to remember," Nisbet (1976:69) explained,

> that the artist, painter, or novelist seeks more than faithful duplication of the individual he is describing ... In Dostoevsky's *Crime and Punishment* ... Raskolnikov is not only a highly memorable individual but also the image of a class or type Dostoevsky was fascinated by: the revolutionary nihilist of his time.

Dostoevsky got inside the head of the character Raskolnikov in order to present a meditative portrait of the inner workings of revolutionary nihilism. The single-church ethnographer moves within the particular religious setting to present it either as a case of some broader phenomenon or as a sign (not a feature) of a broader process. Rather than appearing as attributes of something bigger, institutions in the best of these studies emerge as fully developed, historicized characters that are nevertheless broadly significant. Thus, when we encounter the handful of churches in Arthur Paris's *Black Pentecostalism: Southern Religion in an Urban World,* we really do learn something about Black Pentecostalism and about the ways religious beliefs and organizations conditioned the experiences of southern migrants.

The challenge of my research was to collect information of sufficient breadth and depth to present something combining both landscape and portrait. I wanted to provide a more embroidered ethnographic account of particular church practices and beliefs than Drake while keeping sight of a bigger urban picture that included the multicongregational field, the host neighborhood, and the city. The result is part analysis and anatomy of a local urban system, part religious cultural interpretation: part structure, part meaning. This means I sacrificed some breadth, since I needed to spend enough time in churches to develop an appreciation of complex beliefs and practices. As breadth is concerned, I also sacrificed neighborhood comparative perspective (the strength of Ammerman's *Congregation and Community*) by studying one neighborhood instead of several; this focus allowed me, nevertheless, to portray the range of religious responses to a single context and to depict church interactions within that context (Eiesland 1999; Becker 1999).

On the other hand, I sacrificed some depth as a lone ethnographer trying to approach "saturation" (Glaser and Strauss 1999; Strauss and Corbin 1990) in so many churches. Saturation is the goal of fieldwork in its theory and concept-building mode (although this goal does not preclude the use of ethnographic data to improve existing theory [Burawoy 1991]). Here, the ethnographer observes and compares different social situations and incidents in order to discover general categories of social phenomena and the properties of each category. The ethnographer reaches saturation in a category when additional observations add no further substantive weight to that category. After two years of fieldwork in Four Corners, I decided to pursue saturation in four major categories of religious behavior: the homiletical use of exilic themes, the religious distinction between church and street, faith-inspired conceptions of "activism," and religious institutional "attachments" (and the lack thereof) to the neighborhood. Had this been a study of one, or perhaps even three or four churches, I would have gathered even more detailed data on congregational life but at the expense of a comparative perspective on congregations.

Thus, between summer 1995 and winter 1999 I attended worship services and other church activities, neighborhood organizing and planning meetings, and numerous community events such as Christmas tree lightings and block parties. As could be imagined, Sundays were particularly busy ethnographic periods. Some Sundays I managed to attend two or more services, each of which might stretch to three hours. Other Sundays I would linger in a particular church for much of the day. This allowed me to interact with congregants and clergy in the context of a wide range of formal and informal activities. Weekday mornings and evenings were popular times for community organizing and planning meetings, which I attended regularly. I also spent a good deal of time strolling through neighborhood and sitting in a variety of outdoor spots at odd times of the day and night. I recorded detailed field notes either during or after each of these activities.

I interviewed clergy and laypersons from twenty-four congregations in

Four Corners. I also interviewed representatives from church-based community development groups and from nearby CDCs and health centers. When possible, I tape-recorded interviews; in either case, I recorded extensive interview notes. Archival sources for this study included church records, event fliers, newspaper articles, photographs, statistical information, and documents produced by the city of Boston.

In any ethnographic endeavor, the researcher must negotiate access to people and information. Churches, in this regard, are deceptively easy sites. On the one hand, churches are semipublic places. Most churches welcome outsiders and even reserve a special time in every service for the introduction of "visitors." While these occasions appear to indicate unconditional acceptance of the outsider, they are in fact ceremonial occasions that allow the congregation to "size you up" even as you are doing the same to them. Just as I had been observing their dress and comportment, church members, as practical ethnographers, noticed my India-collared shirt, bookish glasses, battered notepad, and wrinkled khaki pants. Often, the initial reactions of laypersons and clergy to my presence and purpose were useful in helping me figure out the class composition of particular congregations. For instance, in working-class churches my academic appearance set me apart enough to draw stares and glances throughout worship services. In middle-class professional congregations, by contrast, I got fewer curious stares. I stood out least of all at the Good Tidings Church, which contains a large number of young professional African-Americans.

Language differences presented unique access challenges. I understand only enough Spanish and Haitian Creole to make out the broad themes of discussions and sermons. Thus, when visiting Latino/a and Haitian churches, I relied heavily on informants who kindly translated for me. These informants often were church elders, associate pastors, or other authority figures; as such, they were able to provide a good deal of general information about their churches. They also introduced me to and helped me communicate with church members.

Other access issues emerged during in-depth interviews with clergy and laypersons. Frequently people would ask whether I was "saved," either at the outset of an interview or as a "by the way" casually thrown into the discussion. Often this question would precede an invitation to join the church. Sometimes, though, the interviewee was predicating his or her degree of candor on my answer to the question. On these occasions I tried, noting my Catholic upbringing, to turn the question into a discussion of what constituted "salvation." This led to some fascinating exchanges about theologies and religious differences, which simultaneously put the interviewee at relative ease and gave me deeper insight into his or her worldview. More generally, "Are you saved?" situations were instructive because they gave me an idea of the way faith mediated the individual's encounters with unknown others.

All of these situations put me in mind of Robert Park, the early twentieth-century Chicago School sociologist who once told his students to forsake the classroom and "go get the seat of your pants dirty in real research" (McKinney 1966:71). This instruction, of course, ignored the extent to which these would-be fieldworkers had soiled their khakis prior to entering the field. In addition to a host of presuppositions and biases regarding what was happening "out there" and "in the real world," the nascent ethnographers dragged countless attributes (or accidents) of personal biography into the field, including gender, race, ethnicity, and religion. Those in "the field" undoubtedly noticed traits such as these and responded accordingly.

In a sense, the ethnographer dirties the field with his or her already soiled pants. This might particularly be true when the ethnographer attempts to study something as subtle, complicated, and subjective as "religion." I, therefore, continually struggled to notice how my predispositions colored my perceptions of things. I also tried to be sensitive to and honest about the ways my very presence had altered the social situation I wanted to observe. Sometimes, when my own thoughts and actions seemed germane to or inextricable from the narrative or when I simply wanted to remind the reader that I was there, observing not only "the field," but my own judgments, reactions, and notions, I have submitted my proverbial pants to the reader as text. I also found it necessary and helpful to open up to residents, organizers, churchgoers, and clergy when they posed serious questions about my intentions, my background, the state of my soul, and so on.

The hardest question, posed to me in only one interview, was, "How does your asking all these questions benefit my church?" I could only assure her that I certainly did not intend to hurt the church and that I hoped to help people understand neighborhoods like Four Corners and the religious institutions within them.

NOTES

1. Such acts of resistance have multiplied around the country despite the 1993 Federal Religious Freedom Restoration Act, which protects religious practice from government interference in the form of land-use regulations. The Supreme Court subsequently struck down the law as unconstitutional. In 2000, President Bill Clinton restored the law. "Religious liberty," he stated, "is a constitutional value of the highest order . . . This act recognizes the importance the free exercise of religion plays in our democratic society." *Los Angeles Times,* September 3, 2000.

2. Dorchester is the largest and most populous of Boston's sixteen neighborhood districts. The Boston Redevelopment Authority formalized these districts in the early 1970s based on the existing popular social geography. Four Corners and other areas formally are considered subneighborhoods (in Dorchester, residents refer to these as "villages"). The subneighborhood of Four Corners actually straddles two districts, Dorchester and Roxbury. Later in the book I will also refer to Mattapan, a district contiguous with Roxbury and Dorchester.

3. The names of all individuals and organizations operating in contemporary Four Corners are pseudonymous, with several exceptions. First, the Reverend Eugene Rivers, the Azusa Christian Community, Ella J. Baker House, and the Four Corners Planning Committee appear as themselves, since all are named in mass publications that I cite. Members of Azusa and Baker House workers, however, are given pseudonyms. The Four Corners Action Coalition and its director, Marvin Martin, have appeared in mass media and therefore appear here under their real names. I use the real names of city agencies, citywide and cross-neighborhood activist coalitions, and the people who represent these entities. Finally, I use the actual names of Boston neighborhoods, including Four Corners.

4. Population, income, poverty, and unemployment figures are aggregated from 1990 U.S. Census block group data.

5. Scholarly opinion varies as to what constitutes a "high-poverty" area. Studies often reserve the term for census tracts with poverty rates of 40 percent or more. Wilson (1987), however, focused on Chicago community areas with poverty rates of 30 percent or more. Community areas like Four Corners include multiple tracts and are likely to include a wider range of incomes than individual tracts. As such, the 30 percent cutoff, according to Jargowsky (1997: 256), "is probably not different in effect from the 40 percent rate applied by subsequent researchers at the tract level." In any case, I refer to Four Corners as a "depressed" neighborhood rather than as a "poverty" neighborhood. The former intends to capture the economic and social condition of

the area without implying that a particular percentage of residents are poor by census standards.

6. Racial and ethnic figures are aggregated from 1990 U.S. Census block level data.

7. As it turned out, these young Mormons lived in a mission outpost less than a block from my apartment in Codman Square. At the time, six missionaries were assigned to Dorchester. All young adults are encouraged by the Church of Jesus Christ of Latter-day Saints to do two years of missionary work, spending three to four months at each of a variety of sites. The missionaries, known as "elders" despite their youth, are expected to do community service as well as to "witness" to prospective converts. Regarding life in this part of Dorchester, one elder told me: "We love it down here . . . people seem more willing to talk. In other areas, people have more of an attitude—I don't know how to explain it." Sometimes elders found that people were *too* eager to debate finer points of Scripture. Perhaps some prospective converts were ready to convert the missionaries: "Some people let us into the house and pull out the Bible and start saying, 'Well, it says here this and that.' But we're not here to debate and get into arguments about the Bible but to share what we know to be true about Jesus Christ."

8. The findings of this study appear in condensed form in *Black Metropolis,* which Drake co-authored with Horace Cayton and published in 1945.

9. For market accounts of denominational growth and decline, see Roof and McKinney (1987), Finke and Stark (1992), and Iannoccone (1994).

10. In her fascinating study of the religious ecology of Dacula, Georgia, Nancy Eiesland (1999) similarly "localizes" the discussion of individual choice and decentralization in American religion.

CHAPTER TWO

1. The exceptional volume of post-Civil War migration to Boston can be attributed in part to the impact of the Freedmen's Bureau. The bureau, inaugurated in 1864 and dissolved in 1868, created a Black labor pipeline directly linking Boston with the Tidewater region of Virginia. New England was an ideal place to send formerly enslaved Blacks because, according to one Bureau official, "no region . . . [is] more desirable as a home for the negro . . . where colored help is in great demand and where such sympathy is felt for their race" (cited in Pleck 1979:25).

2. Harris was a disciple of Booker T. Washington, whose doctrine of race advancement privileged Black self-help over agitated appeals to the White power structure for civil rights. Unlike Henderson and other "Black Brahmin" commentators, "Bookerite" analysts tended to target snooty elites and scandalized institutions run by a corrupt Black middle class. By 1908, the slant of the *Colored American* itself was decidedly Washingtonian, for in 1904 Washington himself took financial control of the publication and moved it to New York. At its inception, however, the magazine located itself at the middle point between civil rights militancy and Black capitalist accommodationism (Schneider 1995:160).

3. Daniels's treatise differed critically from Dubois's in attitude, if not in design. Dubois blamed Philadelphia's race problem partly on uncouth southern migrants and partly on aloof Black middle and upper classes but was especially critical of White

racial discrimination, which prevented Blacks from all walks of life from entering the primary centers of health, commerce, culture, and education. By contrast, Daniels, a White interpreter of Booker T. Washington's ethic of Black self-reliance, attributed Boston's race problem entirely to Black folks' alleged allergy to the disciplined development of internal organizational capacity.

4. The first Boston City Directory was published in 1789; the last appeared in 1983. Entries, which include personal residences as well as offices, businesses, and other organizations, are based not on telephone subscriptions but on physical addresses. Each year, directory surveyors actually walked the streets and determined what or who occupied each address.

The directory classifies churches by denomination. Sections listing the mainline churches, such as Baptist, Methodist, and Congregationalist, are followed by a section called "The Various Denominations." This is where many of the newer Black storefront churches are listed. The designation "Colored" sometimes followed the names of Black mainline churches. In other instances, I identified Black congregations through a close examination of church addresses and names. Since few Black churches were located outside of predominantly Black residential areas, and few non-Black churches were located within such areas, all churches located within the Black Belt in a given year were considered as candidates for that year. From these candidates, I eliminated churches whose names or denominations indicated a white clientele. Churches with names including the words "Armenian" or "Presbyterian," for example, were excluded (there were no Black Presbyterian churches during the period in question).

I also consulted Boston schedules of the decennial U.S. Census of Religious Bodies published between 1906 and 1945. Unlike the city directory, the census attempted an accurate count of "Colored" churches and even provided denominational breakdowns. Nevertheless, the census clearly overlooked many Black storefront churches and excluded some of the more obscure denominations. Further, the census presents aggregated data only, whereas the task at hand required the addresses of individual churches.

CHAPTER THREE

1. A shortage of Haitian Creole-speaking priests prompted the Roman Catholic Archdiocese of Boston to merge St. Bridget's Creole mass with that already being held at a Haitian Catholic church in Mattapan. In addition to its Haitian Creole mass, St. Bridget's also celebrated an English-language mass, which attracted only about thirty worshipers per Sunday. The forced exodus of the Creole-speaking congregation left the church in financial dire straits. The Archdiocese shut down St. Bridget's Church in spring 1999.

2. The six Witness congregations may be considered a skewing factor. If these were counted as one congregation, the neighborhood would have 39.34 churches per square mile—still 10 more churches per square mile than Grove Hall.

3. In her study of a poor storefront congregation in Chicago, Kostarelos (1995) similarly observed that many members did not come from the immediate neighborhood.

4. This insight draws upon Davis's (1991) discussion of residential property interest groups. He writes that "many of the groups and conflicts that arise within the

place of residence can be explained, to one degree or another, in terms of the multiple cleavages that originate and coalesce around material interests of domestic property" (62). Moreover, the formation of property interest groups can quash any sense of an overarching, monolithic neighborhood identity.

5. For an illuminating discussion of transgression as an aspect of human geography, see Cresswell (1996).

6. For deeper discussions of noncommittal forms of religious commitment, see Eiesland 1999 and Ammerman 1997b.

CHAPTER FOUR

1. Her relatively reserved approach to blessing men is less an expression of gender bias than an attempt to avoid putting off men, who generally prefer handshakes to hugs.

2. The endlessly textured chords of the Hammond B-3 organ evoke raw emotion, especially in the context of intimate churches like the storefronts in Four Corners. This organ can suggest the sound of a roaring tide, then a bubbling creek; it produces rumbling thunder, then induces the vision of sunlight streaking though dark clouds. The B-3 conveys the solemnity, awe, and dread associated with the prospect of confronting God at death or at the moment of conversion. While the traditional pipe organ has a similar awe-inspiring effect, this instrument tends to imply the vastness and depth of God and creation—this is why pipe organs work best in cavernous, echoing cathedrals. They capture the rush of God's movement over the "face of the deep." The Hammond organ, on the other hand, overwhelms one with the *immanence* of God and works best in small, carpeted spaces. It is emotionally intimate rather than vast or distant; its sounds embrace and therefore terrify. See Sanders (1996:55) for a brief history of the Hammond organ in Sanctified churches.

3. Titus 3:1–7 reads: "Put them in mind to be subject to principalities and powers, to obey magistrates, to be ready to every good work, to speak evil of no man, to be no brawlers, but gentle, shewing all meekness unto all men. For we ourselves also were sometimes foolish, disobedient, deceived, serving divers lusts and pleasures, living in malice and envy, hateful, and hating one another. But after that the kindness and love of God our Saviour toward man appeared, not by works of righteousness which we have done, but according to his mercy he saved us, by the washing of regeneration, and renewing of the Holy Ghost; Which he shed on us abundantly through Jesus Christ our Saviour; that being justified by his grace, we should be made heirs according to the hope of eternal life."

CHAPTER FIVE

1. Specifically, it is a metonym. Metonymy is "a figure of speech consisting of the use of the name of one thing for that of another of which it is an attribute or with which it is associated" (*Webster's Ninth New Collegiate Dictionary*). I borrow the idea of the "street" as a trope defined in contrast to the "safe space" of the church from Farah Jasmine Griffin (1995), a scholar of Black migration narratives.

2. Hoodoo is not to be confused with voodoo (*Vodoun*) or any of its numerous cousins, such as *Santeria* and *Candomble*. The latter religions can be traced directly to the Dahomean ancestor religion of West Africa. In the Western hemisphere, voodoo

is masked with the religious imagery of French, Cuban, or Portuguese Catholicism. Hoodoo, on the other hand, is not a religion but a system of magic incorporating elements of African American, Native American, and European American folklore. Moreover, most Hoodoo practitioners are nominally Protestant rather than Catholic.

3. This finding further corroborates Nelson (1997), who heard the pastor of Eastside Chapel compare "the violence of the ghetto streets to the 'spiritual violence' of gossip and discord within the church" (176).

4. Anthropologist Lee R. Cooper (1974) underscored the importance of this training for publishers in the "ghettoes" of north Philadelphia. He noted, after observing Ministry School proceedings at the West View Witness Hall, that "[a]lthough the local congregation must adhere to the prescribed meeting plan, the ghetto illustrations used by West View Witnesses revealed how realistically they face their North Philadelphia environment" (713).

5. Matthew 6:5–6: "And when you pray, you shall not be like the hypocrites. For they love to pray standing in the synagogues and on the corners of the streets, that they may be seen by men. Assuredly, I say to you, they have their reward. But you, when you pray, go into your room, and when you have shut your door, pray to your Father who is in the secret place; and your Father who sees in secret will reward you openly."

6. Similarly, Hannerz (1969) described how some residents of a poor Black neighborhood in Washington, D.C., used religious practice to protect and *distinguish* themselves from what they felt to be a dangerous element. Hannerz, nonetheless did not study churches or religious discourse per se.

CHAPTER SIX

1. Appropriately, the word *ecstasy* literally means "out of place" (Sanders 1996:59; see also Berger 1967:43).

2. I am reminded here of the Bob Marley song, "So Much Things to Say," from the album *Exodus* (Island Records, 1977). In the song, Marley paraphrases Ephesians 6:12: "For we wrestle not against flesh and blood, but against principalities, against powers, against the rulers of the darkness of this world, against spiritual wickedness in high places." There are no Rastafarian congregations in Four Corners. Nonetheless, Christians of more conventional persuasions (i.e., Pentecostal, Holiness, and Baptist) often have taken this verse as a call to attack unjust social systems by becoming "prayer warriors" rather than politicians or secular activists.

3. In the space of one century, Pentecostalism has become the fastest growing religion among Black people in the United States (Lincoln and Mamiya 1990). The predominantly Black Church of God in Christ alone has established nearly six hundred congregations per year since 1982, making it the fastest-growing U.S. denomination in the 1980s (*Yearbook of American and Canadian Churches* 1993). In Boston, Pentecostal congregations outnumber all other churches in the city (Ribadeneira 1996). Most of these congregations are made up of Black Americans, Caribbean Blacks, and Latinas/os and are concentrated in the city's three poorest districts: Mattapan, Dorchester, and Roxbury.

4. One such individual is Evangelist Mary, a member of Jude Church. She joined the church in 1992 after hearing Pastor-"Overseer" Calvin on the radio. "They [refer-

ring to Calvin and, by extension, the church] had everything," she said. "They had a GED program, arts and crafts. Pastor Calvin was registering people to vote. She was working with DYS [Department of Youth Services]. Some people just say 'Jesus, Jesus, Jesus' and that's all; but you gotta be about even more. It's good to deal with everyday things as well. And Pastor Calvin was addressing the everyday things."

5. Ella J. Baker's social justice activism spanned some sixty years, although she is best known for her foundational work with the Southern Christian Leadership Conference and the Student Nonviolent Coordinating Committee. Her style of community organizing, which eschewed strong central leadership in favor of developing leadership among the masses of women and men, undergirded much of what we now call the civil rights movement and inspired many subsequent social movements. See Payne (1995).

6. In 1906, William J. Seymour, a Black preacher with Baptist and Holiness backgrounds, initiated the modern Pentecostal movement with his three-year Azusa Street Revival.

CHAPTER SEVEN

1. This type of scholarship has recently been revived in a flurry of studies on neighborhood crime and youth delinquency (Sampson 1988, 1991, 1999; Sampson and Morenoff 1997; Sampson et al. 1997; Sampson and Groves 1988; Pattillo 1998). This work depicts the local community as a "fabric" (Kasarda and Janowitz 1974) of interpersonal networks formed through public interaction and participation in voluntary associations. The density of the fabric affects the ability of residents to act collectively. The resulting capacity for neighborhood collective action is called "collective efficacy." Residential mobility, in particular, is thought directly to affect this fabric. High residential turnover constrains intraneighborhood social networking, while long-term residence encourages interpersonal contact and neighborhood social cohesion.

2. Actually, not all churches are located in physical space. As growing numbers of people turn to the Internet for social interaction, religious communities and practices are proliferating in cyberspace (Brasher 2001). The conclusions I draw here apply only to those congregations that meet in physical space.

3. Much of the Adventist doctrine, including pronouncements on health and healing, is contained in the writings of the nineteenth-century exponent Ellen G. White. See *The Ministry of Healing* (White 1905).

CONCLUSION

1. Actually, this effort is part of a larger movement to reopen numerous dormant stops along the Fairmount branch of the MBTA commuter rail network. According to Noah S. Berger (2002), a transit policy analyst for the MBTA Advisory Board, many of these defunct stops lie within neighborhoods composed primarily of working poor and working-class African Americans.

2. In their "broken windows" theory of social disorder, James Q. Wilson and George L. Kelling (1982) suggest that physical signs of disorder, such as broken windows, give people the impression that more serious transgressions, such as violent crimes and illicit drug sales, are permissible in those areas. The collaborative effort

described here implicitly agrees, up to a point. The difference between Wilson and Kelling and the Four Corners "trash pickup" campaign is that the latter held municipal services largely responsible for this particular sign of "disorder." They identified the problem not solely with residents who inappropriately disposed of their trash but a municipal system that privileged some neighborhoods over others.

3. Actually, I nearly coined the term "religious *bazaar*," but this seemed to exoticize a phenomenon that appears to be a common feature of urban life—at least as common as voluntaristic religious practice, concentrated poverty, and uneven economic development.

REFERENCES

Abbott, Andrew. 1995. "Sequence Analysis: New Methods for Old Ideas." *Annual Review of Sociology* 21:93–115.

Abu-Lughod, Janet. 1994a. "Diversity, Democracy, and Self-Determination in an Urban Neighborhood: The East Village of Manhattan." *Social Research* 61:181–203.

———. 1994b. *From East Village to Urban Village: The Battle for New York's Lower East Side*. Oxford: Basil Blackwell.

Alexander, Bobby C. 1991. "Correcting Misinterpretations of Turner's Theory: An African American Pentecostal Illustration." *Journal for the Scientific Study of Religion* 30(1):26–44.

Ammerman, Nancy T. 1997a. *Congregation and Community*. New Brunswick: Rutgers University Press.

———. 1997b. "Organized Religion in a Voluntaristic Society." *Sociology of Religion* 58:203–215.

Anderson, Elijah. 1990. *Streetwise: Race, Class, and Change in an Urban Community*. Chicago: University of Chicago Press.

———. 1999. *Code of the Street*. New York: W. W. Norton and Company.

Baer, Hans A., and Merrill Singer. 1992. *African-American Religion in the Twentieth Century*. Knoxville: University of Tennessee Press.

Becker, Penny E. 1998. "Congregational Models and Conflict: A Study of How Institutions Shape Organizational Process." In *Sacred Companies: Organizational Aspects of Religion and Religious Aspects of Organizations*, edited by N. J. Demerath III, Peter Dobkin Hall, Terry Schmitt, and Rhys H. Williams, 231–255. New York: Oxford University Press.

———. 1999. *Congregations in Conflict: Cultural Models of Local Religious Life*. New York: Cambridge University Press.

Bellah, Robert N. 1985. *Habits of the Heart: Individualism and Commitment in American Life*. Berkeley: University of California Press.

Berger, Noah. 2002. "Retrofitting Transportation Infrastructure." Paper presented at the 2002 National Conference of the American Planning Association, Chicago, Illinois.

Berger, Peter L. 1967. *The Sacred Canopy: Elements of a Sociological Theory of Religion*. Garden City, N.Y.: Doubleday.

Billingsley, Andrew. 1999. *Mighty like a River: The Black Church and Social Reform*. New York: Oxford University Press.

Boldon, Dean A. 1985. "Organizational Characteristics of Ecumenically Active Denominations." *Sociological Analysis* 46:261–273.

Boston Globe. 1999. "Turning around Four Corners." November 8, 1999, A20.

Boston Public Facilities Department. 1997. "Four Corners: Fifty Years of Change." Boston: Boston Public Facilities Department, City of Boston.

Boyd, Robert L. 1998. "The Storefront Church Ministry in African American Communities of the Urban North during the Great Migration: The Making of an Ethnic Niche." *Social Science Journal* 35:319–333.

Brasher, Brenda E. 2001. *Give Me That Online Religion.* San Francisco: Jossey-Bass.

Breton, Raymond. 1964. "Institutional Completeness of Ethnic Communities and the Personal Relations of Immigrants." *American Journal of Sociology* 70:193–205.

Burgess, Ernest W. 1969 [1925]. "The Growth of the City: An Introduction to a Research Project." In *The City,* edited by Robert E. Park, Ernest Burgess, and Roderick D. McKenzie. Chicago: University of Chicago Press.

Bursik, Robert J., and Harold Grasmick. 1993. *Neighborhoods and Crime: The Dimensions of Effective Community Control.* New York: Lexington.

Chaves, Mark. 1999. "Religious Congregations and Welfare Reform: Who Will Take Advantage of 'Charitable Choice'?" *American Sociological Review* 64:836–846.

Cisneros, Henry G. 1996. "Higher Ground: Faith Communities and Community Building." Washington, D.C.: U.S. Department of Housing and Urban Development.

Clark, Mathew S. 1989. *What Is Distinctive about Pentecostal Theology?* Pretoria: University of South Africa Press.

Colored American Magazine. 1904. "Boston as the Paradise of the Negro." May:309–317.

Cooper, Lee R. 1974. "Publish or Perish." In *Religious Movements in Contemporary America,* edited by Irving I. Zaretsky and Mark P. Leone. Princeton, N.J.: Princeton University Press.

Cox, Harvey. 1995. *Fire from Heaven.* New York: Addison-Wesley.

Crenson, Matthew A. 1983. *Neighborhood Politics.* Cambridge, Mass.: Harvard University Press.

Cresswell, Tim. 1996. *In Place/Out of Place: Geography, Ideology, and Transgression.* Minneapolis: University of Minnesota Press.

Cromwell, Adelaide. 1994. *The Other Brahmins: Boston's Black Upper Class, 1750–1950.* Fayetteville: University of Arkansas Press.

Cummings, Scott. 1998. *Left Behind in Rosedale: Race Relations and the Collapse of Community Institutions.* Boulder: Westview.

Daniel, Vattel Elbert. 1942. "Ritual and Stratification in Chicago Negro Churches." *American Sociological Review* 7:352–361.

Daniels, John. 1914. *In Freedom's Birthplace.* Boston: Houghton Mifflin.

Davidson, James D., and Jerome R. Koch. 1998. "Beyond Mutual and Public Benefits." In *Sacred Companies: Organizational Aspects of Religion and Religious Aspects of Organizations,* edited by N. J. Demerath III, Peter Dobkin Hall, Terry Schmitt, and Rhys H. Williams, 292–306. New York: Oxford University Press.

Davidson, Powell D. 1985. *Mobilizing Social Movement Organizations.* Storrs, Conn.: Society for the Scientific Study of Religion.

Davis, Allison, Burleigh B. Gardner, and Mary R. Gardner. 1941. *Deep South: A Social Anthropological Study of Caste and Class.* Chicago: University of Chicago Press.

Davis, John E. 1991. *Contested Ground.* Ithaca, N.Y.: Cornell University Press.

Dawson, Michael C. 1994. "A Black Counterpublic? Economic Earthquakes, Racial Agenda(s), and Black Politics." *Public Culture* 7:195–223.

———. *Black Visions: The Roots of Contemporary African-American Political Ideologies.* Chicago: University of Chicago Press.

Demerath, Nicholas J., and Rhys H. Williams. 1992. *A Bridging of Faiths: Religion and Politics in a New England City.* Princeton, N.J.: Princeton University Press.

Denzin, Norman K., and Yvonna S. Lincoln. 1998. "Introduction: Entering the Field of Qualitative Research." In *Strategies of Qualitative Inquiry,* edited by Norman K. Denzin and Yvonna S. Lincoln, 1–34. Thousand Oaks, Calif.: Sage Publications.

Douglass, H. Paul. 1927. *Church in the Changing City.* New York: Doran.

———. 1944. *Missionary Boston.* Boston: Massachusetts Council of Churches.

Drake, St. Clair. 1940. *Churches and Voluntary Associations in the Chicago Negro Community.* Chicago: Works Projects Administration District 3.

Drake, St. Clair, and Horace R. Cayton. 1945. *Black Metropolis.* New York: Harcourt, Brace and World.

Dubois, W. E. B. 1996 [1899]. *The Philadelphia Negro.* Philadelphia: University of Pennsylvania Press.

Dudley, Carl S. 1991. "From Typical Church to Social Ministry." *Review of Religious Research* 32:195–212.

Dudley, Carl S., and Sally Johnson. 1991. "Congregational Self-images for Social Ministry." In *Carriers of Faith: Lessons from Congregational Studies,* edited by Carl S. Dudley, Jackson W. Carroll, and Powell Wind. Louisville: Westminster-John Knox Press.

Durkheim, Emile. 1915. *Elementary Forms of the Religious Life.* New York: Free Press.

Eiesland, Nancy. 1999. *A Particular Place.* New Brunswick, N.J.: Rutgers University Press.

Fainstein, Norman, and Susan Nesbit. 1996. "Did the Black Ghetto Have a Golden Age?: Class Structure and Class Segregation in New York City, 1949–1970, with Initial Evidence for 1990." *Journal of Urban History* 23:3–29.

Fainstein, Susan. 1987. "Local Mobilization and Economic Discontent." In *The Capitalist City,* edited by Michael Peter Smith and Joe R. Feagin, 323–342. Cambridge, Mass.: Blackwell.

Finke, Roger, and Rodney Stark. 1992. *The Churching of America, 1776–1990: Winners and Losers in Our Religious Economy.* New Brunswick, N.J.: Rutgers University Press.

Fischer, Claude. 1975. "Toward a Subcultural Theory of Urbanism." *American Journal of Sociology* 80:1319–1341.

———. 1981. "The Public and Private Worlds of City Life." *American Sociological Review* 46:306–316.

———. 1982. *To Dwell among Friends: Personal Networks in Town and City.* Chicago: University of Chicago Press.

Formisano, Ronald P. 1991. *Boston against Busing: Race, Class, and Ethnicity in the 1960s and 1970s.* Chapel Hill: University of North Carolina Press.

Foster, Brian L., and Stephen B. Seidman. 1982. "Urban Structures Derived from Collections of Overlapping Subsets." *Urban Anthropology* 11:177–192.

Fraser, Nancy. 1997. "Rethinking the Public Sphere: A Contribution to the Critique of Actually Existing Democracy." In *Habermas and the Public Sphere,* edited by Craig Calhoun, 109–142. Cambridge, Mass.: MIT Press.

Frazier, E. Franklin. 1974 [1963]. *The Negro Church in America.* New York: Schocken Books.

Gamm, Gerald H. 1999. *Urban Exodus: Why the Jews Left Boston and the Catholics Stayed.* Cambridge, Mass.: Harvard University Press.

Gans, Herbert J. 1962. *The Urban Villagers.* New York: Free Press.

Geertz, Clifford. 1973. *The Interpretation of Cultures.* New York: Basic Books.

Gibbs, James O., and Phyllis H. Ewer. 1969. "The External Adaption of Religious Organizations: Church Responses to Social Issues." *Sociological Analysis* 30:223–234.

Glaser, Barney G. 1999. *The Discovery of Grounded Theory: Strategies for Qualitative Research.* New York: Aldine de Gruyter.

Goffman, Erving. 1974. *Frame Analysis.* Boston: Northeastern University Press.

Gregory, Steven. 1995. "Race, Identity and Political Activism: The Shifting Contours of the African American Public Sphere." In *The Black Public Sphere,* edited by the Black Public Sphere Collective, 151–168. Chicago: University of Chicago Press.

———. 1998. *Black Corona: Race and the Politics of Place in an Urban Community.* Princeton, N.J.: Princeton University Press.

Griffin, Farah Jasmine. 1995. *"Who Set You Flowin'?": The African-American Migration Narrative.* New York: Oxford University Press.

Guest, Avery, and Barrett A. Lee. 1987. "Metropolitan Residential Environments and Church Organizational Activities." *Sociological Analysis* 47:335–354.

Halpern, Robert. 1995. *Rebuilding the Inner City.* New York: Columbia University Press.

Hannan, Michael T., and John Freeman. 1977. "The Population Ecology of Organizations." *American Journal of Sociology* 82:929–964.

Hannerz, Ulf. 1969. *Soulside: Inquiries into Ghetto Culture and Community.* New York: Columbia University Press.

Hanson, R. Scott. 2002. "City of Gods: Religious Freedom, Immigration, and Pluralism in Flushing, Queens—New York City, 1945–2000." Ph.D. diss., University of Chicago.

Harris, Fredrick C. 1999. *Something Within: Religion in African-American Political Activism.* New York: Oxford University Press.

Harris, George. 1908. "Boston Colored People." *Colored American* 14, no. 1 (January):28–31.

Hayden, Robert C. 1983. *Faith, Culture and Leadership: A History of the Black Church in Boston.* Boston: Boston Branch NAACP.

Henig, Jeffrey R. 1982. *Neighborhood Mobilization: Redevelopment and Response.* New Brunswick, N.J.: Rutgers University Press.

Higginbotham, Evelyn Brooks. 1993. *Righteous Discontent: The Women's Movement in the Black Baptist Church, 1880–1920.* Cambridge, Mass.: Harvard University Press.

Hoge, Dean R., Everett L. Perry, and Gerald L. Klever. 1978. "Theology as a Source of Disagreement about Protestant Church Goals and Priorities." *Review of Religious Research* 19:116–38.

Hoge, Dean R., and Jeffrey L. Faue. 1973. "Sources of Conflict over Priorities of the Protestant Church." *Social Forces* 52:178–194.

Hunter, Floyd. 1953. *Community Power Structure: A Study of Decision Makers.* Chapel Hill: University of North Carolina Press.

Iannoccone, Laurence R. 1988. "A Formal Model of Church and Sect." *American Journal of Sociology* 94(S):S241.

———. 1994. "Why Strict Churches Are Strong." *American Journal of Sociology* 99:1180–1211.

Janowitz, Morris. 1967. *Community Press in an Urban Setting.* Chicago: University of Chicago.

———. 1975. "Sociological Theory and Social Control." *American Journal of Sociology* 81:82–108.

Jargowsky, Paul A. 1997. *Poverty and Place.* New York: Russell Sage Foundation.

Johnson, Benton. 1963. "On Church and Sect." *American Sociological Review* 28: 539–49.

———. 1967. "Theology and the Position of Pastors on Public Issues." *American Sociological Review* 32:433–442.

Johnson, Stephen D., and Joseph Tamney. 1986. "The Clergy and Public Issues in Middletown." In *The Political Role of Religion in the United States,* edited by Stephen D. Johnson and Joseph B. Tamney. Boulder, Colo.: Westview.

Kanagy, Conrad. 1992. "Social Action, Evangelism, and Ecumenism: The Impact of Theological and Church Structural Variables." *Review of Religious Research* 34: 34–51.

Kasarda, John D., and Morris Janowitz. 1974. "Community Attachment in Mass Society." *American Sociological Review* 39:328–39.

Kincheloe, Samuel C. 1964. "Theoretical Perspectives for the Sociological Study of Religion in the City." *Review of Religious Research* 6:63–81.

———. 1989. *Church in the City.* Chicago: Exploration Press.

King, Mel. 1981. *Chain of Change: Struggles for Black Community Development.* Boston: South End Press.

Kornhauser, Ruth. 1978. *Social Sources of Delinquency.* Chicago: University of Chicago Press.

Kostarelos, Frances. 1995. *Feeling the Spirit: Faith and Hope in an Evangelical Black Storefront Church.* Columbia: University of South Carolina Press.

Kramnick, Isaac. 1997. "Can the Churches Save the Cities? Faith-based Services and the Constitution." *American Prospect* (Nov.–Dec. 1997):47–54.

Kyper, John. 1975. "Community Research: Mount Bowdoin and Fields Corner Neighborhoods." Unpublished course paper. Massachusetts Institute of Technology.

Lang, Robert E., and Steven P. Hornburg. 1998. "What Is Social Capital and Why Is It Important to Public Policy?" *Housing and Policy Debate* 9:1–15.

Lasch, Christopher. 1979. *Culture of Narcissism.* New York: Norton.

Leach, William. 1999. *Country of Exiles.* New York: Pantheon Books.

Leland, John. 1998. "Savior of the Streets." *Newsweek,* June 1, 1998.

Levine, Hillel, and Lawrence Harmon. 1992. *Death and Life of an American Jewish Community.* New York: Free Press.

Lincoln, C. Eric, and Lawrence H. Mamiya. 1990. *The Black Church in the African American Experience.* Durham, N.C.: Duke University Press.

Lofland, John, and Lyn H. Lofland. 1995. *Analyzing Social Settings.* Belmont, Calif.: Wadsworth.

Los Angeles Times 2000. "U.S. Restores Special Protections For Religious Groups." September 3.

Marty, Martin E. 1987. *Religion and Republic.* Boston: Beacon.

Massachusetts, Bureau of Statistics of Labor. 1870. *First Annual Report.* Boston: Massachusetts Bureau of Statistics of Labor.

Massey, Douglas S. 1996. "The Age of Extremes: Concentrated Affluence and Poverty in the Twenty-First Century." *Demography* 33:395–412.

Massey, Douglas S., and Nancy Denton. 1993. *American Apartheid: Segregation and the Making of the Underclass.* Cambridge. Mass.: Harvard University Press.

Mays, Benjamin, and Joseph Nicholson. 1969 [1933]. *The Negro's Church.* New York: Arno Press and the New York Times.

McGreevy, John T. 1996. *Parish Boundaries.* Chicago: University of Chicago Press.

McKinney, John C. 1966. *Constructive Typology and Social Theory.* New York: Appleton-Century-Crofts.

McRoberts, Omar M. 1999. "Understanding the 'New' Black Pentecostal Activism: Lessons from Boston Ecumenical Ministries." *Sociology of Religion* 60:47–70.

Medoff, Peter, and Holly Sklar. 1994. *Streets of Hope.* Boston: South End Press.

Mitchell, Rudy, and Jeffrey Bass. 1995. *Boston Church Directory: 1995 Update.* Boston: Emmanuel Gospel Center.

Mock, Alan. 1992. "Congregational Religious Styles and Orientations to Society: Exploring Our Linear Assumptions." *Review of Religious Research* 34:20–33.

Mollenkopf, John H. 1983. *Contested City.* Princeton, N.J.: Princeton University Press.

Morris, Aldon D. 1984. *The Origins of the Civil Rights Movement: Black Communities Organizing for Change.* New York: Free Press.

Myers, Phyllis G., and Powell Davidson. 1984. "Who Participates in Ecumenical Activity?" *Review of Religious Research* 25:185–203.

Myrdal, Gunnar. 1944. *An American Dilemma.* New York: Harper and Brothers.

Nelson, Timothy. 1996. "Sacrifice of Praise: Emotion and Collective Participation in an African-American Worship Service." *Sociology of Religion* 57:379–396.

———. 1997. "The Church and the Street: Race, Class, and Congregation." In *Contemporary American Religion: An Ethnographic Reader.* Walnut Creek, Calif.: Alta Mira Press.

Nisbet, Robert. 1976. *Sociology as an Art Form.* New York: Oxford University Press.

Orsi, Robert A. 1999. *Gods of the City.* Bloomington: Indiana University Press.

Paris, Arthur E. 1982. *Black Pentecostalism.* Amherst: University of Massachusetts Press.

Park, Robert E. 1969 [1916]. "The City: Suggestions for Investigation of Human Behavior in the Urban Environment." In *Classic Essays on the Culture of Cities,* edited by R. Sennett, 91–130. New York: Appleton-Century-Crofts.

Park, Robert E., Ernest Burgess, and Roderick D. McKenzie. 1969 [1925]. *The City.* Chicago: University of Chicago Press.

Pattillo, Mary. 1998. "Sweet Mothers and Gang Bangers: Managing Crime in a Black Middle-Class Neighborhood." *Social Forces* 76:747–774.

Pattillo-McCoy, Mary. 1998. "Church Culture as a Strategy of Action in the Black Community." *American Sociological Review* 63:767–785.

———. 1999. *Black Picket Fences.* Chicago: University of Chicago Press.

Payne, Charles M. 1995. *I've Got the Light of Freedom.* Berkeley: University of California Press.

Phillips, Kevin. 1990. *The Politics of Rich and Poor.* New York: Random House.

Pleck, Elizabeth. 1979. *Black Migration and Poverty.* New York: Academic Press.

Putnam, Robert. 1995. "Bowling Alone: America's Declining Social Capital." *Journal of Democracy* 6:65–78.

———. 2000. *Bowling Alone: The Collapse and Revival of American Community.* New York: Simon and Schuster.

Randolph, Peter. 1893. *From Slave Cabin to Pulpit.* Boston: J. H. Earle.

Ransom, Reverdy C. 1930. *The Pilgrimage of Harriet Ransom's Son.* Nashville: Sunday School Union.

Ridley, Florida Ruffin. 1927. "The Negro in Boston." *Our Boston* 2, no. 2 (Jan. 1927): 15–20.

Rieder, Jonathan. 1985. *Canarsie.* Cambridge, Mass.: Harvard University Press.

Roberts, Michael K. 1990. "Nazarenes and Social Ministry: A Holiness Tradition." In *Faith and Social Ministry: Ten Christian Perspectives,* edited by Powell D. Davidson, C. Lincoln Johnson, and Alan K. Mock. Chicago: Loyola University Press.

Rogers, Mary Beth. 1990. *Cold Anger.* Denton: University of North Texas Press.

Roof, Wade Clark, and William McKinney. 1987. *American Mainline Religion.* New Brunswick, N.J.: Rutgers University Press.

Rooney, Jim. 1995. *Organizing the South Bronx.* Albany: State University of New York Press.

Roozen, David A., William McKinney, and Jackson W. Carroll. 1988. *Varieties of Religious Presence: Mission in Public Life.* New York: Pilgrim Press.

Rowe, Henry K. 1924. *The History of Religion in the United States.* New York: Macmillan.

Sampson, Robert J. 1988. "Local Friendship Ties and Community Attachment in Mass Society: A Multilevel Systemic Model." *American Sociological Review* 53: 766–79.

———. 1991. "Linking the Micro- and Macrolevel Dimensions of Community Social Organization." *Social Forces* 70:43–64.

———. 1999. "What 'Community' Supplies." In *The Future of Community Development: A Social Science Synthesis,* edited by Ronald F. Ferguson and William T. Dickens, 241–292. Washington, D.C.: Brookings Institution Press.

Sampson, Robert J., and Jeffrey Morenoff. 1997. "Ecological Perspectives on the Neighborhood Context of Urban Poverty." In *Neighborhood Poverty: Policy Implications in Studying Neighborhoods,* edited by Jeanne Brooks-Gunn, Greg Duncan, and Lawrence Aber. New York: Russell Sage Foundation.

Sampson, Robert J., and W. Byron Groves. 1989. "Community Structure and Crime: Testing Social Disorganization Theory." *American Journal of Sociology* 94:774–802.

Sampson, Robert J., Stephen W. Raudenbush, and Felton Earls. 1997. "Neighborhoods and Violent Crime: A Multilevel Study of Collective Efficacy." *Science* 277:918–924.

Sanders, Cheryl J. 1996. *Saints in Exile: The Holiness-Pentecostal Experience in African American Religion and Culture.* New York: Oxford University Press.

Scheie, David M., Jaimie Markham, Theartrice Williams, John Slettom, Sharon Marie A. Ramirez, and Steven Mayer. 1994. "Better Together: Religious Institutions as Partners in Community-Based Development." Final evaluation report on the Lily Endowment Program. Minneapolis: Rainbow Research.

Schneider, Mark R. 1995. "The Colored American and Alexander's: Boston's Pro–Civil Rights Bookerites." *Journal of Negro History* 80:157–169.

Sernett, Milton. 1997. *Bound for the Promised Land.* Durham, N.C.: Duke University Press.

Silva, Cynthia. 1984. "Pentecostalism as Oppositional Culture." B.A. thesis, Harvard University.

Simmel, Georg. 1971. "Conflict." In *On Individuality and Social Forms,* edited by Donald N. Levine. Chicago: University of Chicago Press.

Snow, David E., Burke Rochford, Jr., Steven K. Worden, and Robert D. Benford. 1986. "Frame Alignment Processes, Micromobilization, and Movement Participation." *American Sociological Review* 51:464–481.

Stark, Rodney, and Charles Glock. 1965. "The 'New' Denominationalism." *Review of Religious Research* 7:8–17.

Stevens, Walter J. 1946. *Chip on My Shoulder: Autobiography of Walter J. Stevens.* Cambridge, Mass.: Meador Publishing Company.

Strauss, Anselm, and Juliet Corbin. 1990. *Basics of Qualitative Research.* Newbury Park, Calif.: Sage.

Suttles, Gerald D. 1968. *The Social Order of the Slum: Ethnicity and Territory in the Inner City.* Chicago: University of Chicago Press.

———. 1972. *The Symbolic Construction of Communities.* Chicago: University of Chicago Press.

Tamney, Joseph B. and Stephen D. Johnson. 1990. "Religious Diversity and Ecumenical Social Action." *Review of Religious Research* 32:1.

Taub, Richard P., George P. Surgeon, Sara Lindholm, Phyllis Betts Otti, and Amy Bridges. 1977. "Urban Voluntary Associations, Locality Based and Externally Induced." *American Journal of Sociology* 83:425–442.

Thernstrom, Stephan. 1973. *The Other Bostonians: Poverty and Progress in the American Metropolis.* Cambridge, Mass.: Harvard University Press.

Tönnies, Ferdinand. 1957 [1887]. *Community and Society.* New York: Harper & Row.

Troeltsch, Ernest. 1931. *Social Teachings of the Christian Churches.* 2 vols. New York: Harper and Brothers.

Turner, Victor. 1977. *The Ritual Process.* Ithaca, N.Y.: Cornell University Press.

Verba, Sidney, Kay Lehman Schlozman, and Henry E. Brady. 1995. *Voice and Equality: Civic Voluntarism in American Politics.* Cambridge, Mass.: Harvard University Press.

Wacquant, Loic J. D., and William Julius Wilson. 1990. "The Cost of Racial and Class Exclusion in the Inner City." *Annals of the American Academy of Political and Social Science* 501 (Jan.):8–25.

Warner, R. Stephen. 1988. *New Wine in Old Wineskins: Evangelicals and Liberals in a Small Town Church.* Berkeley: University of California Press.

———. 1993. "Work in Progress toward a New Paradigm for the Sociological Study of Religion in the United States." *American Journal of Sociology* 98:1044–93.

———. 1995. "The Metropolitan Community Churches and the Gay Agenda: The Power of Pentecostalism and Essentialism." *Religion and the Social Order* 5:81–108.

———. 1998. Introduction to Gatherings in Diaspora: Religious Communities and the New Immigration, edited by R. Stephen Warner and Judith G. Wittner. Philadelphia: Temple University Press.

Warner, Sam Bass. 1976. *Streetcar Suburbs: The Process of Growth in Boston, 1870–1900.* New York: Atheneum.

Warner, W. Lloyd. 1963. *Yankee City.* New Haven, Conn.: Yale University Press.

Warner, W. Lloyd, and Paul S. Lunt. 1949. *Social Life in a Modern Community.* New Haven, Conn.: Yale University Press.

Warren, Donald I. 1975. *Black Neighborhoods: An Assessment of Community Power.* Ann Arbor: University of Michigan Press.

Warren, Mark. 1995. "Social Capital and Community Empowerment: Religion and Political Organization in the Texas Industrial Areas Foundation." Ph.D. diss., Harvard University.

———. 2001. *Dry Bones Rattling: Community Building to Revitalize American Democracy.* Princeton, N.J.: Princeton University Press.

Waters, Mary. 1999. *Black Identities.* Cambridge, Mass.: Harvard University Press.

Weber, Max. 1993 [1922]. *The Sociology of Religion.* Boston: Beacon Press.

Wellman, Barry. 1979. "The Community Question: The Intimate Networks of East Yorkers." *American Journal of Sociology* 84:1201–1231.

———. 1999. "The Network Community: An Introduction." In *Networks in the Global Village,* edited by Barry Wellman, 1–48. Boulder, Colo.: Westview Press.

West, Dorothy. 1948. *The Living Is Easy.* Boston: Houghton, Mifflin.

White, Ellen G. 1905. *Ministry of Healing.* Washington, D.C.: Review and Herald Press.

Williams, Melvin D. 1974. *Community in a Black Pentecostal Church.* Prospect Heights, Ill.: Waveland Press.

Wilson, James Q., and George L. Kelling. 1982. "Broken Windows: The Police and Neighborhood Safety." *Atlantic Monthly,* vol. 249 (3):29–38.

Wilson, William J. 1987. *The Truly Disadvantaged: The Inner City, the Underclass, and Public Policy.* Chicago: University of Chicago Press.

———. 1996. *When Work Disappears.* New York: Knopf.

Wood, Richard L. 1994. "Faith in Action: Religious Resources for Political Success in Three Congregations." *Sociology of Religion* 55:397–417.

Woodward, Kenneth L. 1998. "The New Holy War." *Newsweek,* June 1, 1998.

Wuthnow, Robert. 1988. *The Restructuring of American Religion.* Princeton, N.J.: Princeton University Press.

———. 1998. *Loose Connections: Joining Together in America's Fragmented Communities.* Cambridge, Mass.: Harvard University Press.

Wynia, Elly M. 1994. *The Church of God and Saints of Christ: The Rise of the Black Jews.* New York: Garland.

INDEX